TUFFERS'

CRICKET TALES

TUFFERS'

CRICKET TALES

PHIL TUFNELL

with JUSTYN BARNES

headline

First published in 2012
by HEADLINE PUBLISHING GROUP

Lyrics to 'The Ashes Song' © Keith Bunker and Richard Melvin

1

Cataloguing in Publication Data is available from the British Library

Hardback ISBN 978 0 7553 6291 2

Typeset in Minion Pro by Avon DataSet Ltd,
Bidford-on-Avon, Warwickshire

Printed and bound in Great Britain by
Clays Ltd, St Ives plc

Headline's policy is to use papers that are natural, renewable and
recyclable products and made from wood grown in sustainable forests.
The logging and manufacturing processes are expected to conform
to the environmental regulations of the country of origin.

HEADLINE PUBLISHING GROUP
An Hachette UK Company
338 Euston Road
London NW1 3BH

www.headline.co.uk
www.hachette.co.uk

To all the captains I caused so much grief to during my playing career. And to my dad for his advice to 'be yourself' (although my former captains might not thank him for that).

Justyn Barnes, who collaborated with Phil Tufnell on the writing of *Tuffers' Cricket Tales*, is the editor and author of more than thirty books, including *The Reduced History of Cricket*, *Freddie Flintoff: England's Hero* and *Four More Weeks: Diary of a Stand-in Captain* with Mark Ramprakash. A Tavare-esque 36 not out in 30 overs for London Schools Under-11s represented the height of his cricketing achievements and his strike rate deteriorated thereafter. He bonded with Phil over their shared interests in quirky human behaviour, fine wines and homemade minced meat-based lunches.

ACKNOWLEDGEMENTS

Thanks to:

Justyn Barnes – for all your hard work, professionalism, excellent choice of wines to fuel our lengthy sessions and basically for being a top geezer. Recalling my past experiences, both good and bad, that had lain dormant somewhere in the back of my mind was very cathartic for me.

Peter 'Reg' Hayter – for getting the project up and running, reminding me of many jolly japes on tour with England, and offering wise advice throughout.

Angus Fraser, Mike Gatting, Simon Shepherd, Shilpa Patel and Andy Sellins – for jogging my memory and helping to fill in the gaps.

Malcolm Ashton – for unearthing some amazing stats (particularly on my lbw hell).

Mike Martin – for organising my life.

Jonathan Taylor and all at Headline – for backing this project all the way.

Dawnie and all the family – for their love and support as always.

Cricket – for giving me a life stranger than fiction.

CONTENTS

Part Two
Just Not Cricket . . . The (Jungle) Trials and Tangos of a
Spinner Turned TV 'Celeb'

Part Three
Infiltrating the Establishment: Cat the Cricket Pundit

INTRODUCTION

Welcome to my book of cricket tales.

Those among you who know me as 'that bloke off the telly' who ate dung beetles in the jungle, foxtrotted around on *Strictly* and reports for *The One Show*, might be wondering what I'm doing writing a book about cricket. Well, I actually used to be a professional cricketer. I played for seventeen years, as a matter of fact, including eleven years for England off and on. Amazing, isn't it?

And if you care to read on, you'll see that it really was a miracle, given that I quit cricket in favour of three years of anarchy in my teenage years and when I took up the game again, my early-career decision not to bother with batting (very dangerous business, you know), my delicate 'hands of a pianist' (© Mike Gatting), which made fielding rather taxing, and my allergy to training (try explaining that to an England coach – I did and he wasn't very understanding), put me at a distinct disadvantage to most pros. Thank God I could bowl and was a fiercely competitive little sod . . . although, come to think of it, the latter attribute got me into a lot of trouble, too.

Anyhow, all you non-cricketing folk, please don't be put off by the term 'cricket tales' in the title because I use it in the loosest sense. While you will find many on-pitch anecdotes, I'm not going to bore on about the technical aspects of the game (although there was that season when I forgot how long my run-up was which was awfully upsetting . . .). No, this is largely a book about people. More specifically, it's about my interaction with the glorious array of colourful/quirky/scary/certifiable characters I've encountered on my travels, some of whom just happened to be cricketers, umpires and coaches, plus spectators, randoms I bumped into on long nights out around the world, and, in more recent years, unique individuals I've met through my work behind the microphone.

In part one I'll be reliving some bizarre incidents from my playing career, and trying to explain what was going through my head at the time. I'm sure this will be of great interest to many of my former captains, teammates, club officials, opponents and umpires who witnessed me, for example, kick a batsman, stand throwing fruit at the crowd when I was supposed to be fielding, square up to an SAS man who could have snapped me in half like a twig, fall asleep during games, attempt to play Shane Warne with my arse, and go mental during a contract negotiation (sorry, Gus).

The second part of the book covers my transformation from cricketer to 'celebrity', via a stint eating wichetty grubs in the Australian jungle, and a new career as a TV/radio presenter without the benefit of training. As with cricket, my time in broadcasting hasn't been without mishaps – doing 'Ring a Ring o' Roses' in front of ten million viewers, calling John Torode 'a burger chef' as I was dragged out of *Masterchef* HQ, and mistaking Jesus for a woman spring to mind – but I think I'm getting quite good at it now.

To finish up, I shall return to my enduring passion, cricket, which I'm very fortunate to be able to indulge as a member of the BBC *Test Match Special* team. I'll take you behind the scenes with Aggers and co. and talk cake, beards and other serious issues in

INTRODUCTION

modern cricket (actually, non-cricketing *One Show* viewers might want to give that last bit a miss, because once I get started on the Decision Review System, I warn you, I will be some time).

From teenage rebel without a clue to unlikely international cricketer to unlikely TV presenter and unlikely *TMS* pundit. How the hell did that happen? Let's find out.

TUFFERS' FIRST XI (PLUS A TWELFTH MAN)

FIRST BAT

It was a Gray-Nicolls, bought from Smith & Sons, a proper old specialist cricket shop down in Enfield run by the father of Mike Smith, Middlesex's opening batsman at the time, who went on to become the club's scorer.

In my pre-teens, my dad and I used to spend all afternoon in Mr Smith's shop. He had all the bats in racks, carefully ordered by brand, weight, length of handle. The place smelt of linseed oil and tobacco. Mike's dad sat there smoking his pipe, knocking in bats with a cricket ball in a sock, talking cricket with my dad while I played around.

I tried out most of the bats until I found one that fitted me, where the handle, weight and balance felt just right – the selection process was rather like internet dating. When I finally bought one, it was like taking home a new girlfriend.

I scored loads of runs with that bat – yes, as a kid, I was a very good batsman – and was heartbroken when it eventually cracked beyond repair.

FIRST CIGARETTE

Over by the swings at the park with my mates, when I was ten or eleven. A pack of Player's No.6 – white box with green and dark blue stripes on it. I think we had either found them or persuaded someone to buy them from the local newsagent's for us.

FIRST GIRLFRIEND

Joanne Hunter, when I was about thirteen. I'd had a couple of little kisses before, but this was my first real girlfriend. She was in my class at Southgate School and it was love. I still remember when I asked her out. There'd been whispers that I was going to do it, and after a geography class I finally plucked up the courage.

'Yeah, I'll think about it,' she replied and I ran off blushing. Always been a smooth operator.

FIRST NUDE MODELLING ASSIGNMENT

Before the Second Ashes Test of 2009, a fifteen-metre-high image of me in the buff was projected onto the side of the hotel where the Aussies were staying. Thankfully, the picture wasn't full-frontal – I was looking coyly over my shoulder and a tastefully placed pot of Marmite protected my modesty.

FIRST PET

A black cat called Trooper, named after a Shetland pony I fell in love with when I went riding during a holiday down in the New Forest. Not sure why I loved that pony so much because he nearly killed me.

It was springtime, and the first proper run out of the year for the ponies. I was eight years old, being led slowly on this pony by an instructor. But when we emerged from the woods into the open heathland, Trooper saw a group of ponies grazing in the distance and bolted after them. He broke the leading rein and I was left clinging on as Trooper charged what must have been half a mile. He'd been locked up all winter and wanted to see his mates. When he finally screeched to a halt, I went flying over his head and landed in a heap.

The lady leading the trek said later I'd done well to hold on all that time. My dad told me years later he thought I was dead when they saw me lying there motionless. But I survived and, er, the name Trooper lived on through my cat.

FIRST CAR

I used to get a lift with my dad to work at his silversmith's factory in Angel, North London, but when I started playing for MCC Young Cricketers at seventeen I needed to be able to get to Lord's. So my dad and I both chipped in some money and I bought a Cortina two-litre Ghia. Black vinyl roof. Fluffy dice. Beautiful it was.

Never get a nice car as your first one, though. Like most teenagers who've just passed their test, I was a dangerous driver. I drove it into bollards, had a couple of nudges parking. Wrecked it.

FIRST FOREIGN HOLIDAY

Benidorm, with the boys, in my teens. We had a fight on the first night with a group of twentysomething, tattooed Yorkshire lads and spent the rest of the week on the run from them. Stayed in an awful hotel, danced, tried to chat up girls and got sick every night on Blue Curaçao. Brilliant.

FIRST COUNTY CHAMPIONSHIP WICKET

Jack Richards of Surrey on a flat one at Uxbridge in July 1986 in my third first-class match. Some would say it was a short delivery. I say I did Jack in the flight. He tried to force the ball through the offside of the back foot, but it got a bit quick on him, caught the edge and flipped off our wicketkeeper Paul Downton's gloves to Roland Butcher at first slip. Butch stuck out a mitt and took a great reaction catch, the likes of which I'd not seen before in Second XI cricket, let alone schoolboy or club games. Butch was one of the best slip fielders I've ever seen. That catch was the first realisation for me that I'd stepped up a level.

FIRST TEST WICKET

Greg Matthews – full toss, hit it straight down Eddie Hemmings' neck at long on – at the SCG, in my second Test match in January 1991. It should have been David Boon in my debut Test when I was denied a perfectly good wicket by a Pom-phobic umpire, but that's a story for later.

FIRST BALL FACED IN COUNTY CRICKET

At New Road on 4 June 1986, Neal Radford bowling for Worcester. My attempt to ask the umpire for the guard of 'Middle, please' came out as a high-pitched squeak, and my teammates told me later that they could see my helmet shaking on top of my head as Neal ran in to bowl. I was in a state of such panic I have no recollection of the delivery, except that it didn't bowl me and long after the ball whistled past I remained stuck in the shot I had attempted. It took the kind words of David Smith, their tough opening bat who was fielding at short leg, to break my trance-like state: 'Who is this ****ing muppet?'

TUFFERS' FIRST XI (PLUS A TWELFTH MAN)

FIRST COUNTY CHAMPIONSHIP CATCH

Lancashire v Middlesex, Old Trafford, 7 June 1986: Clive Lloyd, caught Philip Tufnell, bowled Simon Hughes. The power-hitting West Indian captain smacked it in my direction at deep mid-off. I came running in, realising too late that the ball was really travelling. Not wanting to damage my delicate spinning fingers, I kind of took the ball into my gut, which was padded by two Middlesex jumpers, cradled the ball between my stomach and arms, and fell back as if I'd been shot. I'm not sure I even got a hand on it.

FIRST SINGLE BOUGHT

I'm ashamed to admit it, but I'm pretty sure it was 'I'm The Leader of the Gang' by glam-rocking paedophile Gary Glitter.

PART ONE

A LUNATIC WHO COULDN'T BAT AND COULDN'T FIELD: TALES FROM MY GLORIOUS CAREER

CHAPTER I

PHIL VERSUS LIFE (PART 1)

WINTER TALES

When I was taken on by Middlesex in the spring of 1984 to work on the groundstaff and play Second XI cricket, I was earning £60 a week. In 1986 I graduated to the full-time staff and a grand-a-month salary. Not bad for a twenty-year-old at the time. But it was pro rata and in those days we only got six-month contracts.

Nowadays, county players are paid enough not to have to work between seasons. In return they are expected to keep fit in the off-season and pre-season training starts earlier. It's virtually a full-time job. For me, at the end of the season, it was bye-bye and see you again in six months. Although I tried to save up a bit of money to last me, this meant I had to find work to make a few quid during the winter.

It was a horrible time really, because it was cold and miserable, and I still had no idea whether or not I would make it as a cricketer. And it's very lucky that I did make it, because during those two or three winters of uncertainty, I didn't bother putting anything in place for an alternative career. I wasn't phoning up AXA and asking if I could come in and make the tea and learn how to sell life insurance.

I just floated around doing a few bits and pieces. I did a bit of work for my dad at his silversmith's in North London, until he decided to sell the business. He also got me some silversmithing work down at Hatton Garden with his mate.

I had another sideline driving for the local minicab firm, using my Cortina or the family Volvo. I didn't enjoy it too much and was easily distracted. I'd start the day, get two or three fares, and then see a couple of mates sitting outside The White Hart, pull up, and that would be the day gone.

So I then turned my hand to a bit of building work. Two of my mates were builders, painters and decorators. I was responsible for knocking up the plaster. With plastering it's very important to get the mix right, something I wasn't very good at.

On one job, me and my mate had to render the side of this big factory. A huge wall, so you do it in patches. I'm mixing, he's up the ladder plastering away.

I'm saying to myself: 'What is it, three shovels of cement or four, two of sand? Yeah . . .'

By the time I get to the next batch, I've forgotten what I did before, and it becomes a lottery.

It's only when the plaster dries and we step back and look that we see that every patch is a different colour. The wall looks like a bloody chessboard.

'Phil, I'm not sure you're cut out for this, mate . . .'

Even if you overlooked my plaster-making inconsistency, the job wasn't for me. Yes, I was working with my mates, we had a laugh, and I could nick myself a few quid to pay for my keep and a few drinks in the pub, but it was proper hard work. A lot of freezing cold early mornings, hands freezing to scaffold poles. I soon switched on to the fact I'd better put some effort into my cricket.

PHIL VERSUS LIFE (PART I)

Thankfully, in the winter of 1986 Middlesex brokered a deal for me to play for six months in Australia with Queensland University. That was great for me. Flying halfway round the world meant I really had to stand on my own two feet. I was given a few quid to live on – nothing massive, but enough to get by. I had to get my own food, cook, clean, get myself ready on time. Grow up, in other words, which I did to some extent.

I found myself playing fiercely competitive First Grade cricket, which is just below Sheffield Shield cricket level. We had four or five cricketers in our side who'd played Shield cricket, lost a bit of form and come down to First Grade, so it was a very good standard. Proper cricket on flat pitches against big Aussie men. We won a one-day tournament and I returned to Blighty a much tougher cricketer.

I came back more appreciative of the facilities in English cricket, too. My first match in Oz had been played on what turned out to be a rugby pitch in the middle of nowhere. And when we arrived there, I was somewhat surprised when everyone headed out to the middle with their cricket bags and started undressing. There was no pavilion, so it was the furthest point from the spectators and the nearest the players could get to privacy to get changed!

TROUBLE AND STRIFE AND A STARTLED LAMB

I met my first wife, Alison, while strolling around the back of the stands during the lunch break of a Test match at Lord's. As a member of the groundstaff, I was on duty helping to operate scorebox number two, and I invited her up to assess my scoring skills (how could a girl refuse?).

By the spring of 1986, we're living together in Sidcup, South London, and Alison has brought a level of domesticity to my previously chaotic lifestyle. However, if there's one thing pretty certain for a professional cricketer, it's that during the season you are going to be busy at weekends, playing matches and the like – after all, it is what you're being paid to do – and Alison cannot seem to grasp this concept.

As the first weekend of the new season comes around, she informs me that we will be going shopping for a fridge on Saturday. No ifs or buts, it's happening. There isn't a Middlesex second-team match, but I'm expected for net practice at Lord's in the morning with the first team, who are playing that day, followed by a match in the afternoon for my club, Southgate. Consequently, I'm in a bit of a pickle.

I hatch a scheme. I'll ring up the Southgate skipper, Micky Dunn, on Friday evening and tell him that I've come down with a virus and, unfortunately, will not be able to play. Then I'll go in and do the Middlesex first-team net session, leave around half eleven when their match is under way pretending that I am heading for the Southgate match, but actually go and meet Alison and buy the bloody fridge.

I call Micky. He accepts my story. Everything is going according to plan. The next day I roll up for training bright as a button. Don Bennett greets me

'Hello, Tuffers,' he says. 'Have you got a game for Southgate today?'

'Oh yes, Don. Big match. Top of the table. Really up for it.'

'Good luck, then. See you next week.'

Working like a charm. Clever me.

Once I've completed my net duties, I get changed, jump into my car and head for the North Gate. I'm about fifty yards away when I notice a familiar figure legging it towards the same exit. Bloody hell, it's Don. I've been rumbled.

In a state of panic, my only thought is escape. I kick the accelerator in a bid to make it through the gate before he can cut me off. But Don is more spritely than I thought for an old fella.

PHIL VERSUS LIFE (PART I)

With no thought for his personal safety, he throws himself across the bonnet shouting, 'Stop the ****ing car! Stop the ****ing car!' as I slam on the brakes and come to a skidding halt.

'Right. Get out of that car. Now!'

I'm shaking with fear. Don's face is purple with rage and the effort of chasing me down.

'Would you like to tell me exactly what the **** you think you are doing?'

'Er, I'm off to play for Southgate,' I bleat weakly.

'Really? In that case, who was that ringing me up last night and impersonating Micky Dunn telling me that you'd cried off? Let's start again: where the **** do you think you are going?'

I stammer something about feeling ill yesterday, but now feeling a bit better, before revealing the ludicrous truth: 'Er, well, Don, look, you see, my missus, well, she, er, she says, er, I've got to go with her to buy a fridge.'

Don pauses to take in what this supposed wannabe first-team player is saying to him.

'Look here, son. I don't give a **** about your fridge. Park that car. You are coming with me.'

With my car reparked, I'm then dragged forcibly by the ear back into the pavilion where Don informs me that I have now become Middlesex's twelfth man for the day.

'And if you ever lie to me again, you little bastard, your feet will not touch the floor.'

When I arrive home eight hours later than agreed, Alison gives me my second bollocking of the day. However, during the course of the ear-bashing I think I make it clear that Saturdays are just not great for me to do domestic stuff. Wrong.

A few months later, we're discussing plans to get married. And, yep, you guessed it, Alison is dead set on a summer Saturday wedding: 'I don't give a toss what Middlesex think. They're saying that I can't get married on a Saturday? You ****ing what? Come on, Phil, we're going down to the Middlesex office to sort this. Now.'

Alison is a strong woman, both in mind and body, and there's no stopping her.

Tim Lamb, a former Oxford University boy, then Middlesex's club secretary and the future chief executive of the ECB, doesn't know what's hit him when Alison barges into his office with me skulking in her slipstream.

'What's all this about I can't get married on a Saturday?' she demands, banging her fist on the table. She then leans across the desk, grabs the startled Lamb by his old-school tie, pulls him towards her and repeats the question.

With his face turning purple from lack of oxygen, Tim is initially unable to offer anything more than a gurgle in response. It is only once I've wrestled my wife-to-be off him that he can patiently explain why a Saturday marriage during the season is rather inconvenient. He suggests the first Saturday after the season as an alternative. I cringe at the expected explosion, but amazingly, Alison agrees.

So we get married on the Saturday endorsed by Tim Lamb and live happily ever after . . .

DUMBEST AND DUMBER

. . . Well, we didn't get divorced for three whole years anyway. Which, looking back, was quite a long time given our immaturity, Alison's total lack of respect for the requirements of being a cricketer and, I'm not proud to say, my extra-marital shenanigans.

My big mate at Middlesex coming up was Jamie Sykes, a talented off-spinner and lower middle-order batsman, and also a bit of lunatic like me. Put us together and the potential for trouble was limitless.

Jamie is an East London boy and one evening midway through the 1988 season, we set ourselves the target of drinking in every one of the pubs along the Mile End Road. It's a very long road. After midnight, we finally give up the impossible dream, but we have met a couple of excitable young ladies during our plucky quest.

Stupidly, thinking I'm not over the limit because we had pie and chips earlier to line the stomach, we all pile into my motor and start the journey home. Jamie claims to know the East End like the back of his hand, but, unfortunately, it becomes apparent that he doesn't know jack about the part we're in. Tired, emotional and totally confused, we end up doing lap after lap of the same area.

At about 3 a.m. I'm at the wheel when I spot a police car coming towards us. I try to slow down and act naturally, but achieve nigh on an emergency stop instead. The occupants of the police car take a good look inside our almost stationary car and carry on. For a few seconds, I think we might have got away with it, then I look in my wing mirror and see the police car U-turning.

Jamie then has the dumbest idea: 'Put your foot down. We're going to lose them!'

Dumber, I do it.

The combination of my driving skills and Jamie's navigation – left, right . . . oh, it's a dead end – means the car chase is concluded within approximately thirty seconds.

Leaving the two girls screaming in the back seat, Jamie and I leap out of the car and start running, me pausing only to grab the keys from the ignition and throw them as far as I can (nope, me neither).

Laughing hysterically in our pissed state, we find ourselves running from the law through an industrial estate, jumping over walls and gates as we go. It is only after a few minutes, halfway up an eight-foot wall, with a WPC and a posse of people in their civvies closing in on us, that Jamie has a revelation: 'Hold on a minute. What am I running for? I was the passenger.'

He drops down, holds up his hands and calls out: 'Fair cop.'

Too late to surrender myself, I'm still clinging (cat-like, you might say) to the top of the wall, as a WPC beats me around the ankles with a truncheon. I'm dragged down, pinned on the ground and cuffed. Out with the breathalyser and we're under arrest.

It turns out the plain-clothes policemen were so quickly on the scene because there's been a spate of warehouse robberies in the area, but they soon establish that we are idiots rather than professional criminals.

We spend the rest of the night in a cell at Poplar nick in the company of two winos. At one stage, it seems likely I may be charged with carrying an offensive weapon and, understandably, they take some persuading that the cricket bat in the car boot is a tool of my trade (many of my Middlesex teammates might not have backed me on that one either).

I'm released at 6.30 a.m. Time to go home. Except I can't. It takes me three hours retracing my steps to find my car keys.

When I finally slink in through the front door, an irate Alison has news for me. Her father, a policeman, has phoned. News does travel fast.

I end up going to court and being banned for a year from driving. Thankfully, I hadn't caused an accident with my stupidity. Lesson learned.

For the next year, I regret it even more every time Mike Gatting drops me off on the North Circular after a match or training with my coffin to carry and two buses still to catch to get home.

CAUGHT CATNAPPING

In my youth, it was a delicate balance to maintain the standards expected of a professional cricketer alongside my hectic social life. Sometimes I got it very wrong.

August 1988. We're up in Headingley for a Championship match. Our skipper Mike Gatting has asked us to be out on the pitch for training at half past nine. After a late night, I run out at quarter to ten, hair everywhere, kit half on half off, and apologising profusely to Gatt.

He goes to do the toss and when he gets back to the dressing room, he breaks the news that I'm not playing.

'Oh, what do you mean, Gatt? Come on.'

'Phil, I told you, if you turned up late this time, you weren't going to play.'

Gatt has a rule: if you turn up late once, you get a warning. Twice and you're out of the side. And this is not my first offence.

Although he's right and my preparation hasn't been ideal, I always want to play. I'm pushing for an England place now and I don't want to miss out.

Annoyed and admittedly a bit knackered, when the boys take the field I find a quiet corner in the dressing room and curl up for a nap.

It's pretty cold at Headingley, but I'm told later that the number of extra sweaters requested from the dressing room during that morning was more due to the boys trying to get me running around for a laugh. I'm totally oblivious to this, though, as I'm fast asleep through the entire session. Meanwhile, a disgruntled Don Bennett is forced to take on twelfth-man duties instead, fetching drinks and sweaters for fielders.

At lunchtime, as I awaken from my slumbers, I'm confronted by Gatt.

'What're you doing? You're supposed to be twelfth man. Why's Don running out with jumpers?'

I don't have a very good answer to that one.

'Right, that's it,' he says. 'Disappear. I don't want you here. It's ridiculous.' Gatt is furious.

'Can I borrow one of the lads' cars, then?' (I didn't bring mine up to Leeds.)

'No! Get a ****ing train!'

'How will I get to the station?'

'Get a ****ing cab! This is a punishment, Philip. Get your own cab, your own train and give me a call in seven days' time if you want to play, because at the moment it doesn't seem like it.'

Turning up late, falling asleep for an entire session and then asking the captain who's sending me home in disgrace if I can borrow a car. Not my finest day and it earned me another bollocking and a fine from the club committee.

At least one good thing came of it, though – after that, I would forever be known as 'The Cat'.

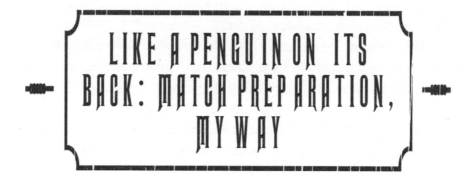

CHAPTER 2

LIKE A PENGUIN ON ITS BACK: MATCH PREPARATION, MY WAY

PUKING IN EALING...

Nowadays, international and county players are on contracts which pay sufficient that they don't have to do other jobs in winter. In return they are expected to keep fit all year round. In the early years of my career, it was somewhat less professional. We were on six-month contracts and, like most players then, I didn't do any exercise in the off-season. Absolutely nothing. Although by the time I returned to the club my darts-throwing/pool-cue-wielding/pint-lifting left elbow was nicely oiled.

Luckily, I've always been quite a skinny fella; a bit flat-footed, but light on my feet. And as a kid and teenager, I'd been very active, played a lot of sport, so I had that basic fitness that just about got me through.

When I first started at Middlesex, Graham Barlow took charge of pre-season fitness training, by virtue of the fact that he was our fittest player. We didn't have any sort of specialist coaches working with us or technical data to refer to. We used to do pre-season training in Ealing, in a gym off Hanger Lane, next to Barclays Bank. In this windowless, cheerless box marked out with a badminton court, we did loads of shuttle runs punctuated by bunny hops, press-ups, sit-ups, star jumps – old school exercises. Run, run, bunny hops, star jumps, breather, run, twenty press-ups, run, sit-ups, run, run, run . . . Repeat to fade.

My overriding memory of pre-season training is of mass puking. Especially on the first day back. There was a push-bar fire-exit door in the corner of the gym and every five or ten minutes you'd hear it creak open, then: 'Bleeearrggghhh!'

Our reward for throwing our guts up might be a nice little game of five-a-side football before stopping for a nutritious lunch of sandwiches and crisps.

In the afternoon we might do a weights circuit, but more often we'd go on the dreaded five-mile run around Ealing, which is quite hilly. Horrible – just like the old secondary school cross-country run. And, of course, just like at school, I used to skive it. Me and Jamie Sykes or Neil MacLaurin (son of future ECB chairman Lord MacLaurin) would hide, cut across to the end of the route, splash a bit of water on our faces and T-shirts to look like we were sweating, and jump out from behind a fence after the leading group of runners had gone past.

. . . AND PORTUGAL

We raised our game when a ten-day stint of warm-weather training in Portugal was introduced as part of our pre-season preparations. Well, that was the theory. One year – 1994, I think it was – we arrived in the afternoon, and immediately embarked on an epic drinking session that went on well into the night.

I'm still a bit lashed when I come down for breakfast, but manage to force down some scrambled egg on toast and a pint of orange juice before practice. The coaches want us to do some middle practice, but when we get out to the pitch, the astroturf wicket is a bit dewy and too dangerous for the seamers to risk running on.

'Tuffers, do you mind bowling the first few overs?'

This wasn't part of the plan; I was hoping to ease myself gently into training down at third man. But no worries, should be okay if I take it easy.

First ball, I rock up, slip on the greasy top and land awkwardly on my right hand. I look down and three of the fingers on my right hand are hanging off at odd angles. Argh!

Our physio, Simon 'Shep' Shepherd, runs onto the pitch to help. Unfortunately for me, I'd had my accident just as he was applying his suncream for the day, so his hands slip off when he attempts to relocate my digits, which only increases the volume of my screams.

He wraps his hand in his shirt and manages to put them back at the second time of asking, but the feeling of the fingers popping into place proves too much for my dicky stomach.

Suddenly, I can feel the bile rising, I break away from Shep and vomit violently. With a big puddle of orangey-yellow chunder just back of a good length on the wicket, the session is called off after one ball, much to the delight of the rest of the boys who want to go and play golf.

My week in the sun is over before it starts. The management decide that having me out there unable to train and leading everyone astray each night might not be beneficial to the overall fitness of the squad, so I'm packed off home.

BUCHANAN OUT!

Having huffed and puffed through pre-season, we didn't like to do much physical training during the season, as the now legendary

Australian coach John Buchanan discovered when he came to coach Middlesex in 1998.

A radical cricket thinker (he once proclaimed that cricketers would soon become ambidextrous, bowling and batting left- and right-handed), John's previous form included leading the Queensland Bulls to two Sheffield Shield titles – the one in 1994/95 was the first in their history – and two triumphs in Australia's major domestic one-day tournament, then known as the Mercantile Mutual Cup.

We got rid of him within a year.

The county cricket schedule with one-dayers and four-day Championship matches meant you often only had one day spare between games. But rather than let us have that time off at home to recuperate, John decided we should travel to the games that day, so we could have a long training session at the ground followed by a proper meeting at the hotel to discuss tactics.

We'd all be sitting there, moaning about him, saying: '**** that, I want my day off.'

Our club had recruited one of the best coaches in the world, who would go on to steer the Australian national team to unprecedented success, and all we could do was bitch about his methods. It was like Jose Mourinho coming in as manager at a football club, and the players going: 'Pah, what does he know?'

Funnily enough, by the end of his season with us, John and I got on all right. I could see where he was coming from and I think he could see that there was some logic in my arguments, too. The match schedule in the English county season is much more congested than on the Australian domestic scene, so that you are just constantly knackered and you need all the rest you can get. And I didn't feel the need to sit down the night before the match and discuss how to get out Derbyshire's top six when we'd got them out cheaply a million times before.

John had a Plan A, B and C for every situation, but we didn't buy into his ideas, and he headed back to his home country to oversee probably the greatest Test team ever.

THE EVOLUTION OF GUS

We used to have to drive ourselves to away matches; all we did was drive up and down the country. You might be up in, say, Yorkshire for a week, so you needed some wheels to get around.

It was quite normal for me to bowl 40 overs on a sizzling hot day at the end of a four-day game, have a shower, a quick pint of lager, then get in my car with a couple of teammates and drive for four-and-a-half hours home. We used to swap driving duties about a bit but how there weren't more pile-ups involving cricketers on the motorways of Britain I don't know, because we would all be absolutely shattered.

However, if we were staying over, in my younger days, alongside other of the more, um, spirited boys, we might ignore the distress signals from our bodies and head to the local discotheque. There we'd indulge in a couple of beers, which seemed to lubricate the joints enough to do some bad dancing, only to wake up as stiff as a board the next day: 'Oh my God, I can't move my bloody legs!'

The stiffness could be agony. It was bad enough for me as a spinner tiptoeing in to bowl off a few paces, but I've roomed with seamers Gus Fraser, Devon Malcolm and David 'Syd' Lawrence and virtually had to peel them out of bed in the morning.

Gus looked like he was knackered every ball he bowled in his life, but somehow he would grind through long spells day in, day out. In the morning, I'd hear him mumble: 'Tuffers, can you run a bath for us, please?' I'd do that and then watch as Gus winced and hobbled his way to the bathroom. Every morning it was like the evolution of man as, via a soak in a hot bath, his crumpled body gradually straightened up. Then he'd go out and do it all again.

Weirdly, although it was painful, I actually seemed to bowl a bit better when I felt stiff. It made me stand taller and kind of 'hold me' in my action.

In the absence of warm-downs, ice baths and the knowledge that modern coaches and players have about recovery, the go-to guy among the backroom staff was the physio. But earlier in my career, getting a rubdown from the club physio to ease aches and pains was almost impossible. If you asked, the response would usually be a rather sniffy: 'Excuse me, I'm a physio, not a masseur. If you've got a strain or pull, I'll treat you, but I don't do rubdowns.' Even though that was exactly what you needed.

Instead, we mostly relied on daily handouts of painkillers to get the stiffness out. There was the big pink one, which was the Brufen. We'd have Voltarol.

'Pink and a green one for you today, Frase. One for you, Norman.'

Being true professionals, we also used to ask the physio for Brufens before a night out, so the headache wouldn't be so bad the morning after!

Later, with England, there would be two or three masseurs available who would be constantly working to loosen the boys up, leaving the physio clear to deal with injuries. When Shep came in as Middlesex physio, he brought in 'rubbers' as part of our regular routine, too, because he could see that after a few matches we were falling apart. He also craftily reduced our painkiller consumption. When I complained about some ache or other, he'd give me a pill, telling me it was the strongest painkiller available.

'Don't tell anyone, Tuffers. I don't normally give these out.'

'No worries, thanks, Shep.'

So I'd take this tablet and an hour or two later, I usually felt much better.

It's only recently he told me that they were either vitamin C or folic acid tablets, better known for their health benefits for pregnant women. He just gave me them to stop me bugging him!

LIKE A PENGUIN ON ITS BACK: MATCH PREPARATION, MY WAY

GOOD INTENTIONS

Physical training was never really my bag. However, on my debut Ashes tour, having glimpsed the life of an international Test cricketer – staying in beautiful hotels, going to glamorous parties, etc. – I did get motivated to work out. Briefly.

One day in Adelaide I joined my mate Gus Fraser for a bit of extra training – some running and weights – before going up to the roof of our hotel where there was a Jacuzzi, with a magnificent view across South Adelaide towards the cricket ground.

We're sitting there for half an hour chatting away while the tiredness bubbles out of our bodies. It's my first tour, Gus' second. This is the life.

I say to Frase: 'I want to be doing this for the next ten or fifteen years, and I'm going to do whatever I can to make sure I do.'

As Gus is always quick to remind me, I was not seen in the gym again for the rest of the tour.

FITNESS FREAKS XI

Adam Hollioake
Graeme Hick
Alec Stewart
Graham Gooch
Jack Russell
Chris Lewis
David 'Syd' Lawrence
Ronnie Irani
Graham Barlow
Justin Langer
Mike Gatting

Adam Hollioake

A fitness fanatic. You'd see 'Smokes' heading to the gym wherever we stayed, running on beaches, doing chin-ups from tree branches. A good party boy, too, but even when he was out with us in a bar, he might suddenly drop and give you twenty push-ups.

'What are you doing?'

'Just fancied squeezing out a quick twenty.'

Not only was Smokes fitness-mad and strong as a bull, he was also tough. During the 1998 West Indies tour, he dislocated his shoulder in a warm-up game against West Indies 'A' and still played in the First Test, which I'm not sure is medically possible.

His party trick was to invite people to punch him in the stomach as hard as they could. I had a go and it hurt. Me.

Graeme Hick

A big fellow and super-fit. Graeme earned his nickname 'Arnie', as in Arnold Schwarzenegger, after we witnessed him doing his own impromptu fitness session at Pukekara Park, a beautiful ground in New Plymouth, on England's 1992 tour of New Zealand.

At Pukekara Park, spectators sit on big man-made steps cut into huge grass mounds surrounding the pitch. I remember us knackered at the end of a day's cricket going for a warm-down jog around the boundary. By halfway, Ian Botham, who had just joined up with the tour party ('Beefy' had been delayed by recording *A Question of Sport* or something), said '**** this' and we all decided we would be better off having a sit down. Apart from Hicky, that is. Next thing we know, we can see him striding up these big steps to the top of the grass 'stand' and hear his grunts of effort echoing round the now empty ground. And once he got to the top, he jogged down and did it all again and again. Relentless, like the Terminator.

LIKE A PENGUIN ON ITS BACK: MATCH PREPARATION, MY WAY

Alec Stewart

The ultimate pro. Absolutely fit as a fiddle. He loved his training and took pride in his appearance. Stewie was the sort of bloke who if you roomed with him, you had to get in the bathroom first because if you didn't you'd find it filled with all his moisturisers and pampering products.

Graham Gooch

Goochy loved to run. You didn't see him do much weight training (he probably had enough upper-body exercise carrying that heavy bat of his), but I think he ran so much to increase his endurance for long innings. He'd run whenever he could on top of our normal training and all the extra work took its toll sometimes. On one tour, Beefy banned him from running because he kept falling asleep at the bar!

Goochy was not a natural runner; in fact, it is probably the exercise his body is the least suited to. But what he lacked in style he made up for in bloody-minded determination and stamina. Many's the time I'd be wandering round a town somewhere and see Goochy staggering past – 'All right, Skip!' He looked like he was on his last legs, but he could keep going for mile after mile.

Jack Russell

Jack was super-fit, ran every day. We called him 'The Beeswing', speculating that his all-action style on the pitch might translate to the bedroom!

His preparation for the West Indies tour was as extreme as it comes. As acclimatisation training, he used to go in the sauna fully kitted up – whites, boots, thick socks, pads, jockstrap, shirt, short-sleeve jumper . . . the lot. The thing is I don't think Jack had a sauna at home so he must have rolled up at his local gym looking like that. Mental.

Chris Lewis

Possibly the first real athlete to play for England – his nickname was 'Carl' after the legendary American Olympic athlete Carl Lewis. Chrissy had an incredible physique and wasn't afraid to show it off. Unsurprisingly, he holds the distinction of being the first cricketer to pose naked for *Playgirl* magazine.

David 'Syd' Lawrence

Not so much a fitness fanatic, just a massive, powerful unit. If there was ever someone you'd want on your side in a punch-up, it was Syd – in fact, he used to spar with professional heavyweight boxers. If ever I got into sticky situations on nights out, you'd often hear me cry 'Sydddd!' and anyone bothering me would immediately back off when they saw him approaching.

We called him 'Hissing Syd' for the noise that he made as he approached the crease on his run-up, but it was more like a steam train – choo-choo-choo-choo – before this explosion of whirling arms and legs at the crease. Standing at the non-striker's end could put the fear of God into you.

Ronnie Irani

I was rooming with Ronnie in Bulawayo on his first tour. Half asleep on my bed one afternoon I heard him phone down for room service.

'Can you send me up four buckets of ice, please.'

I'm thinking, 'Wahey, party tonight!'

When they arrive, he starts pouring the cubes into the bath.

'Are you going to put all the booze in the bath then?' I say.

'No, I'm getting in it!'

'You ****in' what?'

'Ice bath, Tuffers.'

That was my first introduction to the modern and very effective method for warding off stiffness and strains.

Ronnie was another bloke who liked a party, but he also enjoyed keeping fit. Perhaps it was Goochy's influence at Essex.

I roomed with him on another England warm-weather training camp in Portugal, and while I'd be getting up in the morning moaning about the prospect of training, Ronnie couldn't wait.

'You've got to love it, Tuffers. You're being paid to get fit. Get up at eight o'clock and love it.'

'I hate it.'

'You've got to enjoy running up that sand dune. I love it. Love it.'

A fantastic attitude . . . and it almost rubbed off on me. Almost.

Ronnie's knees are buggered now, mind. Luckily, he's got a nice job sitting down presenting one of the most popular radio shows around.

Graham Barlow

Another fitness fanatic who led pre-season training at Middlesex back in the day as I said before. The measure of his fitness is that while the rest of us all threw up, he never did.

Justin Langer

Justin, who captained Middlesex in 2000, is a black belt in Zen Do Kai, and martial arts or boxing were part of his daily fitness regime. I'm a lover not a fighter, so I never joined in.

Mike Gatting

I'm going completely left-field here, but despite appearances, Gatt was one of the fittest people I played with. He ate well, but he worked on fitness, too. He couldn't do bleep tests, he couldn't do sprints, but he could knock anyone off a squash court, pedal for hours on an exercise bike, and run for miles – slowly, but just kept going.

We used to call him 'The Bread Van'. He was like a little cube. He knew he only had little legs and he was a little fat man, naturally, but he had great stamina and was as strong as you like – forearms like hams. Like a prop forward. You wouldn't want to run into Gatt. You would bounce off. Proper solid physique.

TRAIN LIKE AN OLYMPIAN (SORT OF)

I once went with the England team for warm-weather training at a complex in Lanzarote, in preparation for the 1996/97 winter tour of Zimbabwe and New Zealand (which, incidentally, was the longest tour I ever went on, lasting six months including this little jaunt). We walk out first day, wearing ill-fitting T-shirts and shorts. There's Goochy, Gatt – quite old fellas by then, bit of a gut on them. I'm smoking a fag, moaning to Gatt about the breakfast at the hotel: 'Worst scrambled egg I've ever had.'

The contrast between our ramshackle crew and the real athletes training there could not be greater – Olympic pole vaulters, hurdlers and sprinters, ripped physiques, doing proper stretches, leaping about with balletic grace. All of them take a break to watch our aerobics sessions, though. It's the first time I've ever known us to do aerobics with England and it becomes the must-see spectacle. We've got no rhythm whatsoever, we're stumbling around, bumping into each other. Quality viewing. All these athletes are just shaking their heads and laughing at us.

We also do a mini-triathlon. There's a few bets flying about and, believe it or not, quite a bit of money going on a Tufnell win. Probably because I'm paired with the fittest player we've got, 'A' team player Dougie Brown. We all have to do a swim and then laps of running and cycling. Dougie overtakes me running when I'm on the bike! I'm only saved when I realise there's a good spot to thumb lifts from passing tourists. Get in, lie down on the back seat and say, 'Drive, drive!' Take at least half a mile off a lap that way. Despite my best, um, efforts, we still come dead last. Dougie is waiting for me as I cross the finishing line pushing my bike.

LIKE A PENGUIN ON ITS BACK: MATCH PREPARATION, MY WAY

On the plus side, there's a nightclub at our resort in Lanzarote, so after a hard day's embarrassment in front of the athletes, we can go and get smashed there.

Madness, but it was just a different game back then: get drunk, up at seven the next morning with a pounding head, and sweat it out in training. No doctors would recommend it, but in a strange way, it hardened you up.

During a match, the bowlers went out when the batters had to bat the next day, and the batters could go out when a fielding day was coming up. However, as a slow left-armer who couldn't bat or field, possibly the laziest role in a cricket team, I felt obliged to go out with the batters too on occasions . . . to give them advice on how to play the opposition's bowlers, of course.

As a top player in those days, you were expected to prepare yourself. There was no support or guidance. It was almost as though, if you did ask for assistance, it would be seen as a sign of weakness. Nowadays, it's all 'Team England', we'll tell you what's good for you. The attitude then was, 'You're an England international, you should know yourself what to do.' The problem was, as a young fella, who'd got into the England team while regularly going on the piss, I thought that was best for me!

So, yes, when I was young, I did take a liberty or two, but don't get me wrong, as I got older, I became more sensible without going to extremes. I tried going to my hotel room at half past nine, but I'd end up staring at the ceiling till half past midnight, wasting mental energy thinking about the enormity of the task the next day. If I went out for a meal, had a glass of wine or two, a chat about cricket and got back to my room by eleven, that way, I still got a good night's sleep.

'PENGUINING' FOR INSPIRATION

During my playing career, it's fair to say that I wasn't known for being one of cricket's greatest thinkers. And if people had an image of my nocturnal activities, it was more likely to involve drinking and carousing than sitting around discussing tactics. Ironic, then, that I believe my success as a bowler was mainly due to intense mental preparation and visualisation for games. And I did some of my most effective work late at night just before I fell asleep. In fact, I think I was even better when I was asleep. No, really – stay with me on this . . .

Although I might not have been the most disciplined of players when it came to physical training, I was always very intense when it came to focusing on my primary role in the team as a wicket-taking spinner. Being a slow left-armer with just three stock deliveries, plus variations on the theme, I relied on outwitting batsmen to get them out, and this is where my night-time, one-man brainstorming sessions came in.

I believe that one of the main reasons I became a cricketer in the first place was that as a kid I used to go to sleep thinking about how I was going to bowl the following day. My mind was buzzing and these thoughts seemed to carry through into my dreams. By the time I came to bowl the next day, everything seemed clear as a bell in my head. I'd done all the work when I was asleep.

As a pro cricketer, I just carried on doing it. I used to lie there, like a penguin on its back, shuffling my arms about under the covers, as I tried to visualise how I might bowl, work out field placings and how the batsmen I'd be up against might play me. How does he shape up to play a good-length ball? If it's outside off stump, does he look to sweep? Does he tend to play pad or bat first? That sort of thing.

When I shared a room with someone for the first time on away trips, they could be a bit confused about what I was up to.

'Do you mind? I'm trying to get some sleep.'

'Sorry, mate – I'm not actually knocking one off the stump, I'm trying to work out how to get Mark Waugh out!'

Maybe all the thought that went into my bowling is why, even now, I can visualise just about every one of the 1,057 wickets I took in first-class cricket (and quite a few from my youth cricket days). It's strange, because I haven't got the best memory in other ways, but if you ask me about the four wickets I took when we beat West Indies at the Kensington Oval, Bridgetown, in 1994, for the first time in years, I can reel them off:

Shiv Chanderpaul – little arm ball, caught by Ramps off the outside edge.

Keith Arthurton – bowled him trying to leave one outside leg stump. Got the ball to turn out of the rough and he dragged it on.

Dessie Haynes – bat/pad, caught at silly point. As I appealed, the West Indian umpire didn't raise his finger and, from experience of home umpires, I feared the worst, but when I turned round Des had walked. Respect due. Des was a proper sportsman.

Winston Benjamin – big slog, caught at deep mid-off by Alec Stewart.

So there you go. No cricket fan's ever accused me of being a thinker before, but the truth is out. And now, when I die and the MCC commission a statue of me to go outside Lord's (stop sniggering at the back), rather than going for an obvious pose like me unsuccessfully appealing for lbw for the millionth time, I trust I shall be immortalised under the bed covers, like a penguin on its back. It'll be like cricket's answer to Rodin's 'The Thinker!'

BRAINIAC XI

Mike Atherton
Andrew Strauss
Simon Hughes
Mike Gatting
Nasser Hussain
Ed Smith
Derek Pringle
Imran Khan
Phil Edmonds
Frances Edmonds
Keith Fletcher

Mike Atherton

A Cambridge University graduate, Athers soon gained the nickname of 'FEC', as in 'Future England Captain' although his Lancashire teammates jovially suggested an alternative meaning: '****ing Educated ****'.

I must have been a nightmare for him when he achieved his destiny and became skipper of the national team. Before he took the job, I roomed with him. One time a little party was in full swing in the lounge area of the hotel suite we were sharing. Drinking, carousing and girls.

Then I hear a noise, look round and there's Athers sitting up in bed reading, oblivious to the debauchery.

'All right, Mike. Sorry about the noise, mate. What're you reading?'

He gives me a brief synopsis of the weighty tome, which goes quite a way over my head. Seeing my blank expression, he says kindly: 'Might be a few too many long words for you, Tuffers.'

It's a defining moment in what will be a long, tempestuous, but mutually understanding relationship.

LIKE A PENGUIN ON ITS BACK: MATCH PREPARATION, MY WAY

Andrew Strauss

Ex-Radley College and Hatfield College boy and Durham University graduate. I played a year under Straussy as captain at Middlesex in 2002 when he was a mere fledgling, and he was a bit of a jazz hat – 'All right, old chap' – but very steely and a good lad with it.

Simon Hughes & Mike Gatting

Yosser and Gatt are both in the XI by virtue of the fact that they both used to do the *Daily Telegraph* crossword when we were sitting up on the balcony at Lord's and they always finished it. Impressive. I used to sit there and say, 'Gissa clue,' which they dutifully did and of course it usually went right over my head.

Nasser Hussain

Another Durham University boy. He pretended to be one of the lads, but when it came to a cricket brain, he was as sharp as they come, which he showed as a captain and now as an eloquent pundit for Sky.

He was a member of the brat pack in his younger days – him, Ramps, Thorpey were all bat-throwers when things didn't go their way – and a punchy little fighter.

Ed Smith

Nickname: 'Two Brains'. Say no more.

Derek Pringle

Huge man, brain to match. 'Suggs' (or 'Suggo', so-called because of his vague resemblance to the Madness lead singer when he wore his little glasses) was ex-Cambridge Uni.

I loved rooming with him because he taught me a lot of new words and whatever town we were staying in he always had a book on it. I'd say, 'Suggs, what are we doing today?' and he'd reel off a list of interesting places to visit.

While the other lads went to McDonald's and wandered round a clothes shop, our itinerary would involve visiting castles and museums and stopping off for lunch at a restaurant that had been reviewed well. Suggs was my personal tour guide.

Imran Khan

A man of impeccable breeding, he spoke in a very posh Oxford-educated/Pakistani accent and walked around as if he was the Prince of Pakistan. Which, essentially, he was.

Phil & Frances Edmonds

I've included Philippe Henri and his wife Frances as a double act. When I met Frances, a journalist and an author, at club functions as a youngster, she scared the living daylights out of me, because she was so clever. And Phil was a very educated Cambridge boy and had a superior bearing about him, too.

Not many people argued with Mike Brearley over tactics, but I saw Phil and him have a couple of big arguments over field placings. They were so well spoken, it was like witnessing a jolly fierce Cambridge Uni debate.

Keith Fletcher

A great thinker on the game. He started the Essex dynasty as captain and then coach, and was the brains behind the era when they vied for trophies with Middlesex.

He got a bit maligned because his slightly gnomic manner (well, his nickname was 'The Gnome') didn't play well publicly, but he was great in the dressing room. Gave players a lot of confidence.

LIKE A PENGUIN ON ITS BACK: MATCH PREPARATION, MY WAY

TAKING THE MIDDLE GROUND (BRIEFLY)

At Middlesex, we never practised on the main square at Lord's. At other clubs, they'll do a bit of practice on the centre wicket to get a feel for it. Not allowed at the Home of Cricket, though. But during his year with us, radical-thinking coach John Buchanan pushed hard to get the head honchos at the club to allow us to do it and he got his way. Things did not go according to plan.

I start off bowling to David Nash, our wicketkeeper. In matches, Nashy is always a blocker, and we like to take the mickey saying he can't get it off the square. But he likes to wind me up too, and he catches me on the wrong day today.

First ball he comes down the track and hits me straight back over my head for six.

'What you doin', Nashy? You're supposed to be playing like it's a match situation. You never do that in a match.'

'Oh, leave off, Tuffers.'

He keeps doing the same thing, though, just trying to smash me out of the park. We have a couple more verbal spats to and fro. Then he smacks me for another four, playing a shot he'd never dream of playing in a match situation. I've had enough. I kick down all three stumps at the bowler's end and storm off, effing and blinding at Nashy all the way to the Edrich Stand where I sit down, sulk, and refuse to practise any more.

I found out later that MCC Chief Executive Colonel Stephenson happened to look out of the window of his office at the precise moment I kicked the stumps out of the ground. And in my time at Middlesex, we never had another middle session at Lord's.

THE FCW

What is 'FCW' an abbreviation for? Well, just take three well-known swear words, add an 'ing' to the first two . . . Got it? And, believe me, if you'd ever had to do Duncan Fletcher's FCW fielding drill (as the players christened it), you'd have been spitting expletives yourself.

Fletcher introduced it after becoming England coach in 1999, as part of his tough new training regime. I didn't mind the extra fitness stuff, believe it or not, and I tried my best, but I don't think someone with my reputation really fitted into his vision of a highly disciplined squad. And he pushed me too far with this FCW business.

So what was the FCW? Basically, at the end of a training session, Fletch would grab one of the players and make him catch ten balls before he could go back to the dressing room. Simple. Of course there was a catch (if you'll pardon the pun).

Now, I never saw Fletch bat in his playing days, but I'm guessing he probably wasn't all that, because he batted number six. For Zimbabwe. However, he was a grandmaster with the small fielding-practice bat in his hand, boasting a Lara-like ability to hit the ball just out of reach of the fielder, seemingly at will.

As anyone who recalls his bullfrog-swallowed-a-wasps'-nest demeanour in England press conferences will testify, Fletch is not naturally one of life's smilers, but the sight of a cursing fielder sprinting and diving fruitlessly after the elusive cherry was guaranteed to make him chuckle. And the longer his little game went on, the more the fielder's tired legs burned, the less likely he was to get to the ball, and the more Fletch laughed.

During the 1999/2000 tour of South Africa, for those players lucky enough not to be nominated for the FCW, watching Fletch make his victim sweat his nuts off became a highly amusing spectacle. All through the series, I bobbed and weaved and managed to avoid getting collared by Fletch for it. Come the Fifth and final Test at Centurion Park, I wasn't even in the eleven, so I felt pretty confident that I'd got away with it. But at practice on the day of the game, as I wombled off the pitch with the boys, I got the dreaded call.

LIKE A PENGUIN ON ITS BACK: MATCH PREPARATION, MY WAY

What? Oh, FFS . . .

As Fletch grabs his beloved little bat, mitt and some balls, I can see all the other boys taking their places on the balcony of the dressing room high up in the stand to get a good view. Lined up as if they're at the cinema. Take your seats for this morning's feature presentation: Phil Does The FCW Drill.

So I say to myself, 'Okay, let's have a go.'

First three bombs go up. Boom, boom, boom – catch them all, over my shoulder. Good start. Three in the bag, seven to go.

Next one he tickles short, though, and I can't get to it. Then he lobs another one, which goes to ground.

Now I can see the boys sitting up there laughing and I know what they're saying: 'Look at Tuffers – his legs are going, his legs are going . . .' And they're right.

I feel like Fletcher's trying to humiliate me in front of everyone – my teammates, a load of English fans and the South Africans who are having a net – and the anger is starting to bubble.

If you want me to do catching practice give me a ball to catch. Don't just keep lobbing it. If you want me to do running, I'll go to the track, but this is your way of breaking the wild horse, right?

All of a sudden, I have an idea. I can see that he's got one ball in his mitt and just three balls within bending down distance. If I throw all the balls over his head, he ain't going to have no more balls, is he?

So he's hit the next one and I've gone, 'Oh, well done, just out of my way.'

'C'mon Tuffers, keep going!' he yells.

I pick up the ball and beam it in over his head. Whoosh. He's only jumped up and caught it!

'Sorry, sorry,' I say for the 'bad' throw. 'I'm tired, you're wearing me out, Fletch. You're doing a great job. Fantastic job. Really good. Really, really good.'

He hits another, and this time, my underarm flick return is perfectly judged: just beyond his reach.

So we go on like this, and soon I've got him down to his last ball. He booms one up over my head, I make the catch and without turning round, windmill the ball back over my head a country mile from where Fletch is standing. Now that pisses him off.

'I've done my ten,' I say.

'You're only on five.'

'But you ain't got no more balls.'

'Don't worry, you stay here and I'll go and get the ****ing balls.'

By now, it's degenerated into a battle of wills: you hit the ball just in front of me, which is no use to me because it's not going to happen in the game, and I'll pick it up and throw it over your head. Okay, you can keep going to get the balls, but I'll still be ****ed, because you won't hit me ones I can actually catch, so I'll keep throwing them back over your head.

I get to about seven catches before I storm off, saying, '**** you, **** your drill. I ain't bombing it. All you're trying to do is prove a point. If you wanted to get me onside, have a chat to me. Don't try to make a mug out of me.'

'Huh, I thought that would be your response,' he nods. It's almost as if he's proved his own point to himself.

So while most will remember the Fifth Test at Centurion for the infamous Hansie Cronje match-fixing scandal, and some, even, for Darren Gough playing the final day with a raking hangover after a long night at the hotel bar with golfer Ian Woosnam, to me it shall always be 'The FCW Test'.

LIKE A PENGUIN ON ITS BACK: MATCH PREPARATION, MY WAY

THINGS NOT TO SAY TO THE ENGLAND COACH, NO.1: 'I AM ALLERGIC TO TRAINING'

At the start of the following season, Middlesex put me in the Second XI for a match against the Army at the RAF ground at Vine Lane, Uxbridge, to get some overs in.

We win the toss and bat. Me being the senior pro, I take that as my signal to retire to the bar upstairs, assume the position on the sofa, get a fag on and a bacon sandwich and tune in to daytime television. Imagine my surprise when the door opens and Duncan Fletcher walks in.

I'm simultaneously stubbing out my cigarette, wiping brown sauce off my chin and turning off *Richard & Judy* while Duncan explains that he's here to discuss how the South Africa tour went. After our FCW fall-out, I guess it's a good sign that I'm still in his plans.

His first question is about training. With the benefit of hindsight, I don't think my response did me a lot of good.

'Well, Duncan, I think I may be allergic to it.'

He looks at me, bemused. 'Are you ****ing joking?'

'No, no, I'm not. I think I'm allergic to training.'

As I say it, his habitually hangdog expression droops into extreme hangdoggishness.

After that he glazes over, probably feeling that all his suspicions about me being a total waster have been confirmed. So I'm not sure he really hears my explanation, which I mean sincerely.

When I go to countries like South Africa and Australia, I get a physical reaction to the heat and the grass. I get a bit of eczma, lumps under my skin, a prickly rash up my neck and my eyes get puffy. It's so uncomfortable that I just want to get off the pitch and have a cool shower and I pop a lot of antihistamine pills for it.

I also get terrible hay fever. I had to have jabs in January/ February and boosters during the season every year for ten years

45

to allow me to play cricket, because otherwise, my eyes would be itching and nose running uncontrollably. Maybe my average daily intake of three pills accounted for the drowsiness that earned me my nickname of The Cat? With a violent allergy to grass pollen and heat, a career that involves running round for hours on grass fields, often in tropical climates, probably wasn't a great choice, but there you go.

So what I try, and fail miserably, to articulate to Fletch is that working up a sweat in the sunshine, then running, diving, catching and rolling around on the couch grass in training brings me out something rotten.

Whatever, he clearly isn't impressed. Without a word, he gets up and leaves.

There's a seventeen-month gap before he selects me again in what proves to be my final Test match, and that's only because, as Fletch tells the press, he doesn't have any other option!

CHAPTER 3

SMELLS LIKE TEAM SPIRIT

THE BENCH OF KNOWLEDGE

I could be quite a 'challenging' teammate. In my younger days, I was quite a needy character who couldn't shake off problems on my own. I really needed someone to boost my confidence, tell me I was bowling well or give me some advice that would help me get out of a rut. And it's well documented that I had more than my fair share of off-pitch issues, too. Indeed, my old Middlesex mate Gus Fraser reckons he should have got paid a bonus in recognition of his extra-curricular services as an amateur psychiatrist and relationship expert.

Gus and I got changed next to each other in a corner of the Lord's home dressing room commonly known as the 'Bench of Knowledge'. The joke was that if you wanted to know anything about cricket, you'd come over to speak to Gus, and if you wanted to know where the party was happening later, speak to me (although my ex-skipper Mike Gatting says I could also be relied upon to supply the odd pearl of cricketing wisdom when required). Anyone passing by the Bench could be forgiven for thinking it was also the unluckiest corner in world cricket as Gus and I were forever bemoaning our bad luck and the wickets that had been criminally denied us by terrible umpiring decisions.

My role as unofficial social secretary at Middlesex and with England fitted me well. Yes, all right, sometimes too well, but I think a team does need characters who can take the pressure off. That's especially true when you are away on a long tour. If you just have a load of introverts, when you have a bad result the enthusiasm can ebb away. You need some people in the dressing room who'll pep you up after a bad defeat, who'll say, 'Oh well, let's have a drink and put it behind us. Next time we'll do better.'

And I've always been a very loyal boy. I played hard for my team, for my mates. A lot of observers might have thought different when they saw me arguing with umpires and booting my cap all the way down to fine leg. That might have looked like a selfish tantrum, but the reason I was doing it was because I wanted my team to win and I hated letting the team down. I was upset because I wasn't contributing to the side. It was many years before I realised that behaving like that just created another problem for my captain to deal with. Luckily, I had some brilliant (and very forgiving) skippers.

CAPTAINS I HAVE LOVED (AND PISSED OFF)

Mike Gatting

I have a lot to thank Gatt for. He was my Middlesex captain for most of my career, and the best captain I played under. He taught me what was expected of you as a Middlesex player. He would tell me, 'As a Middlesex player, you have got the best opportunity. You're playing at Lord's, you could play for England. Don't waste your talent and the chance you've got here to fulfil it. Set your goals high and try to achieve them. Don't sod about.'

To me as a youngster, often he seemed quite harsh, but looking back I know it was for the right reasons. He had every opportunity to get rid of me. I was a nightmare and must have been a headache for him to deal with. But I think he saw that aside from having a talent for the game, I did bowl with passion for Middlesex and I bowled for Gatt himself. He saw beyond all my messing about on and off the field that I cared. Sometimes, I'd drive him around the bend – sulking, saying I wouldn't do this and that, swearing at umpires – but he always had that ability to get me back onside and wanting to play for him. I always wanted to impress him.

He was also very kind to me through my personal troubles – and there were many – even going as far as letting me stay at his house. He'd be a hard taskmaster, but when the shit did hit the fan, he was the first to say, 'What can I do to help?'

One of Gatt's greatest qualities is that he never held a grudge, no matter how big the fight we'd had on the field. He'd say I bowled shit. I'd have a go back at him even though he was right and we'd have stand-up rows, until I eventually backed down because he was the captain.

When I walked into the dressing room the next morning, he'd give me a cheerful, 'Hello, Tuffers,' as if nothing had happened.

If I bowled badly, he didn't always ram it down my throat, but if he felt I'd let myself down through not preparing properly or whatever, he would let me know in no uncertain terms. He said what he had to when it needed to be said, but it was nothing personal and once he'd done that, it was over as far as he was concerned. I know from talking to other players that that wasn't always the case in other dressing rooms – people would stop talking to each other for two weeks. The dressing room was always quite loud at Middlesex. People were encouraged to say what they thought. Not be a quiet little boy in the corner. If you had an opinion, air it. This led to some monumental arguments, but the next day was a fresh start.

For Gatt it was always about what was best for the team and I really respected him for that. Even though he was 'the Establishment',

I realised that he wanted me to do well. And he was very good fun socially, too – he didn't mind people enjoying themselves when the time was right.

Another quality which endeared him to me greatly, was his ability to marmalise opposition spinners. He was one of the best players of spin bowling I've seen – great cutter of the ball, great sweeper, would come down the pitch and smash them over the top. County spinners couldn't bowl to him. He'd murder them. He made all the competition for my England place look bad. I'd be sitting there watching, saying, 'Go on, Gatt. Kill him. Get a hundred. Get two hundred.'

And being a great player of spin, he also had a great understanding of field placings for spinners. He was a big help to me in every way.

Mark Ramprakash

Ramps was Middlesex captain from 1997 to 1999, a time of great upheaval for the club. After nineteen years as club coach, Don Bennett retired, then John Buchanan came in with a lot of new ideas for one season, which some of the old guard like me were all complaining about. He was replaced as coach by Gatt, who probably hadn't had quite enough time away from the captain's job. Middlesex was a funny old place at the time; there was a lot of politics and Ramps had to deal with that.

Gatt set very high standards, but could understand when players who weren't as good as he was weren't able to reach those standards. I think Ramps found it more difficult to tolerate players who lacked his ability – 'I want you to bowl just outside off stump on a length, so why do you keep bowling legside?' I liked playing for Ramps, but he was probably rather intimidating to some of the younger guys, because he was so good.

Ramps has a great cricketing brain, but perhaps he was better suited to the vice-captain's role, where he could pass on his knowledge but not have to be so much of a politician as is the case when you're captain. I got the impression that he didn't really enjoy that side of it.

Justin Langer

We had just one season with Justin as Middlesex captain, in 2000, but he made an impact. Another focused character, he was a winner who epitomised the Australian approach to the game. I shall always remember him for 'Eclairgate'. It happened like this.

It's a County Championship game, we've been bowled out for well under a hundred, and the opposition batting are now eating us alive in the field. They're something like 300 for 2. As tea's called, while most of the players are slowly trudging off the pitch absolutely pissed off, a couple of the younger lads who shall remain nameless are already sprinting up the pavilion steps, laughing and shoving each other out of the way. They are determined to secure their pick of the fantastic cream cakes we have for tea at Lord's.

By the time Justin walks into the dressing room, the boys are already eating and joking: 'I've got the ec-lair-airs', 'I've got the van-illa slice'.

Justin walks over, picks up the entire tray of cream cakes and bellows: 'You're never going to win ****ing anything eating cream cakes,' and throws the lot across the dressing room. There's cream, jam, chocolate dripping off the walls, and the place has gone silent. 'Right, from now on, we're not having ****ing cream cakes for tea. We were bowled out for nothing, we're getting killed out there and all you're worried about is running up the stairs to get ****ing cakes.'

He was right, of course – they didn't give a toss about the game, all they wanted was their eclair – and after that the Lord's tea consisted of a cuppa and a sandwich.

That was the difference between an Australian Test player caring about the state of the game and these kids who were treating it like amateurs. He was trying to get across, like Gatt had before to me, that this was their opportunity to do something with their lives. They should be dying for the club and all they were doing was bowling a load of shit, collecting their money and asking: 'Where's me eclair?'

Angus Fraser

My mate Gus did a couple of years as Middlesex skipper before his retirement in 2002. He led by example. Honest hard graft, desire, work ethic and, um, 'ploddingness' in the best sense of that made-up word.

He was a good captain. Good on the tactical side, good with people, but perhaps a bit soft for the job. We might crack up when Gus threw a strop because he's a big, nice guy, is Frase.

He was reminding me recently what a pain in the arse I could be to captain, and how he employed reverse psychology to get me to do what he wanted. I'm sure he's making this up, but he claims that some days I got so frustrated with my lack of luck/success, I refused to bowl any more.

'I've had enough, I don't want to bowl. Let someone else have a bowl.'

Gus's strategy in these situations was simple.

'Come on, Weekesy, have a bowl. Tuffers has given in.' That always worked.

'I ain't given in.'

'Yes, you just told me you don't want to bowl. You've had enough. You've given up.'

'Give me the ****ing ball . . .'

Andrew Strauss

He became captain in my final year, 2002, at the age of just 25, and I could see even then that he was England captain material. He could achieve that balance between putting an arm round youngsters and laying down the law when required. And he had the steel to assert his authority over grizzled veterans like me. The best example of that was during a very bad-tempered match against Essex at Southgate.

At drinks in the afternoon session on the last day, the Essex boys sit down on the pitch and have ice-creams. It's a hot day, but they're making a point because they feel we've batted on too long and should have eclaired . . . sorry, declared, to keep the chance of a result alive. But the talk on our side is that Essex have created the situation themselves by batting on too long in their first innings.

By the tea interval, we're four down, and if we declare, we're not going to bowl them out on this flat pitch. I kicked Essex batsman Darren Robinson in their first innings (that's a whole other story I'll tell you later) and I'm not in a charitable mood: '**** 'em, keep them out there. We don't need to go and bowl.'

A few of the other guys, riled by Essex's antics, are in vocal agreement. But Straussy has the steel to stand up to us: 'I know what you mean. But we might win the game and we've got to try to do it.'

So he declares and we go out and bowl for a couple of hours and the game peters out to a predictable draw. But he was right to do that. However unlikely the odds were of winning, it only takes ten balls to get ten wickets and rather than going tit for tat with Essex, he made a clear-minded decision.

Graham Gooch

My first captain with England. He was always very encouraging, telling me I was a good bowler and just to knuckle down, but I think he got a bit disenchanted with the job. He was a great player, and it meant so much to Graham to captain his country. He took the responsibility very seriously and lost a bit of *joie de vivre* when he didn't get the backing of the senior players for the new fitness and diet regime he was trying to implement.

He had a big tear-up with David Gower because David was off flying aeroplanes, drinking champagne and not setting a particularly disciplined standard. He must have looked round and thought, right, who's my other senior pro? Lamby. Oh no! Okay, who else? Wayne Larkins. Argh! And what about the younger players . . . Tufnell. God help me!

We had some great players and some exciting young players, but the success we did have, like getting to the World Cup final in 1992, was achieved by pure boys-on-tour bunfight. He felt we could do better. He was a little bit before his time in that respect, because it was the early days of fitness training being taken more seriously in cricket. On tour, England had a manager who would sort out the travel and accommodation, a coach, a captain, a physio and that was it. Nothing like the support staff Andrew Strauss and the boys have today, so it was left to Graham and coach Micky Stewart to try and change the culture.

Embers, who was big mates with him, told me that Goochy once was a mod, a bit of a boy, who used to turn up to training on a Lambretta. Then he became England captain, which was a poisoned chalice back then, the worst job in the world. It just made you go grey and become a very miserable man. We didn't see him in the evenings any more. We'd see him at practice, at the hotel, and perhaps he'd go out with the hierarchy for a bit of dinner. And this was someone who genuinely is a bit of a card and a great laugh.

Allan Lamb

Lamby was England captain for a couple of series, which was great fun. I'm not sure why they gave him the captaincy – I think he was just the only senior pro left who was guaranteed selection at the time!

Obviously, Lamby was a great player who led by example on the pitch, but let's just say he ran a relaxed ship off it. He'd say, 'I don't know what you lot are doing, but I'm off to the winery now. You amuse yourselves.' He liked to enjoy himself as much as anyone, so it was quite hard to take him seriously as a disciplinarian, and I did take advantage of his easy-going nature.

On my first tour, with Graham Gooch injured, Lamby came in as acting captain. Goochy was none too impressed when Lamby and David Gower, his two senior players, accepted an invitation from billionaire Kerry Packer and former England captain Tony Greig to join them at the Jupiter's Casino on the second evening of the Brisbane Test. I was among the few who tagged along, too. The papers were full of it, including a very creative back-page image of our heads superimposed on a roulette wheel. Peter Lush, the tour manager, gave the media the party line that Lamby had returned to the hotel in good time, around 11 p.m., which would have required him to have left almost as soon as he arrived!

A few days later in Adelaide for a World Series Cup one-dayer against New Zealand, I'm not in the running for selection so I commit to another big night out. I start with a few of the boys, but one by one they drift back to the hotel, leaving me to my own devices. And, very kindly, a couple of lovely ladies in a bar invite me back to their place. As the team won't be leaving for the ground until around nine the following morning, I think, 'Why not? They say they live ten minutes away, so should be fine.'

Forty-five minutes, and a couple more beers in the back of the car, later, we arrive. Some more drinking, a little dancing, and I find myself in bed frolicking around with my two new chums. A while later, two of their flatmates come knocking and jump in, too. It's a tight squeeze to fit four strawberry blondes and me in a double bed, but we all bravely make the best of the situation.

Finally, when things have calmed down, I identify the girl whose bed we're in. I tell her I need to be back at the hotel by 8 a.m., on pain of death. She tells me it's just fifteen minutes' drive from here: 'No worries, I'll set the alarm for 7.30.'

This only allows for a couple of hours' sleep, but it's better than trying to get back there now.

I don't know what wakes me up, but it isn't the alarm clock. Half asleep, I check the time. It's half eight.

'Oh my God. Oh my God. Wake up. I am in so much trouble.'

She barely stirs.

'Oi! What happened to your ****ing alarm clock?'

'Huh. Oh, I dunno. You see, sometimes it just doesn't work.'

'I've gotta go. Come on, get up!'

I grab my scattered clothes, we dive in the car and floor it back to the hotel.

Unbeknown to me a couple of the boys are busy cooking up cover stories for me, although I'm not sure anyone would believe the one Robin Smith tells coach Micky Stewart: 'Sometimes he likes to jog to the ground early.'

I mean, really.

I arrive at the hotel about ten past nine in a panic. The lads have already gone. If I can somehow get to the ground in half an hour, I might be able to get away with it. I grab my key from reception, sprint for the lift.

New shoes on polished marble. Whoah. I slip, take out a couple of rubber plants, an information board and a nice vase, before sliding to a stop in front of the lift.

Ding.

The doors open. Looking down at me are tour manager Peter Lush, Micky and Goochy. They are obviously going their own way to the ground.

'Not a word,' says Goochy. 'Get your arse upstairs, have a shower and get yourself to the ground. I will talk to you later.'

By the time I make it to the dressing room, the story is out among the lads, who struggle to stifle their giggles in front of the management. Lamby is among those biting on his hand.

No, Lamby wasn't really cut out for the disciplinary side of captaincy, bless him.

Mike Atherton

I'd played quite a lot with Athers before he became captain and got on well with him. He was a completely different fruit, but he'd go out and have a good time. He'd enjoy his successes with the boys, but was equally happy to go for a nice dinner and a glass of wine with the hierarchy, or retire to his room for the evening and read.

As a captain, he wasn't motivational in terms of rousing speeches, but set a standard in the way he played and applied himself. I had massive respect for him as a batsman. He went out there, a Cambridge University boy who you might think was a bit soft. But he was the opposite. Proper brave.

In cricketing terms, he could be tough and didn't shy away from his responsibilities as a captain. Once he was staying round at Robin Smith's house and casually informed 'Judge' over breakfast that he was dropped for the next Test match. And, of course, there was the time he declared with Graeme Hick on 98 going for his first Ashes century in Sydney, 1995, because he felt Hicky was scoring too slowly and holding the team up. Athers said later he might have made a mistake there and it was a bit harsh. Indeed, Gus Fraser reckons partner Graham Thorpe was at least as much to blame for the slow run rate, because he couldn't get it off the square and kept pinching the strike.

He's also a nice fella, and I think sometimes people took advantage of that a little bit – 'Oh, come on lads, I've got to give you a bollocking here.' Generally when he told me off, I just wanted to ruffle his hair and tweak his nose. Ah, it's only Ath . . .

He did give me a couple of serious dressing downs, though, one of the biggest being during the First Test of the 1994 West Indies tour when my social whirling got way out of control.

Not selected for the First Test, and having spent most of the previous night (and indeed the previous few weeks) partying, I turn up at Sabina Park on the first day in desperate need of some shuteye. So while Athers and Alec Stewart bravely meet the challenge of fending off Curtly, Courtney and co. on a fiery pitch in the morning session, I'm fast asleep in the physio's room. When Athers finds out at lunchtime, understandably, he goes ballistic.

'This is pisshole,' he begins. 'Alec and me are out there busting a gut for this side, a side that you are part of, and your idea of supporting us is buggering off for a kip. I put myself on the line to get you on this trip, you've been on the piss for a month and now you can't even be bothered to stay awake to watch the first morning of the series. That is out of order and I'm very, very disappointed.'

My weak attempt to make a joke out of it – 'You know, that's why they call me The Cat' – is met with a withering stare.

He's absolutely right. My behaviour is poor. And amazingly, it gets worse.

Four nights later, another evening of drinking sees me return to my room in the company of a couple of attractive ladies for a jumping and bumping party. The sun is rising when I finally pass out, and when my alarm goes off an hour later, I'm in no fit state to move. I ring our physio Dave Roberts and tell him I'm suffering from a stomach upset (technically true). With the West Indies needing just eight runs to win, I suggest that my services as twelfth man won't be required.

'Well, you sound dreadful,' he says. 'Don't worry. Just stay in bed and get yourself better. I'll let Athers know you're not well.'

When informed of my predicament, Athers does not take the news well: 'You've got to be ****ing joking. Three hours ago, he was in the room next to mine swinging from the ****ing chandelier.'

Despite all the grief I caused him, I've heard from those present at the team selection meetings that most of the time Athers batted for me. In his autobiography he admitted that he cut me a bit more slack than the other lads because he reckoned I could bowl no matter what was going on in my usually turbulent personal life.

'Tuffers,' he'd say, 'I'm not saying go to bed at 9.30 every night. Don't worry about having a net, if you don't want to. But just give me this in return.'

I didn't quite twig at the time how pro-me he was. I can remember the disbelieving looks on his face on occasions when I was hauled up in front of him, like he was at a loss to know what to do to pull me into line – which was understandable because I gave him kittens.

I can take a little credit for extending his reign as England captain, though. Athers endured a torrid home Ashes series in 1997, and went into the final Test with the team three-nil down and his captaincy under threat. I'd been picked in the squads all summer, but been told my services weren't required on the first morning of each match. Athers had backed Robert Croft instead, but apparently Athers' Lancashire teammate Wasim Akram of all people had been championing my cause for a recall and eventually managed to sway Athers' thinking. So I was in and I justified my selection by taking 7 for 66 and 4 for 27 on the way to England's solitary victory of the series.

Nasser Hussain

I actually advised Nass to take the England captaincy. We were sitting on a coach back to Barbados airport after the Test matches had finished in 1998 because our services were not required for the one-dayers.

Nasser turned round to me and said, 'They've asked me to be England captain. What do you reckon I should do, Phil?'

We had quite a long conversation about it. He was uming and ahing, worried whether it would affect his game, how he'd cope with the extra pressure.

I said, 'Listen, mate. Go for it. You'll never know if you don't try. You're going to be picked and dropped if you're not captain. At least if you're captain, you've got a better chance of not being dropped!'

Another good lad, Nass. Chippy, edgy and feisty. When he walked out to toss a coin in company with big names like Steve Waugh, he didn't bow down to them as some captains do. He was what England needed at the time.

He was a scrapper. Sometimes, if anything, he was a little bit too feisty, a bit too snappy. It became too much of a siege mentality. He liked to fire his team up by reminding his players of what the opposition had done to us or negative things they'd said about us before.

Duncan Fletcher didn't want me, but Nass vouched for me and got me on my last tour with England, to South Africa. He got me in and stuck by me as long as he could, but eventually came to the conclusion that I was not going to go along with Fletch's way of doing things. Nass knew I was England's best spinner, but Fletch was all about three-dimensional cricketers: people who could bat a bit and field, as well as just bowl. He'd sacrifice a touch more extra bowling threat for the all-round package. It was a change of psyche about who should get picked, with more emphasis on bits-and-pieces players, good trainers who added value in all aspects of the game. To be fair, it worked, because England started winning!

THE WONDER OF BUMBLE

Aside from the captain, the coach is a key character in galvanising team spirit and when it came to that, David 'Bumble' Lloyd was in a category all of his own.

Great lad, Bumble, and so passionate. 'Coum on, lads,' he'd say in his broad Lancashire accent, like Gromit's owner. 'Just dooo sumthing. Get a wicket, fuh God's saaayke.'

When he and Nass got together, they'd be playing 'Land of Hope And Glory' and 'Jerusalem'. Bumble would be saying, 'Remember Agincourt!' It was all 'Cry God for Harry, England and Saint George . . . Chaaaarrrrge!' Sometimes it got a bit too much for me. Can we just calm down a bit and play cricket?

He was a very knowledgeable coach, someone you could talk to easily and have a laugh with. If he had a fault, it was that he was maybe just too much one of the lads. But when he came in as England coach, he was just what we needed after Ray Illingworth's grey, uninspiring regime. At least, with Bumble, we felt like there was someone who cared for us, and was with us all the way. Never was that more apparent than during the infamous 1996 winter tour to Zimbabwe.

In Bulawayo for the First Test, we're watching our second innings unfold from a tent on a mound overlooking the pitch because the dressing rooms are miles away. Zimbabwe start deliberately bowling the ball wide so we can't hit them, and the umpires aren't calling it.

Up on the mound, the players are getting increasingly irate, with shouts of 'That's a ****ing wide!' filling the air. Bumble is doing an Arsène Wenger on the sidelines: 'Youuu cahhn't dooo that!' Hearing our vocal complaints, the Zimbabwean supporters at the bottom of the mound start shouting insults and marching up the hill towards us. It's getting a bit heavy, and a few of the boys are looking round for means of self-defence. I pick up a teacup. How very British.

The Zimbabweans' dubious tactics pay off, and when the match finishes drawn with the scores level, a first in Test match history, it really kicks off. There's us lot and the Zimbabwe fans arguing, pushing and shoving each other, and Bumble right in there amongst it.

At the post-match press conference he's still fuming, prompting his, ahem, emotional summary of the match:

'We murdered them. We got on top and steamrollered them. We have flipping hammered them. One more ball and we'd have walked it. We murdered them and they know it. To work so hard and get so close, there is no praise too high. We have had some stick off your lads. We flipping hammered them.'

Got him in trouble, but as a player it was great to have someone who you felt was living and dying with you like that.

THE DEMISE OF DON CADDICK

Acquiring a nickname is a very important rite of passage for a cricketer. When you are joining a new team or coming up from the youth side, there's always that iffy period when you don't have one. The danger is that some established member of the squad might say: 'Ooh, I know, let's call you "Twat".' Steady on, not sure if I like that one.

Everyone eventually gets a nickname, but some are more imaginative than others. For the many Thorpey-type monikers, there are a few wilfully obscure ones, such as 'Pigeon' – a nickname given to Glenn McGrath as a youngster with New South Wales, where they reckoned there was a pigeon flying non-stop around the world who couldn't land because McGrath had nicked his legs.

I feel quite lucky to have been blessed with the relatively creative nickname of 'The Cat' as well as the more obvious 'Tuffers'. Mike Gatting came up with my feline handle for my tendency to curl up and have a doze on the aforementioned Bench of Knowledge when our boys were batting. As for Tuffers, in my experience of English cricket, you tend to get more 'ers' nicknames down south, whereas if I'd played up north, I think I would have more likely been a 'Tuffo'.

What you don't want is opposition players coming up with

nicknames for you. Past sledgemaster Shane 'Warney' Warne was great at stitching people up that way. He started calling Ian Bell 'The Shermanator', after the red-haired, nerdy, virgin character Chuck Sherman in the *American Pie* films. That got picked up by the press at a time when Bell was struggling to assert himself against the Aussies and it can't have helped his self-esteem. Warne also tried to get under Paul Collingwood's skin by dubbing him 'Caddyshack', saying he was only in the England team because he'd caddied for Michael Vaughan at a pro-am golf event. Talking of golf, I once tried to give Andy 'Caddy' Caddick the nickname 'Don', as in 'Don' Caddick. Quite flattering really and I thought this play on words was hilariously funny at the time, but despite my relentless efforts to drop it into conversation, Don Caddick didn't stick.

IT HELPS TO HAVE A LEGEND ONSIDE

When you are the new boy in a team, it takes a while to settle in, so it helps to have an experienced pro looking out for you. Allan Lamb was the person who first made me feel like I was really part of the England side on my debut tour of Australia.

In a warm-up game against Victoria in Ballarat, I've bowled all right, but got a bit of tap from Dean Jones who's hit a century, and I'm feeling a bit downcast at the prospect of being outbowled by Victoria's left-arm spinner Paul Jackson just when I'm hoping to be selected for the First Test. But Lamby gives me a wink before he goes out to bat and then proceeds to smash this guy all round the park.

When he comes back into the dressing room after scoring 143 off 129 balls, he says: 'Tuffers, he's not a patch on you, son. He's not a patch on you. I had to just ****in' deal with him.'

Made me smile and, more importantly, I felt that this guy who was a legend of the game had my back.

THE BUFFALO CLUB

In my day, when we went on international tours, a lot of team bonding took place in the local hostelries, and it often revolved around drinking games. One of my favourites originated in Miller's Beach Bar, Antigua, when Robin Smith and Alan Igglesden instituted a left-handed-drinking-only rule. Don't know why – just something to do – but this Masonic ritual carried on throughout the entire 1994 West Indies tour. If you caught someone drinking right-handed, you called them – 'Buffallllllohhhh' – and the forfeit was to neck whatever was left in the glass. Robin was absolutely hopeless and by the end, he was just Buffaloing himself.

In theory, being a leftie, I was pretty safe, but when you are drinking Caribbean-style rum punches, which are 90 per cent rum, 10 per cent punch, your sense of orientation can soon deteriorate. Sometimes I'd be chatting to someone, pick my glass up right-handed and suddenly hear the cry from a teammate I didn't even know was in the same bar. And wherever and whenever you were called, you had to drink up. That was the Buffalo code of honour.

WIN WHEN YOU'RE LOSING!

In 1993, by the time we got to our final match at Worcester, Middlesex had already clinched the County Championship title. Hadn't lost a game all season. Pre-match, there's a dressing-room debate on how to approach the task in hand.

Option one: get our heads down and graft hard for four days to maintain our spotless record.

Option two: start the celebrations now and hope for the best.

It goes to a show of hands. Worcester win the toss, put us in and skittle us out for 68 on the first morning of the match. Guess which option we plumped for?

In the second innings, as we are crashing joyfully to an innings defeat within two days, Mickey Roseberry bets all the tail-enders a bottle of champagne that we can't hit our first ball for six. God knows what the Worcester bowlers are thinking as a succession of dodgy batsmen try (and fail) to lamp the first delivery they receive over the top.

When my turn comes, it's 142 for 9. Last-chance saloon. I'm not known for my six-hitting prowess (well, I'm not known for my hitting prowess, full-stop), but set me a challenge and the old competitive streak comes out, so I'm psyched up for it as I march out to bat, windmilling my bat like Ian Botham in his pomp (sort of).

I'm facing medium pacer Stuart Lampitt, who rocks up, plops it on a decent length. I drag my left foot out of the way and slash the ball over point with everything I've got. Right out of the meat of the bat. I'm willing it over the ropes . . . and, yes, it's a six!

I leap up and punch the air like I've scored the winning runs in a World Cup final. On our dressing-room balcony, my teammates are whooping and cheering and Mickey Roseberry is already popping my prize bottle of champers. God knows what the Worcester members must think.

For the record, we lost by an innings and 36 runs, with me left undefeated, six not out. Champion-es, champion-es, la-la-la-la!

DIFF'RENT STROKES XI

As a great philosopher once wrote, it takes diff'rent strokes to move the world. And it takes all sorts to make up a cricket team as this select eleven show . . .

Jack Russell
Alec Stewart
Peter Such

Graham Thorpe
Andrew Strauss
Andy Caddick
David Ward
Adam Hollioake
Neil McKenzie
Geoff Boycott
Anonymous

Jack Russell

So many quirks, so little space. So let's start with his diet. All he ate on tour was Weetabix, beans, plain, cremated chicken and steak and chips. With his Weetabix, which he ate for lunch with a mashed banana, he insisted that the biscuits were soaked in milk for eight minutes before he ate them.

One time, I'm twelfth man, having a little 'Catnap', and only wake up just before the players come off for the lunch break. I quickly rush to get Jack's Weetabix ready, as is my duty, but he appears before it has had his optimum soaking time.

'What's this?' he says, knowing on sight that something's wrong.

'For ****'s sake, Jack. Just eat your Weetabix.'

'But it's only been soaking for five minutes.'

'Well, just wait three more minutes, then!'

If you ever went into Jack's hotel room, there'd be massive Y-fronts, which he'd washed out in the sink – massive skidmarks, because all the stumpers had piles from jumping up and down all day – hanging off the lamps. Then you had the inners from his wicketkeeper gloves, which used to stink, on the bed, plus the pungent odour of his oils and turps for his painting (he's a very accomplished artist) . . . and, cowering in the corner, some innocent youngster rooming with him, crying, 'Let me out of here!'

Alec Stewart

All his kit would be immaculate and kept in regimental order. He had his fielding and batting shoes numbered 'Alec 1' and 'Alec 2'. Then there was 'Bat 1', 'Bat 2', 'Bat 3'; Monday shirt, Tuesday shirt . . .

Everyone else's stuff was all over the place, but Stewie's corner of the dressing room would be an oasis of order amid the chaos. To start with, of course, we used to mess around with his stuff for a laugh, but after a while we just left him to his OCD ways.

Peter Such

Suchy used to iron his jockstraps. I'm not sure even Stewie did that.

Graham Thorpe

Thorpey was forever playing with his bat handles. He'd be shaving bits off, putting tape round and changing the rubber to get the feel right. I'd ask Aggers to describe his method for putting on rubbers in more detail, but this is a family book . . .

Andrew Strauss

You wouldn't peg Straussy as a tabloid newspaper man, but he used to be obsessed with doing the *Sun* crossword when he was a youngster. Him and Jamie Dalrymple would do it together. Wonder if he still does it now?

Andy Caddick

I remember Ian Botham organised for us all to go out on an incredible boat owned by one of his rich friends off the coast of Auckland. It was the kind of fishing trip I like. We all sat there supping Sauvignon Blanc and chatting to a few very attractive ladies, while some high-tech camera equipment and sensors scanned the surrounding waters. Every now and then we'd hear the shout, 'Hooks in!' and you'd catch a fish, just like that!

Meanwhile, I could hear Caddy talking to the captain about the boat's security – 'Has it got an alarm system?'

Caddy was a geek, really into how things work, and very handy for all us technophobes who needed anything fixed. On a plane and your Walkman (remember them?) broken? 'Caddd-eeee!'

Air con in your hotel room on the blink? 'Caddd-eeee!'

And, bless him, he always came to help: 'Yeah, I know how to do that . . .' We kind of used him, but he loved it.

David Ward

On Red Nose Day once, Wardy came out and fielded at short leg wearing a red nose. All day. Maybe he took it off for lunch, but very commendable all the same.

Adam Hollioake

Adam liked tipping things over. Sleeping cows, parked cars, whatever. On tour in the West Indies in 1998, a few of us were wandering back to the hotel after a few drinks and suddenly Adam bombs off at full pelt and shoulder charges into an old car, about the size of a Twingo. Bang! Knocks it on its side and stands there brushing his hands together as if it was the most natural thing in the world to do.

Neil McKenzie

The South African batsman, I'm told, insists that all the loo seats have to be up in the dressing-room toilet before he goes out to bat.

Geoff Boycott

If you'd knocked on my *TMS* colleague's hotel-room door in his playing days, you might have got a big surprise. Legend has it that on one of Ian Botham's early England tours, Beefy popped round to check up on Boycs, who was going through a lean spell with the bat. Boycs answered the door wearing nothing but his pads, told

Beefy to sit on the bed, then picked up his bat and demonstrated his immaculate forward defensive stroke.

'Now tell me what's wrong with that,' said Boycs. 'Nothing, that's what.'

Welcome to the team, Boycs.

Anonymous

Last but not least, there's a player who shall remain nameless who liked to relieve tension by heading to the toilets and, um, 'knocking one off the stump' before going out to bat.

CHAPTER 4

'I'M BUILDING AN IDIOT': AN EXPERT'S GUIDE TO GETTING THE FANS ON YOUR SIDE

THE THIRD MAN

People may think that fielding at third man is the easiest position on the pitch, but as someone who spent most of his career down there, I can tell you, it has its own special challenges. Six hours standing on the rope waiting for edges through gully is just the start of it. I mean, sometimes you are even called upon to jog across to fine leg and that is quite a distance. But most demanding of all, you are up close and personal with the paying members of the general public and often fans of the opposing team.

There's no real separation from the crowd when you are fielding on the boundary. In the old days, they allowed people to sit on the grass by the boundary rope and you sometimes had to knock spectators out of the way to make a catch or stop the ball going for four. Even now, when they stay behind the advertising boards, they are close enough to lean over and ask for an autograph. They are right there, so you've got to sharpen up your people skills as much as your long throw to the wicketkeeper.

A lot of so-called competent fielders who spent their careers at slip never had to deal with the complex social/sociopathic issues I had to. In fact, I know of a few close fielders who were scared to enter this cricketing no-man's land. Occasionally, in a one-dayer or when the shit hit the fan in a Test match, they did get posted on the boundary and afterwards they were begging, 'Please don't send me out there again. I don't want to go back there.'

So for more reasons than one I was always top of the list to field on the boundary behind the bat. To be fair, if I wasn't going to practise my batting or fielding, taking care of customer service on behalf of the team was the least I could do.

Having fielded on the boundary from the year dot, I've decided to plough the benefit of my international experience into a survival guide for budding third-man fielders or, indeed, any cricketers who find themselves stationed on the boundary within sledging distance of opposition fans.

1. If you turn around don't expect a round of applause
Quite often I'd hear a shout of 'Oi, Tufnell!' from the crowd. Your natural instinct is to turn around, but the sight of your caller standing there, making an obscene gesture and shouting 'Yer w******' may cause offence. Which brings me to my second point . . .

2. Don't take insults personally
Abuse is an occupational hazard for the boundary fielder, so you've got to take it in your stride. See the good in people and appreciate that deep down, they love you really (well, probably). Thin line between love and hate and all that.

I learned this lesson on my first tour of Australia at the Fifth Ashes Test in Perth, January 1991.

'I'M BUILDING AN IDIOT'

I'm sent down to field at third man in front of the hill. As I walk down there for the first over of the first day, I see an Australian bloke – vest, big fat gut, corked hat – sitting on his camping chair.

'Morning, Tuffers,' he says cheerfully.

'Oh, mornin''.

He then proceeds to spend the next six hours calling me a 'Pommie bastard', telling me I'm '****in' rubbish', 'You ain't got no ****in' bowlers', etc etc.

At the end of a very long day's abuse, I'm relieved to see him packing his gear up.

'Tuffers, see ya tomorrow, mate,' he chirps. 'Lovely to see ya.'

'All right, mate. Bye.'

Amazing, but he'd obviously had a great day. That sums up my relationship with the Aussie fans – they would sledge me all day long, but it was generally good-natured, relentless abuse.

There were times when their comments got a bit close to the bone, though. For instance, the less sensitive members of the crowd had a field day following the newspaper headlines that my first wife was on the game:

'Eh, where's yer missus, Tuffers? I've got 25 quid. Have you got her number, mate?'

All you can do is laugh at them, otherwise they know they've got you.

I used abuse as a spur and I gave as good as I got, which I think they liked. When I was fielding, I'd sometimes give my tormentors a sly two-fingered salute behind my head, or in front of my chest if I was running back down there after getting a wicket. That would get a reaction – 'Rarrrrr!' – and then I'd give them the handbags mime – 'Whoooo!' – which made them smile.

Although I shipped more abuse from Aussie fans than any others during my career, I think they did warm to me. They thought I was a 'larrikin', as they say. I knew they loved me really.

73

3. Beware of 'gifts' from the crowd

New Zealand fans must have loved me, too. The more generous spectators showered me with gifts. During a one-day international in Auckland, in January 1992, mangoes, bananas and peaches were flying in my direction. On a hot day, a juicy piece of fruit to nibble on is quite welcome. However, when an unripe peach hits me square on the back of the head, at first I think someone has run on the pitch and punched me. And when a couple of miniature bats, the kind people get autographs on, are lobbed in my direction (they only needed to ask and I would have signed them), I have to get the umpires to stop the game.

My experience will be immortalised in a cartoon by Jak in the following day's *Evening Standard* (I've got the original on my wall at home), but when I proudly list the array of missiles I've braved to my teammate Derek Pringle at the end of the day's play, he is surprisingly unsympathetic.

'What do you know about being pelted by the crowd? The last time I fielded down there, someone threw a bat at me.'

He means a full-sized bat. Cripes.

India could also be a hazardous place to play when it came to 'gifting'. Devon Malcolm had a screwdriver thrown at him there. On twelfth-man duty, I got a bowl of noodles on my head. Splat! I had to walk the last quarter of a lap back to the pavilion with noodles and gravy down my face. And sometimes I did think, right, enough's enough. You're getting it now. Like at Madras in 1993.

I'm fielding at deep midwicket and getting fruit chucked at me constantly. Luckily, it's only soft fruits, but in quantities enough to make a very respectable fruit salad. It's searing hot as usual, and when I get hit for the second time by a satsuma I finally lose my rag with it. As the game continues, I gather up all the fruit, turn around and start hurling it back at them while screaming expletives.

Spotting that I'm not actually facing the right way while the ball is being bowled, I can hear the voice of one of my teammates: 'Tuffers, would you concentrate. We've got a game on here.'

'All right, just hang on a minute . . .'

I was told later that the TV commentators picked up on it too: 'What's Tufnell doing? Tufnell appears to have gone mental.'

When it came to missiles, it wasn't all bad, though. In the West Indies, some well-meaning punters used to throw spliffs. The last over before lunch, I'd gather them all up from the outfield and, ahem, hand them in to the authorities.

4. Don't take advice from spectators

Dealing with Australian fans provides the ultimate test for a third man, because they will do anything for a laugh. A favourite of theirs on my first tour was to claim that the captain was telling me to shift position.

'Oi, he's telling you to move to the left, mate.'

This was a particularly good ruse during the day-night games. When we were wearing coloured clothes, it was really hard to see the other players, who were fielding close to the wicket, because they were miles away on the big Australian grounds and they rather merged into the crowd behind.

On a couple of occasions, I couldn't see Goochy, and the locals tried it on. I'd turn round and ask, 'Where? . . . How far left? . . . Here?'

A few seconds later, out of the multi-coloured mirage appeared Goochy, running towards me.

'OI, I SAID ****ING THAT WAY!'

'Oh, sorry.'

Once I got wise to that trick, I could still get it wrong, though.

'Tuffers, he says move five yards to the right, mate.'

'You winding me up?'

'No, mate, he's telling you.'

'You're not getting me this time. I'm staying right where I am.'

They carried on pointing and then their expressions changed. I'd look round to see an irate moustachioed man approaching.

'I SAID ****ING FIVE YARDS THAT WAY!'

Oh no. I'd trudge, head down, into position and they'd be pissing themselves. I learned very quickly always to watch carefully for the captain, rather than rely on second-hand advice from the Pom-baiters.

5. Never go commando

During the First Test of the 1996 series against Zimbabwe, I was fielding at fine leg. I was standing there, and all of a sudden, someone jumped over the fence and yanked my trousers down. Trousers round my ankles, just my jockstrap to protect my dignity. Debagged in Bulawayo.

6. Persuade the captain to let you field somewhere else

As the team's acknowledged specialist third man (aka worst fielder), this will be a tough sell, but when the opposition team has a mix of right- and left-handed batsmen, do whatever you can to persuade the skipper to swap you to the infield. A righty-lefty batting partnership is the third man's worst nightmare, especially on the supersize Aussie grounds. If they get four or five singles an over Down Under, you could end up running miles back and forth between third-man positions. And how the crowd loved watching me huff and puff: 'Wahey – c'mon Tuffers.'

7. Remember where you are

I actually learned this lesson doing twelfth-man duty at Kensington Cricket Club, Kingston, Jamaica, in 1998. In one corner of the ground there was a group of cricket-mad locals coming out with some fantastic comments on the action in front of them.

When Gus Fraser bowls, one shouts: 'Fraser! You bowling like a cow. You ready for milking.' When Jack Russell is batting, he gets a beauty: 'No, Russell! You jammin' it like Bob Marley. You got to beat it like Michael Jackson.'

As I meander past, a couple of them are having a chat about the relative merits of Carl Hooper and Jimmy Adams. I get the call.

'Tufnell . . . who better: Hoops or Jimmy?'

'Well, they're both very good players. But perhaps Hoops is slightly more of an attacking batsman—'

I'm trying to be diplomatic, but before I can finish my sentence, they absolutely go off on one. Schoolboy error. I've forgotten that Hoops is from Guyana and Jimmy is from Jamaica. Jimmy is their boy.

I can still hear them shouting at me when I get back to the pavilion.

8. Don't be intimidated by scary-looking hecklers

In Port Elizabeth, December 1999, I spent some quality time on the boundary in the company of eight South African blokes. Absolutely massive, shaven-headed, they all look like prop forwards. They're sitting at the bottom of the hill about six feet away from me, chowing down on eggs and sausages cooked on their 'braai' (the Saffer version of a wok) and 'drrrinkin' thi Castle beer'.

When I turn in their direction, one guy goes to me: 'Y'fickin' Inglish winker, Tuffers. Ye shud play a rrreal man's game. Ye shud play rrrrugby. Nun of this pansy crickit shit.'

'All right, yeah, thanks . . .' I reply, trying to stop my legs from shaking.

The compliments keep on coming.

Me being me, when an over ends and I can get away, I turn around and say, 'Why dontcha just **** off?'

That eggs them on even more for the next time I'm back there, but even though they cane me all day, and could break me in half like a cream cracker, I never feel threatened. Abusing me is just their idea of fun.

9. Have a laugh with the punters

Most important of all. Like it or not, you are going to spend quite a bit of time in the company of opposition fans, so it's worth trying to get them onside.

Even after being conned into changing my field position in Oz, if I heard a voice behind me saying, 'Tuffers, can you move a bit to your right, mate? I can't see,' I'd shuffle across a bit although I knew it was a wind-up. They appreciated that I'd mess around with them, and it went down well.

I think I played in a great era for cricket crowds. It may have calmed down a bit now, but it was like football at times, especially over in Oz. And amid the abuse there were some comments that made you laugh: 'Tufnell! Can I borrow your brain? I'm building an idiot' was my all-time favourite.

It helps if you like playing to the crowd. Funnily enough, I was actually quite shy as a kid. My mum used to get me to sing 'Is This the Way to Amarillo' at parties – 'Look what Phil can do' – and I always kind of dreaded that. But as I got older, I found that I could make people laugh at school. And if you can't fight, make 'em laugh to stop yourself getting a right-hander. I carried that through to my cricket career.

My general tactic when I was down at third man was to give a bit back and hope that no one punched me, and I just about got away with it.

THE MELBOURNE SIDESTEPPER

Fielding on the boundary, you are on the frontline, but you're not always safe out in the middle, either. For instance, I'm bowling in a one-day game at the MCG, and as I get back to my mark, I see a golf ball bobbling across the wicket. Must have been a good hit with a four-iron.

Another popular one at Melbourne was for plucky punters to

try and make a run for it right across the pitch without being caught by the stewards. Nowadays, the fine has got so expensive very few are willing to risk it, but I saw a couple try and fail. One time, a kid comes running on the pitch who has a few moves on him. The crowd roars their approval as he sidesteps the increasingly desperate lunges of stewards converging from all corners of the ground to try and intercept him.

I'm standing at the end of my run-up, when he comes running past me, arms and knees pumping, cheeks puffed out. I'll never forget the look of intense concentration on his face. Think Eric Liddell in *Chariots of Fire*.

'Go on, son! Nearly there!' I say.

For a split-second, he looks round at me – 'Cheers, Tuffers!' – before resuming his sprint for glory. Sadly, after a couple more nifty sidesteps, and with the boundary rope in sight, he gets scythed down, bless him. So close.

XXXX SHOWER

While the nearest I got to a fight with spectators was a fruit fight, I did witness the odd incident of fan-on-fan violence over the years. I can remember a couple of brawls at Sydney, which spilled on to the field and caused the game to be stopped. It was like an old Western film with three or four big Aussie bruisers throwing haymakers while the whole crowd chanted 'Fight! Fight! Fight!' and burly stewards tried to break it up. But the most bizarre display of anarchic behaviour I witnessed was the traditional beer-can fight down at Brisbane in 1994. People had told me about it, but it has to be seen to be fully appreciated.

I'm fielding down at fine leg, close to fans sitting watching on the old hill. It's the evening session, red hot, everyone's well lubricated. All of a sudden, all the empty cans of XXXX people have been drinking during the day are launched. It continues for about three minutes solid, XXXX cans fizzing through the sky like a swarm of bees. It's not exactly the Northern Lights, but the scene has a strange kind of beauty.

This is on the back of another surreal moment a bit earlier.

Two attractive girls, wearing bikini tops and hot pants, have been parading up and down at the bottom of the hill all day, a spectacle that has drawn many appreciative whoops and whistles (not from me, obviously, as I've been fully focused on the game). Not everyone is enjoying their distracting display, though. Just after tea, as they sashay along, I see an irate bloke running down the hill towards them. The next thing I know, he's picked up one of the girls and deposited her head first in one of the big yellow bins. All you can see is her legs kicking about. A bit harsh, but very funny.

PLAYING IN A WASHING MACHINE

When it comes to sheer numbers of cricket-mad fans, there's no place like India. When I toured there in 1993, the place just blew my mind.

Lying on my bed in the hotel room on a Test match day, ready to go down to the lobby to get to the ground, it's nice and peaceful. Then the time comes to leave, so you pick up your bags, go out the door and take the lift down to the lobby. The lift doors open on the ground floor, and you're hit by a cacophony of noise. And it's non-stop from that moment on, everywhere you go. Volume turned up to 11 for the whole day.

Even the coach journey to the ground offers no respite. We run over three people on the way – knock a couple of people off their bike, clip a tuk-tuk – and I'm looking out the window saying, 'Is he all right? . . . Ooh, there's another one on the floor,' but no one seems to bother.

When we eventually arrive at the ground, there are so many

people everywhere. At Lord's, everyone queues up. Here, it's just a massive bundle like you used to have trying to get through the door at school break-time, but multiplied by thousands.

I feel like a boxer making his way through a very rowdy crowd to the ring. Huge crowds crushing in on you, police everywhere absolutely lacing the spectators with these huge bamboo batons, and stricken supporters hobbling away.

When we are finally spat out from this crush into the safety of the pavilion dressing room, it's with a mixture of shock and disbelief that I'm looking at the veterans in our squad who've toured India before: 'What is going on? Is this normal?'

'Oh yeah, that's how they control it.'

Absolute chaos and we haven't even started playing yet.

Out on the pitch, the huge crowds are penned in by high wire fences. The only way I can describe it is like being in a washing machine. You can't actually see individual faces in the crowd, just a seething mass of life in constant motion. Like amoebas.

They set fire to all the rubbish and let off bangers when someone scores a fifty or a hundred. Bang. Bang. Flares flying over your head as you stand at third man. I wouldn't call it intimidating, but it's just a huge culture shock.

When the time comes to bowl, my mind is buzzing like a fridge. It doesn't seem possible to stop, take a deep breath and refocus, it's like everything's out of control.

Cheers. Bangs. Flares. Fires . . . Whaaat! Stop! I'm trying to bowl!

The whole day passes in this confusing, swirling fog of colour and noise. It's only at night when you finally get back to your hotel bedroom and close the door that the mute button is hit. And relax.

WHERE I WANT TO BE

For great stadiums and passionate, knowledgeable, hostile crowds, Australia takes some beating. It was such a buzz to play there. I think back to January 1991.

A day-night game at MCG in the Benson & Hedges World Series Cup (I always used to enjoy Benson & Hedges-sponsored games as the nice Benson's rep used to leave boxes of free cigarettes and cigars, which I squirrelled away in my coffin). Huge stadium. Full house. Everyone's lively. Beautful evening. Wearing the blue kit. Everything shimmering under the lights. Wow! Never played in anything like this.

When it's my turn to go out to bat, we're 176 for 9 and need 47 to win with overs running out. I make my way nervously out of the dressing room into this incredible arena. It's about a two-minute walk out to the middle. Miles away. And as I start the long walk down the steps to the pitch, 90,000-odd people serenade me: 'Tufnell's a w*****', ch-ch-ch-ch-ch, 'Tufnell's a w*****', ch-ch-ch-ch-ch- . . .

Talk about entering the bullpen.

I've had a bit of a warning about what to expect earlier in the day during our warm-up. Doing some shuttle sprints, we made the mistake of running down towards the notorious Bay 13 section in the Great Southern Stand. All of a sudden, they started chucking things at us. Retreat, Captain Mainwaring, retreat! The game hasn't even started.

Later, when I was fielding, I was pelted with eggs. By the time we get to bat, a good percentage of the spectators are well-oiled and the atmosphere is crackling.

When I finally reach the middle, I see my mate Angus Fraser, who's just put on a gutsy 30 partnership with Martin Bicknell, and we just start laughing – at the chanting, the atmosphere, the perilous match situation, and us two Middlesex boys playing in these awe-inspiring surroundings. And I will always remember the first thing Gus says to me: 'This is where I want to be.'

I know exactly what he means. I'm more used to playing in front of one man and his dog on a cold Tuesday in Cardiff. This is it. This is ****ing it. This is cricket. This is what you play for.

We're so inspired Gus and I almost eke out an unlikely victory. Almost – the Aussies can't get us out, but we're three runs short when our 50 overs are up.

Defeat, then, but an unforgettable experience. And I'm later advised that being called a 'w*****' by an Australian means they love you really . . . Hmm.

A BARMY KIND OF LOVE

As an England player, to balance out the sledging from opposing fans, I was lucky enough to have the backing of the Barmy Army, who first mobbed up during my debut tour of Australia in 1994/95 and have followed the team all over the world ever since. Men and women of all ages and backgrounds, from teenagers to pensioners, labourers to lawyers, united by a love of cricket and having a drink and a laugh in the sun.

It's so great to have that support when you're a long way from home and things aren't going well for you. It might be 400 for 2, it's been a long hot day in the field and they're still singing and encouraging you. It made me feel that there was a little corner of England's green and pleasant land close by even when I was thousands of miles from home.

Some of the Barmies were travelling around on a shoestring – sleeping on beaches, etc. – and they'd sacrificed a lot to come and support us, so we'd always try to help them out. In Sri Lanka in 1993 we let them into the dressing room to take any mementoes they wanted. They stripped it in about three minutes; nicked all our beer.

The last few years they've been rewarded for their support by getting to watch a winning England team. But there were times during my international career when they could go for weeks of a tour with only a warm-up game victory against a Numpties XI to savour, and yet they were still supporting us. Even when we were getting absolutely slaughtered by the press. During those lean times they needed to have the mentality of a bottom of League Two football club fan travelling to away games in the vain hope that one day we might triumph. I think some of the Barmies took a perverse pleasure in our defeats – 'I've been on three England tours, never seen them win a game. One day I'll see us win away!' – and when we finally did win a game, it made it all worthwhile.

They'd always find a bar to use as their headquarters for the duration of their stay in each town, and they'd take over. In Jamaica and Guyana at the start of the 1994 tour to the West Indies, there were just a few hardcore fans watching us, but by the time we arrived and won in Barbados, Barmies outnumbered locals in the rumshacks around the island.

If we won, we'd join them. By the time we reached them, though, they'd be hammered after a day's drinking in the sun while we toiled. After we beat the Aussies in Adelaide in 1995, the Barmies went, er, barmy. They'd had a ten-hour start on us, but we did our patriotic best to catch up during the ensuing all-nighter.

CHAPTER 5

THE CRÊPE SUZETTE PAN OF UNCERTAINTY

I began playing cricket with my elder brother Greg and our mates in our garden at home in Hadley Wood, North London. My dad built a net so we could play with a proper cricket ball and dug up the rockery to create space for a run-up. The rose garden was sacrificed to allow us to indulge our other passion for playing football without fear of punctures. The garden turned into a mudbath, but my parents loved sport too, so they didn't mind. In fact, they were usually out there with us, joining in our games.

At that time, I showed some potential as a fast bowler. However, to build up sufficient momentum within the limited dimensions of our garden required some creativity. My run-up was more eccentric than Bob Willis' in his prime. I would start by doing a loop of the summer house before disappearing under the hanging limbs of a weeping willow tree, emerging suddenly to deliver the ball (with a textbook action, if I say so myself) as hard as I could at my intended victim. At such lightning fast speed (well, it seemed fast to me), I lacked control and more often than not my deliveries arrived around head height.

To educate me in the virtues of line and length, and stop me killing someone, my dad came up with a Heath Robinson-esque training device. He built a contraption consisting of a free-standing frame from the top of which he hung an old crêpe Suzette pan. He calculated the correct trajectory for a good-length delivery and placed the pan in the centre of the target area. Hit the pan and it meant I'd bowled it straight and on a length. I'm certain that aiming at that crêpe pan of uncertainty stood me in good stead for the future.

At the age of nine I went for a trial with Middlesex Under-11s and got picked. It was there I was coached by Jack Robertson, the former Middlesex and England player, and during a net at Lord's a couple of years later, we had a conversation that may have changed my life.

'Phil,' he says, 'you're a good bowler, but there are lots of fast bowlers. Have you ever thought about bowling spin?'

He lays out the advantages for me – I'm a lefty so I can move the ball away from right-handed batsmen and bowl into the rough against the left-handers – and also for the team. It will give our attack a bit more variation.

At first I don't fancy the idea at all. I love charging in and trying to frighten batsmen, and even as a pre-teen I'm not inclined to take advice from people in positions of authority. But Jack persists.

'Okay, can you show me how to do it?'

He shows me the grip and bowling action and puts a ball in my hand.

I run up – almost with a seamer's run-up – bowl it. Whoom. It plops on a good line and length and it spins. Easy as that. All feels very natural.

For a while after that, I bowled a bit of quick stuff mixed up with a few spinners . . . like a young Garry Sobers! However, I soon discovered that schoolboy batsmen used to a diet of medium-pace bowling hadn't got a clue how to deal with a left-arm slow bowler who could spin it. I also came to the realisation that it was bloody hard work pounding in only to get hit back over my head – I could do that slow spin bowling off a couple of paces (yes, the infamous Tufnell work ethic was kicking in at a young age).

SPINNER WITH ATTITUDE

Even though I turned to spin, I think my early years of trying to be a fast bowler helped me. From the start, as a spinner, there was always energy and aggression in my bowling. I might have been tossing the ball up slowly, but I kept the same attitude. I was an in-yer-face character and I'd sledge batsmen like nobody's business, which got me into a lot of trouble as a youngster at Middlesex. I'd get fined all the time.

If I didn't get an lbw decision from umpires, I'd be saying, 'You ****ing what, you blind ****?' It took me a while to realise this was not the smartest way to get any decisions in my favour. After giving them a volley of abuse, you could guarantee that when a batsman nicked one behind, the ump would just stand there and smile at me.

I'd be swearing at batsmen to the point I often ended up squaring up to them. Small boys, big boys, made no difference . . . mind you, if they came back at me, I'd be calling for our wicketkeeper Keith Brown, who was also a useful amateur boxer: 'Oi, Brownie, Brownie, he says he's going to see me afterwards.' Lot of mouth, but lacking trousers, I was.

Although my rebellious streak got me into trouble and cost me money, I think it also helped me get wickets. Slow bowlers are very reliant on will to get batsmen out, beating them mentally. Batsmen didn't quite know what to make of this lunatic stamping around, swearing at them. I was trying to get inside their heads and I wanted them to be the ones worrying about me. I put across the impression of aggression and self-belief and that gave me an edge. That's why

I never liked it when opposing players came into our dressing room after the game. I didn't like them in my bubble. I didn't want them to know what I was about.

It was only later, when I started Test cricket, that the mystique ebbed away. Playing alongside players from other counties, they'd get to know and understand me, see me at my low times. They'd go back to their county teammates and say, 'Tuffers isn't as confident as he looks.' Playing alongside overseas professionals at county level had the same effect – they'd tell their international teammates about my weaknesses. Over time, they work you out. 'He's not all that – if he doesn't get a wicket early, his head goes.' I always felt a bit cheated by that at the time – like I'd opened myself up to people and then they used that against me – but, of course, they were no different from me, because you take any advantage you can get.

I'm a bit tricky by nature – a little bit wherrr, a little bit whayyy, like that character on *The Fast Show* – and I think that was also an asset. As a spinner, you have to build spells of bowling, be able to think on your feet and lure batsmen into traps. I enjoyed that side of the game. You don't have the luxury of extreme pace to whistle ball after ball past their lugholes. If you've got a flat pitch with no turn, you can find yourself bowling slow, straight deliveries to the best batsmen in the world, which is quite a scary situation. So you have to find some way of tricking them into thinking it's harder than it actually is, using variations in flight, changes of pace, clever field placings and the like.

Some batsmen weren't easily fooled, though. The great Viv Richards used to have a very cool way of letting me know that he knew I was trying to wing it on a dead pitch. Rather than smash me out of the ground immediately, he'd play an overly studious forward defensive shot, then look up and smile. I'm thinking, 'You could have hit that for six!' It was his way of saying, 'I'm in no rush, I can take you any time I like.' And the next ball – boomp – he'd flick it over the ropes, easy as you like.

SPINNING YARNS

TUFFERS' TEN: MY TOP BUNNIES

Mark Waugh
Chris Cairns
Ian Healy
David Boon
Daniel Vettori
Mark Taylor
Stephen Fleming
John Wright
Curtly Ambrose
Viv Richards*

Mark Waugh (7 Test dismissals)

It might surprise a few people to hear that the younger of the Waugh twins is my top bunny in Test cricket. Surprised me too, because he's one of the best players of spin bowling I ever played against. Lovely soft hands.

Mark and me had a bit of a running feud, which originated in our Essex–Middlesex rivalry. When we played Essex, he liked to try and knock me out of my stride with a few comments – 'Just bowling to keep the runs down, eh Tuffers?' that sort of thing – and, naturally, I'd give it right back to him.

I have carefully avoided checking the stats to find out the total number of runs he scored off me against those seven dismissals. I prefer just to remember getting him caught and bowled (beat him in the flight, he looked to work me through the offside, leading edge) at Old Trafford in 1993 in my first home Ashes Test and that time at The Oval in 1997, when I got him out in both innings for 19 and 1. I also stopped a punter winning big money when I bowled Mark for 99 with a beauty at Lord's in 1993. This guy had bet on their top four all scoring centuries, and with Mark Taylor, Michael Slater and David Boon all reaching three figures, he was just one run away from hitting the jackpot. When I played with Mark later for Lashings, he told me the guy came to see him in the dressing room, and he wasn't a happy bunny!

Chris Cairns (5 Test dismissals)

I'm pleased that Chris is on the list, because all people seem to remember about me bowling to him is when he hit me for a massive six at The Oval in 1999 as New Zealand beat us to win the series 2–1 and our skipper Nasser got booed. Perhaps that is because this one moment was immortalised on the front cover of *The Cricketer* magazine, with Cairnsy mid-follow-through and me curled up like a foetus.

That was the only time he tagged me, though.

I have Robin Smith – more specifically, his foot – to thank for one of these wickets, in Auckland, 1992. I bowl one a bit short, and as Chris goes back to cut it, 'Judge', fearing the worst, jumps up. Chris hits the ball straight onto Judgey's boot with such force that it ricochets all the way to extra cover where Graeme Hick takes a simple catch. We all run over to congratulate Hicky while Judgey writhes around on the floor in agony, ignored: 'Aaaarrrggghh, I think I've broken my foot!' Brutal business.

Ian Healy (5 Test dismissals)

Wicketkeepers are usually good players of spin, probably because they spend more time than anyone else watching it up close, and Heals was no exception. So it's nice to have him up near the top of my list.

David Boon (4 Test dismissals)

I got Boonie out four times. Really? I did get him out with a fantastic delivery at the Gabba in January 1991 – bowling over the wicket, the ball pitched outside leg, hit the top of off stump. A bit Warne-ish, it was. Ball of the century? Well, maybe *my* ball of the century.

SPINNING YARNS

Daniel Vettori (4 Test dismissals)
Always nice to sort out the opposition's spinner.

Mark Taylor (3 Test dismissals)
My most memorable dismissal of Mark was at The Oval in 1997 when I got one to turn a bit out of the rough, took the inside edge and Adam Hollioake fielding at short leg caught the ball in his groin. Sure Adam remembers that one well, too.

Stephen Fleming (3 Test dismissals)
Good batsman who came and played with us at Middlesex. Another leftie . . . the 'omelette' of rough, as I called it, outside their off stump always came in handy in the second innings. My close fielders used to call out to me: 'Plop it in the omelette, Tuffers. They don't like it in the omelette!' No wonder, because if I didn't have any idea what the ball was going to do when it pitched, they certainly didn't.

John Wright (3 Test dismissals)
. . . And another leftie. In the pre-DRS era, I felt I had a much better chance of getting them out than the right-handers. If the ball didn't turn, I had a chance of an outside edge to slip. If it did turn, I could get them bowled or lbw; I certainly got more lbws against left-handers. With the right-handers, I really only had the outside edge to play with. I'd try to get them caught in the covers or playing across the line, but if they played across the line and missed, they never seemed to be given out lbw.

At the end of the 1992 New Zealand series, when I took a load of wickets, Wrighty came up to me and said, 'Can you change your boots because I'm sick of the sight of them!'

I always remember getting him out for 99 at Christchurch during that tour, when they were battling to save the game. He came down the pitch, realised he'd misjudged the flight, and before the ball had pitched, yelped, 'Oh no!' Stumped.

Curtly Ambrose (3 Test dismissals)

The strategy was quite simple against Curtly. Big, macho West Indian coming in at number nine, bit of rough outside off stump, post a deep square leg and a deep midwicket, toss the ball up in the air and I knew he couldn't resist having a swing!

Viv Richards* (1 Test dismissal)

Big asterisk against the great Sir Viv's name, because there are fifteen players I got out twice in Test matches who, statistically speaking, could be in my top ten above him. However, I'm including him on the basis that dismissing the legendary batsman, my boyhood hero, just once is worth ten normal wickets. And I never tire of telling the tale of how I got him.

The Oval, Saturday, 10 August 1991. Day three of the Fifth Test against the West Indies; 2–1 down in the series. Viv is suffering from piles, so I'm told, and is batting down the order. But when I have Malcolm Marshall caught by Ian Botham at slip to reduce the Windies to 161–6, the destroyer of a thousand bowling attacks belatedly makes his way to the crease. And how. The way he swaggers to the crease, muscles bulging, carrying his bat like a club, is enough to strike fear into any bowler's heart let alone a mere stripling like me in only the fifth Test match of my life, and my first of the summer. He-e-elp.

I look to Beefy for encouragement and perhaps even a bit of advice. He's known Viv for years, playing together for Somerset and against each other in Test cricket. Unfortunately, he's too busy laughing at the prospect of me bowling to his mate. Nothing to do but bowl the ball, and I serve up my best loopy, spinning, ball-on-a-string on a perfect length. Viv pats the ball away and looks up from under his peaked West Indies cap with barely disguised contempt at my effort. Jesus Christ, this bloke is going to whack me ****ing everywhere.

I wobble back to my mark on jelly legs. For a split-second I think I might actually faint. Pull yourself together, Philip. Come on. If he's going to come after me, there's nothing I can do about it. Just bowl.

As I reach the crease to bowl the next delivery, Viv is already on the move. All I can do is hold the ball back a fraction, try to mess with his timing. He's coming for me full pelt, crossing his legs in midair so high that I can almost see the sole of his leading boot, bat held grandly at the top of his backswing. As I follow through I'm in survival mode, assuming the cricketing version of the crash position. If he hits it as intended, I won't be attempting a heroic caught and bowled.

But he doesn't hit it the way he was shaping up to. Instead, out of the corner of my eye, I see the ball pitch, turn, nick the outside edge of his bat and go through safely to Alec Stewart. Through previous bad experience of umpires not hearing nicks, I shout, 'Stump him!'

Alec whips the bails off. Umpire Mervyn Kitchen, confused by Alec's stumping manoeuvre, is looking across to the square-leg umpire John Holder who raises his finger.

Merv then raises his finger for the caught behind.

I look back at John. Then back at Merv again. Two fingers aloft. It takes a second for my brain to process what has happened. It's a sunny day at The Oval, England v West Indies, and I have just got Viv Richards out. Blimey.

In my moment of triumph I somehow muster Viv-like cool in my celebration, strolling down the wicket and shaking hands with Alec Stewart as though Viv's fate had never been in doubt. My true feelings are reflected better by my brother Greg and his mates, who are up in one of the corporate boxes jumping around, punching the air in delight. It's only later as I walk off having taken 6 for 25 that I even realise Greg is at the ground – apparently, it's his stag day celebration. Bastard could have told me!

As for King Viv, the Masterblaster, he was no one's bunny, but

I'm very proud to say I got him out in a Test match, even if it was just the once.

MY TEST WICKETS: COUNTRY BY COUNTRY

Against	M	balls	wkts	bowled	caught	ct wkt	ct field	c&b	hit wkt	LBW	stumped
1 Australia	12	3230	36	7	26	4	20	2	0	1	2
2 India	2	483	4	0	3	0	3	0	0	1	0
3 New Zealand	10	2703	37	5	26	3	22	1	0	3	3
4 Pakistan	1	204	1	0	1	0	0	1	0	0	0
5 South Africa	4	1360	10	2	6	1	4	1	0	0	2
6 Sri Lanka	2	493	8	2	4	1	3	0	0	1	1
7 West Indies	9	2318	18	1	14	2	12	0	0	2	1
8 Zimbabwe	2	497	7	0	6	1	5	0	0	1	0

DUCK AND CHURN

As an international bowler, you experience disastrous moments and passages of play that stay with you for days, weeks and even years. Just a flicker of the memory of the most extreme cock-ups can cause a physical reaction – your stomach tightens, your hands clench into fists and your teeth grind. The only way I can describe the feeling is a churning, and two incidents can still give me 'The Churn' to this day. The first occurred during the First Test against New Zealand in Auckland, January 1997.

Coming off our failure to win an acrimonious series in Zimbabwe, the boys bounce back well with our under-pressure skipper Mike Atherton making a gutsy 83 and both Alec Stewart (173) and Graham Thorpe (119) notching centuries on the way to a first innings total of 521. New Zealand, who've batted first, mustered 390 in their first innings and half an hour into the afternoon session on the final day, they're just 11 runs ahead with one wicket of their second remaining.

The only batsmen standing between us and victory are Nathan Astle and Danny Morrison. In Danny's case, I use the term 'batsman' loosely, for he is the ultimate number 11, the proud holder of a world record 24 Test noughts who glories in the nickname 'Danny the Duck'. So proud is Danny of his achievements, he has even endorsed a range of 'duck callers', which are sold at the ground. I like to think I'm no mean number 11 myself, but I can only dream of attaining such depths of hopelessness. He chooses today to play the innings of his life, though, occupying the crease for 166 excruciating minutes, scoring 14 runs off 133 balls in an unbroken last-wicket stand with Astle of 106 to clinch a draw.

Danny never looks in trouble on a pitch that is as dead as a dead duck. And the longer he stays in, the busier the vendors selling Danny the Duck callers become. As Athers switches the bowling around, and we try desperately to get just one single ball to move off the straight, let alone create a chance, the Kiwi fans' quacks reach a deafening crescendo.

For me, the moment when I know we're not going to win comes when I bowl the last ball of an over to Morrison. It gets lodged between his bat and pad, before rolling in slow motion past his off stump by the width of a duck feather. Deflated, I fall back on the pitch and close my eyes. After a couple of seconds, I slowly open them and think about standing up. But it's such a beautiful blue sky, just a few wispy clouds. And then a couple of gulls pass over-head. And the grass is soft and springy. Actually, I quite like it here.

My blissful interlude is only broken when the shadow of umpire Steve Dunne looms over me. He pats my shoulder, gives me my cap and says: 'Tuffers, I think that's just about it.'

The other lasting churner comes from the Third Test against South Africa at Durban between Christmas and New Year 1999. We're losing the series 1–0, but we've got a 210-run lead after the first innings and have enforced the follow-on, leaving us two-and-a-bit days to bowl them out and knock off any runs by which they get ahead. This is my chance to show Duncan Fletcher, who clearly has doubts about me, that I am a match-winning bowler. This is my chance to shine. In the past, I've usually produced in this situation.

When he's scored 30-odd, I have their opener Gary Kirsten plumb lbw . . . but it's a no-ball. Kirsten hasn't changed his shot, and he's caught right in front of the sticks. Even the umpire turns to me and says, 'Oh Phil, I'm sorry.'

I try to tell myself, it's okay, I'll get him soon, but deep down I know this could be a turning point.

Two days later, with close calls and possible catches falling short off my bowling, our occasional off-spinner and keen guitarist Mark Butcher finally bowls Kirsten round his legs for 275. Yes, 275 runs scored over fourteen-and-a-half hours, the last twelve of which I have spent replaying the lbw that wasn't over and over in my head.

South Africa grind out a miracle draw. I seek out the umpire in the bar after the game, looking for some crumb of comfort.

'Would you really have given it lbw if it wasn't a no-ball?'

'Yes, Phil. He was nailed on.'

At our New Year's Eve party the night after the match, I can't bring myself to celebrate. I'm absolutely destroyed. I keep prompting my teammates to say something that will make me feel better.

'It wasn't just down to that one no-ball that we didn't win, was it?'

'No, of course not.' But the way they look at me tells me different.

Deep down, I know it's the beginning of the end of my Test career. I know Fletch thinks so, and I can feel that even my most loyal teammates think so, even if they don't say as much. In the past they could justify my maverick tendencies, because I'd come through when it counted on the pitch. But this is exactly the sort of situation I'm in the side for and if I can't deliver a victory now, why am I in the team?

It's not just me stepping one inch the wrong side of the popping crease that has cost us. Yes, if Kirsten had been out then, I think it would have given me and the team the momentum to go on and win the game. But the fact is I couldn't fight back from that error and find another way to win the game, as I have done before. That's the point.

Reliving what happened now, twelve years later, still makes me double up in pain.

That is 'The Churn'.

THE DAY I STOPPED SLEDGING

On day two of the Fifth Test against West Indies in April 1994 I said to Brian Lara, 'You lucky bastard,' after he thick-edged – almost manoeuvred deliberately – a ball from me past slip for three. He smiled at me with pity, probably because he was on 284 at the time, gliding effortlessly towards a chanceless world-record innings of 375. At that point, I thought, 'Hmm, yeah, better shut up.'

Mind you, Brian was a little bit lucky later on. When he swivelled to hook Chris Lewis for four to go past Garry Sobers' previous record mark, his foot hit the stumps and the bail lifted up slightly without falling off. That's right, we could have had him out for a mere 365, the jammy sod.

TUFFERS' TEN: SPINNERS I HAVE ADMIRED

Shane Warne
Muttiah Muralitharan
John Emburey
Phil Edmonds
Anil Kumble
Daniel Vettori
Graeme Swann
Saqlain Mushtaq
Derek Underwood
Jim Laker

Shane Warne

I was playing in that game at Old Trafford in June 1993 when Warney bowled 'The Ball'. We'd bowled them out for 289. I'd got 2-78 off 28 overs – Mark Waugh, caught and bowled, and Ian Healy. Spun it a little bit. Very respectable stuff.

In our first innings we're doing all right, 70-odd for one wicket. Up in the dressing room it's pretty relaxed, people having a read, eating a bit of toast or whatever. Then the shout goes round: 'Here's this boy Warne.'

It's his first Test match in England. We've all heard about him, but never seen him bowl before. In future, England players will watch footage of new players before matches. For us, it's more, 'Who is this geezer? Some blond kid who bowls leggies? Oh, he'll be shit.'

There are two or three rows of cinema-style seats in front of the telly, which is attached to the wall, so we all sit down and look up at the screen.

Mike Gatting, a brilliant player of spin, is facing. Warne strolls up, the ball bananas through the air, bringing a whole new meaning to the word 'drift', landing outside leg stump, biting viciously and fizzing the other way past the outside edge of Gatt's bat to hit off. Boomp, boomp.

Gatt doesn't even know it's bowled him at first. We're all going, 'Has that bowled him . . . ooh, Gatt's walking off. Must have.'

For a few seconds there's just stunned silence. Total disbelief. Then my mate Robin Smith turns round and says, 'Tuffers, what were you doing yesterday?'

I let out a little sigh, like the last breath of a dying man. Straight away, it's obvious that this boy is special and he's going to make life very difficult for me by comparison.

At team meetings, one of the things they used to do was challenge each of the players to outdo their opposite number:

'C'mon, Athers – you get more runs than Taylor and Slater,

we'll win the game . . .', 'Caddy, if you can get more wickets than McDermott . . .' – that sort of thing.

Then they got to my name: 'Tuffers, you're up against Warney . . . Er, best of luck with that.'

It really pissed me off at the time, because I'd made a good start to my Test career, got my first 50 wickets in 15 matches and was considered one of the top two or three spinners in the world. But, deep down, I knew I couldn't compete with him. Yes, I gave the ball a decent tweak, spun it, had my little variations, but I always wanted to spin it like he did, and that was impossible. He was a leggie, got more revs on it, simple as that.

However, rather than the backroom staff telling me not to beat myself up about it, I was compared directly. In fairness, spinners ourselves were like that in my day. At Middlesex I used to tell our batters not to get out to the spinners who were after my England place, like Richard Illingworth. In return I promised to destroy all the young batsmen who wanted their spot. It could be a good way to sharpen up your competitive edge.

I outbowled Warney about three times in ten years, and then only later on in my career when the approach changed and coaches wouldn't try to pit the spinners against Warne in the same way. Instead, it was more a case of, 'This is what you do, do what you do to the best of your ability.' And if the alternative is being compared to the player I consider the greatest spin bowler of all time, that's definitely a better option.

Muttiah Muralitharan

I first came up against 'Murali' in Colombo, Sri Lanka, March 1993, in only his fourth Test match.

We win the toss and choose to bat first. It's baking hot, pitch as flat as a pancake. 'Judge' Robin Smith, opening the batting, scores 108, Graeme Hick and Alec Stewart get 60-odd each, but in the conditions, our total of 380 all out is below par. And the reason for that is this kid Muralitharan. Like Warney, we've only heard about him before, never seen him bowl. He's spinning it all over the place, getting incredible bounce.

With eight wickets down, I trundle out to have a bat with my mate John Emburey. I take my guard. There's a gaggle of Sri Lankan fielders crowded round the bat, jabbering away. Muralitharan runs up and bowls. Ooh, good length ball – big stride Philip, press forward, cover the spin. It's a dead pitch. No problem.

The ball hits me under the armpit. 'Ow!' Where's that come from?

A couple of balls later he gets me lbw for his fourth wicket, and returns with figures of 4-118 off 45 overs on a dead wicket.

When it's our turn to bowl, Embers and I toil away for 30-odd overs each, and manage three wickets between us at a cost of over 200 runs. For us, the ball is going through shin-high and straight . . . and we're quite good bowlers. We're convinced they'd taken the stumps and moved us to another pitch!

Another England squad member, Dermot Reeve, who isn't playing in the game, is suspicious. He even gets a video camera to film Murali's action and concludes, 'The boy's chucking it.'

I have to admit that when we first saw him, it looked like he was running up and throwing it at you. Of course, it was revealed a year or two later that Murali can't straighten his arm and has a freakishly mobile wrist, which made him the first wrist-spinning off-spinner in history. I think the Sri Lankans could have headed off the accusations a lot earlier if they'd come out and explained straight away. Instead, we saw photographs of him bowling with a bent arm and it tarnished him.

The ICC tested him a couple of times in his career, and revised the limits on bending the elbow of the bowling arm when they discovered that a lot of other bowlers exceeded the existing limits, too. Some bowlers I have seen just run up and fling it at you – when a fast bowler tells you he's got a 'mummy bouncer' and a 'daddy bouncer', the daddy is a chuck – but there's a difference between an out-and-out chuck and a straightening of the arm in delivery.

You can argue about whether or not Murali was bending his arm too much, but to bowl with the control he did for long spells takes incredible skill. Ultimately, I think the authorities took the view that Murali, Brett Lee and Shoaib Akhtar – who were all accused of throwing it at times in their careers – were three of the players people loved to watch and they all had hundreds of Test wickets to their names, which couldn't just be wiped from the record books for the sake of a few degrees of bend in the arm.

If it was left to all the old farts, we wouldn't have bigger bats, we wouldn't have Twenty20. Okay, it mustn't become like baseball, where some bloke can just stand there and chuck it at you, but I think the authorities made the right decision to tweak that rule to allow for individual flair. And Murali had buckets of that.

John Emburey

Great bowler, one of my mentors. Embers is from Peckham, a good lad who always enjoyed a laugh, but also a top professional who knows the game inside-out. I played a lot of cricket with him at Middlesex and then with England. He was a senior international, quite a bit older than I am, and he took me under his wing.

He used to field at first slip for me, and together with Mike Gatting used to set the fields when I started out, but they both encouraged me to think about the game so I could eventually take on the responsibility. They told me to analyse each batsman: how does he hold the bat? Does he stand square on? Does he close the face of the bat? Are there certain types of shots he struggles to play? You've got to work that out within the first couple of balls you bowl, if not the night before (the old 'penguin on its back' routine). Both Gatt and Embers were very good at that. After a while, Embers said, 'Come on, mate, you've got to start believing your own theories and strategies and putting them into place.' That was one thing I actually became quite good at – working out a batsman's strengths and weaknesses and setting fields appropriately – and Embers takes a lot of credit for that.

Phil Edmonds

Six foot three, barrel-chested, big spinner of the ball. Like Embers, Philippe Henri Edmonds was big and strong and would crunk the ball into the pitch and get deep turn, whereas I was more of a flighty bowler. He could even bowl a bouncer off a couple of steps as a surprise ball.

A Cambridge graduate with an aristocratic air about him, it was Phil's business interests that eventually ended his playing career and made way for me in the Middlesex team. He'd have meetings during matches at Lord's and get our lunch lady, Nancy, to send down food and a bottle of wine for him and his clients in the dressing room.

Once we'd eaten in the lunch room, we'd all filter back down to go out again and he'd be sitting there chatting away, sipping a glass of wine. Seeing us, he'd get up, shake hands with his guests and then stroll back out to play the afternoon session!

Another time, he walked on to the pitch clutching a mobile phone (this was in the days when few people had one and they cost a fortune). He handed this brick of a phone to one of the umpires, saying, 'I'm expecting a call. Just give me a shout when it comes through.'

The final straw came against Somerset in Bath in June 1987. In the middle of a bowling spell Phil asks Gatt if he can go off to make an important phone call.

'I forbid you to leave the field under any circumstances,' replies Gatt.

A couple of overs later, Phil tells the umpire he needs to change his boots. Gatt is fuming.

Twenty minutes later Phil reappears, and his first contribution after his 'boot change' is to try to field the ball one-handed down at third man. He makes a complete Horlicks of it and then slowly jogs after the ball.

'Get that ball in, Henri,' bellows Gatt from his position at first slip. He does, bulleting a throw directly at Gatt rather than the wicketkeeper. Gatt can't stop it and the batsmen run two further overthrows. Cue an epic stand-up row.

After that Phil asked if he could play as an amateur. He didn't want to play away matches, but just turn up for games at Lord's, which was more convenient for his office. Unsurprisingly, the committee weren't having that, so Phil went off to make his millions as a corporate executive, and I became Middlesex's first-choice, first-team, left-arm spinner.

However, five years later, at the age 41, Phil did play for Middlesex again up at Trent Bridge. I was away playing for England, he came in to cover for me, took four wickets and bowled beautifully by all accounts. But, having not played for years, his body was not used to the strains of three-day cricket and he shovelled down painkillers to numb the aches and pains. Rather too many it seems. Eye-witnesses recall him falling face-first attempting to jump across the wicket at the end of an over in the second innings, and sitting in the dressing room after the game looking absolutely pie-eyed!

Anil Kumble

Ah, Anil Kumble – I whacked him back over his head for four in my magnificent Test-best innings of 22 in Chennai, February 1993. Have I mentioned that? Yes, probably . . .

Before we played him, the England coach Keith Fletcher had done a lot of work on him. 'He doesn't spin it,' he told us. 'You should play him as an indrift bowler.' Kumble ended the series as top bowler on either side with 21 wickets and we lost all three games!

Fletch was right to say Kumble didn't spin it much, but he had subtle changes of pace and bowled little skidders. Often, you'd see his wrist action and think the ball was going to turn, but instead it skidded on straight, which got him a lot of clean bowleds and lbws.

He was also so tall you didn't feel as if you could go forward to him, because he could generate that bit of extra bounce. You'd end up on the back foot, so he got a lot of lbws that way, too. He was very difficult to sweep, cut or drive, and that cuts off a lot of potential scoring strokes.

On that tour, Richard Blakey got out to Kumble three times in three Tests, for six runs (bowled), one (lbw) and a duck (bowled). I remember sitting next to Richard on the plane home, and Richard shaking his head, saying over and over: '****ing Anil Kumble'. Ruined him, he did!

Daniel Vettori

Another left-arm spinner. I first met Daniel on tour to New Zealand, when I was an established cricketer and he was still a young boy. We had a couple of little chats and I could see he had great potential. Huge fella – six foot three. Great arm ball, good flight. A change of pace bowler very similar to myself. Another one who could bowl it quickly at you and keep you in your crease.

I remember he got Darren Maddy out in Darren's first Test innings, at The Oval in 1999. Darren's opening with Athers and doing okay, batting for an hour for 14 runs. At the tea interval, I warn him to be very, very careful about Daniel's arm ball, though. 'He disguises it really well,' I say. (When I bowled my arm ball, my little finger always used to poke out, so you could see it coming last Tuesday – mind you, I did use that to my advantage as well, bowling fake arm balls!)

Darren replies, 'Yes, Phil, yes, Phil,' but I can see that he's a bit tense.

First ball after tea, Daniel bowls him the arm ball, Madds shoulders arms and is bowled. Oops. When he walks back in to the dressing room, I resist the temptation to say, 'I told you so,' because I know how well Daniel bowls that delivery.

Graeme Swann

Swanny was on my last tour to South Africa back in 1999/2000. He was a lively lad – reminded me very much of myself. I took him under my wing, which I'm sure the management were delighted about. He didn't play for England for another seven years after that, which some people seem to blame me for. As influential as I am, I'm not sure what I could have done in a three-month tour of South Africa to have had a bearing on the next seven years of his career!

I thought the days of the orthodox off-spinner had gone – you have to have a 'doosra', you have to have a 'top-spinner', you have to have so-called 'mystery' – but Swanny has proved that's nonsense. He's an old-school bowler who tosses the ball up, varies his pace, spins it hard and enjoys the challenge of luring batsmen into traps he's set for them. Very good at setting his fields and working out how players play.

Saqlain Mushtaq

The pioneer of the doosra. My first sight of him was in a Middlesex–Surrey game at Lord's in August 1997. He's got a slip and a gully, and more of an offside field. We haven't seen the doosra before, so when he pitches it on middle stump, the batsman, playing for off-spin, looks to clip it legside, and the ball either hits off stump or takes the edge. Each of his wickets falls in just about the same way and he ends up with two five-fers in the match.

No one's got a scooby what's going on. We're all chuntering to each other in the dressing room as a succession of bamboozled batsmen trudge back in: 'It's not possible to do that.' 'Is it an arm ball or a top-spinner?' It's not like a good arm ball that pitches and sort of nips away from you, or a top-spinner, which accelerates and bounces up on you. 'No, this pitches and actually goes the other way. Whoosh!'

Derek Underwood

His prime was a bit before my time, so I didn't really see a lot of 'Deadly' Derek except for on TV when I was a kid. He wasn't really a spin bowler; instead, he bowled these little left-arm cutters, which were lethal on uncovered wickets. If you played forward to him, the ball might likely whizz past your earhole.

I was fortunate enough to bowl against Deadly in a County Championship game between Kent and Middlesex at Canterbury in August 1987. He was 42 by then, but still an excellent bowler. In our second innings he took 5 for 43, but I managed to outbowl him, taking 6 for 60, which were the best figures of my career up until then.

After the game, he made a point of coming up to me and saying, 'Very well bowled,' and 'Good luck with your career.'

To have that recognition from a class bowler like him really meant a lot, and, probably for the first time, made me believe that maybe I could be an international player myself.

Jim Laker

I never saw him play, but he must have been pretty good, because he got 19 out in one match!

HOW NOT TO SET THE FIELD

As I've mentioned, my apprenticeship served at Middlesex under a great spinner (Embers) and a great player of spin (Gatt) helped me become quite canny at setting fields for batsmen. But the most glaring exception to that rule came in Madras in February 1993.

It's deep into the second day, steaming hot weather, India have millions on the board in their first innings. Navjot Sidhu and Sachin Tendulkar have hit centuries. Poor old Gatt, who has missed most of the day's play with a stomach bug, crawled off his sickbed to field at short leg for Ian Salisbury, only to drop an absolute dolly lobbed up from Kiran More's glove. Kapil Dev has just run down the wicket and hit the first ball from Devon Malcolm – bowling the second new ball – into the crowd for six. All in all, things are not going well.

I come on to bowl again. Glorious figures of nought for a hundred-plus in the bank. By now, our fielders are spread far and wide. All notions of attacking fields have gone out the window. Damage limitation is the priority, but I'm still trying to do the right thing and think about my field. So I go up to Graeme Hick, a good player of spin himself and usually good for a bit of sage advice.

'Got any ideas how we're going to get this geezer out?'

'Don't ask me, Tuffers, I've lost the plot.' And when I hear Hicky, who is Mr Cricket, say that, I know the game's up.

From then on, I was on my own and setting what were, looking back, some of the most ludicrous fields in the history of Test cricket. At one stage I had two men on the drive, a couple of blokes on the reverse sweep and a bloke 'over there' in a position that hadn't been invented yet and didn't need to be.

Unsurprisingly, I failed to add to my tally of no wickets, finishing with 0 for 132 when India mercifully declared on their way to a crushing innings victory.

HOPPITY SKIP, I'VE GOT THE YIPS

One thing all spinners dread is getting the 'yips', when you lose all sense of timing of when to release the ball. Most commonly, this results in hanging on to it too long and bowling double bouncers, but it can also lead to wides, beamers flying over the wicketkeeper's head. It's embarrassing and can be career-ending.

I've been told that for some reason left-handers seem to get the yips more than right-handers do – indeed, Phil Edmonds, my southpaw predecessor at Middlesex, suffered a bout of it. I never suffered with the conventional yips. I think that was partly because I always had very good muscle memory and also because I'd been a fast bowler and I kept that fluidity in my action as a spin bowler. A lot of spinners have quite stilted actions, but I ran through the crease more like a seamer – it was a very repeatable, smooth, fluid action.

No, it was another bizarre mental block that hastened my passage to the spinners' knacker's yard. It's embarrassing to admit it, but during my last season I couldn't for the life of me remember how long my run-up was supposed to be!

Rather than a carefully marked out run-up, mine had always been an instinctive thing. At the start of a bowling spell, I would step it out and grind out a mark with my spikes, but after that I'd never really look at the mark. I'd just get into a rhythm and almost feel my approach to the crease: turn, boomp, boomp, hoppity-skip-boomp-boomp-boomp-boomp-boomp-boomp, bowl.

This less-than-scientific approach probably contributed to me bowling a few no-balls over the years, but come the 2002 county cricket season, I just could not remember if my run-up was ten or eleven paces.

On a typical matchday, my first over would start something like this:

Hand my cap to the umpire. Pace out ten steps, mark it, run in, bowl.

Hmm, feels okay, but a bit wrong. I'll add a step.

Bowl the next one off eleven steps. Yep, that feels, better.

Walk back to my mark, just about to turn and think to myself, 'Oh ****, did I start off my left foot or my right?'

And it degenerated from there.

I asked teammates to keep an eye on me, had a look at videos of me bowling in the past, but soon, whether I went off ten or eleven paces, I'd still mess up and bowl no-balls because it never quite felt right. Something that had come so naturally, suddenly became a problem. The Middlesex wicketkeeper David Nash could always tell that I was struggling; I could see him shaking his head as I did a mini-riverdance at the start of the run-up trying to decide whether to push off my left or right foot.

I still bowled reasonably well that season – took 45 first-class wickets, including an eight-fer – but this daft problem really started to nag away at me. After sixteen years as a pro, how could I forget my own bloody run-up?

PHIL TUFNELL: MYSTERY BOWLER

When I was playing for England, Saqlain Mushtaq and Shane Warne were inventing all these new deliveries. Saqlain had his doosra and, later in his career at Surrey, claimed to be working on a 'chotra' and a 'teesra' without ever really explaining what the hell they were (although Pakistan's current star off-spinner Saeed Ajmal of course has now added the teesra – a backspinning ball – to his armoury).

Shane had the leggie, the toppie, the zooter and made up names for other variations on fairly standard deliveries, a ploy he later admitted was just part of his mind games to scare the opposition. It worked because it got everyone saying that England also needed a 'mystery' leg-spin bowler if we were going to compete . . . which filled me with confidence as I was the spinner they had to make do with in the meantime ('We need a leg spinner or we'll have to keep Tufnell in the team . . .').

In English spinners' desperation to be seen as more, er, mysterious, people started trying all sorts and claiming they'd reinvented the wheel. For instance, off-spinner Robert Croft developed one where he paused mid-action before bowling it, a bit like a penalty-taker at football pausing mid run-up. The 'Croft Pause' wasn't a bad ball, it made the batsman think, but I think Crofty would admit it was no doosra.

Then there was old muggins here. What have you got, Tufnell? Er, well, I've got an arm ball, a slower ball and a quicker one.

So imagine my surprise when recently, almost a decade after I retired, I realised that I actually was a mystery spinner after all. All it took was a brainstorming session with a team of top brand consultants (well, a couple of mates). Between us we came up with a few names ending in 'ra' for my various deliveries to discover that I had more, um, mysterious balls than Warney, Mushtaq, Murali and Ajmal put together. I just hadn't marketed myself effectively.

So here, revealed for the first time, the mysterious Tufnell bowling repertoire:

Tuffra

Your bog standard left-arm spinner's delivery, but sprinkled with some indefinable (possibly, non-existent) Tufnell magic dust.

Redwigglera (aka Blackgnatra)

This one I used to call my 'Ball on a string'. Basically, it involved varying the flight to get the ball to drift in the air before pitching and spinning sharply. Bamboozled many a fine batsman, and clearly deserves a better name, which comes courtesy of my old England chum Allan Lamb.

When I was bowling it well, Lamby, a keen fisherman, used to say to me, 'Don't change the fly, Tuffers. They're rising!' – meaning I was dropping the ball on an awkward length, like dangling the bait in front of a fish's nose (do fish have noses?) to lure them in, and the batsmen were rising to the bait. He'd say to me conspiratorially, in his thick South African English accent: 'What fly have you got on today, Tuffers? Is it the red wiggler or the black gnat? Whatever it is, keep using it.'

The North London Swinger(a)
The delivery formerly known as the arm ball – bowled by holding the ball like a seamer rather than across the seam – which curves into the batsmen's legs.

Milfra
A bit like a teesra, only better. I used to call it the 'Finger ball' but 'Milfra' adds a touch of class. I came up with this filthy delivery, frankly, out of desperation, when everyone was banging on about England needing a 'mystery bowler' to match Warney and spinners up and down the country were trying to invent new deliveries. After a bit of fumbling around in the nets, I tried holding the ball across the seam, which made the ball skid on. Quite literally, bowling porn.

Bouncing Bomb(ra)
The bouncing bomb (add 'ra' for extra exoticism) is a slight top-spinner where you roll the wrist over the top of it to get a bit of extra bounce.

Labradora
Now we're getting into the realms of desperation. The last three variations in my repertoire would usually be deployed deep into the second day of the opposition's innings when utter despair had set in (for instance, Durban, Gary Kirsten, 1999).

The labradora one is bowled 'blind' by turning your face away from the batsman in the delivery stride. I've named this one in tribute to all the guide dogs doing a great job up and down the country.

Bloodvessel(ra)

A very complex delivery, which required me to propel my tongue out of my mouth at the point of delivery in a vain attempt to put off the batsman. Named in tribute to the legendary Buster Bloodvessel, because it was terribly bad manners.

Whirlertwirler(a)

A frankly ludicrous delivery, which is delivered front on to the batsman with both arms windmilling over at the same time. As I say, desperation stuff.

See? That's eight whole mysterious balls! If only I'd known this at the time, I could have saved myself all those years of feeling inadequate while the England selectors, pundits and fans searched fruitlessly for another Shane Warne, and got myself another forty or fifty Test caps.

CHAPTER 6

BATTING AND ME: WHERE DID IT ALL GO WRONG?

I started playing cricket at seven and, believe it or not, I was a very good batsman from the off. I was captain of my primary school a couple of years early and opened the batting or batted number three. In 20-over games I was getting fifties, nearly getting up to hundreds. Smashing it around. The idea of playing yourself in and building an innings was alien to me. I just wanted to whack the ball.

My problems with batting came because I completely stopped playing cricket (for reasons I'll explain in Chapter 8) between the ages of fifteen and seventeen, a crucial time in the development of any young sportsperson.

When Dad finally persuaded me to play again, I picked up where I left off with my bowling, but batting was a different matter. In the years I'd missed, the boys had got bigger, the bowling a lot faster and I couldn't deal with the extra pace.

It was a different game. No more dolly-drop bowling you can step back and wallop. Instead, balls delivered at pace, swinging and seaming, or spearing at your head before you've got time to get out of the way. And cricket balls hurt.

With the ball whizzing past my nose, I didn't have that resolve to defend, take a few blows, to wear down the bowler and build an innings. I just tried to hit every ball for four, and as soon as you do that in the county game, they bowl one at your head. At which point I realised I couldn't play the short ball.

As my scores got lower and physical fear of facing fast bowling heightened, I stopped bothering to practise and gradually my batting just fell away. Nowadays, everyone's got to be three-dimensional cricketers, able to bat, bowl and field, but that wasn't the case back then. The batters were expected to bat, the bowlers to bowl and if they scored a few runs at the tail end of an innings, happy days, but no biggie. The wicketkeeper was a specialist, too – he wasn't expected to bat. So I decided to be a specialist left-arm spinner and no one, er, batted an eyelid. When they started seeing me running away to leg at Middlesex my teammates just went 'Ha-ha-ha' so I went 'He-he-he' back and didn't bother having a net. If you had to pick the laziest role in a cricket team, a left-arm spinner who doesn't bat or field would be top of the list, so you could say that I manipulated my position rather nicely!

I joke about my batting (and will continue to do so in this chapter) but, looking back, I do regret not working on it. I had natural aptitude with a blade, I could time the ball sweetly, and I wish I'd had the mental application to overcome my fears.

I was always a very aggressive bowler, and if I could have translated that attitude to my batting I might have got somewhere. Bowling twenty overs straight, getting in batsmen's faces was no problem for me, but the idea of spending four hours at the crease building an innings with bowlers bombing in brought out my yellow streak. I was happy to be the intimidator with the ball in my hand, but when bowlers gave me the same medicine, I couldn't hack it.

In fairness, plenty of coaches tried to encourage me to improve my batting. They'd say, 'Tuffers, it'll be another string to your bow,' but I'm a stubborn so-and-so: 'I'm quite happy with my "ball on a string", thank you very much.'

Towards the end of my career, England brought in the 'buddy system', pairing up a batter with a bowler, to try and improve tail-enders' batting. Poor old Mark Ramprakash was lumbered with me but I was too far gone by then. Although when Ramps did throw-downs with me, I could look a million dollars. I was fine when I had time to play my shots. Front foot, bang. Swivel onto my back foot, hook. Ooh, lovely. The problem came when they were bowling 90mph at my head out in the middle. I could never quite see the connection.

I was never going to make a Test match hundred, so at the time I thought, why go through all the agony of worrying about it? It was the wrong attitude.

ANTICIPATING AMBROSE AND CO.

Waiting to bat was torturous for me. At the start of my team's innings, I might sit on the balcony to watch our openers, but once I'd seen a couple of balls whizzing past their earholes, that was enough for me. If the pavilion was positioned to the side of the pitch, it was even worse, because you couldn't even see the ball when a bouncer was delivered at speeds of 85, 90mph, just the blur of the bowler's arm and almost instantaneously our batter weaving out of the way and the wicketkeeper taking the ball.

Whoosh. Thud.

'I ain't watching this!'

Instead, I'd sit inside just hoping our batsmen would get on top. But if we had a little collapse the feeling of dread would soon build.

It was the roar of the crowd when a wicket fell that I hated most. I might be in the physio's room, and hear a 'Yeeeeeeeaaaa-aaahhhhhh'. Another one gone. Each roar caused a physical reaction. I could feel the adrenalin surging through my body, every muscle in my body tightening.

I hated those minutes and hours of anticipation. I was known as The Cat because of my tendency to sleep in the dressing room, but that was just a way of trying to shut out this creeping dread. Other people had their own ways of dealing with it – reading, working out, watching a bit of telly . . .

When it reached seven or eight wickets down, I'd start to put my pads on with all the enthusiasm of a man awaiting the guillotine. And eventually my time would come.

I can only relate the experience of going out to bat in a big game to being a gladiator. You're walking out into the arena, all eyes on you, and there's a bloke there waiting for you who wants to knock your block off. And the worst thing was I wasn't equipped to defend myself. I knew it, the bowler knew it. I wasn't on the same level. And in those situations, the only thing that can save you is courage, something I'd left on the second step down from the dressing-room door.

Playing away from home, you often had fans screaming abuse: 'Kill him', 'Tufnell's a w*****' – pleasantries like that. Then you've got the slips giving it to you as well: 'Come on Curtly, knock his ****ing head off.'

You started to feel very alone out there.

As I stood at the crease, the old right leg wobbled, desperate to step away from the line of fire. The next thing, you've got a great big bloke like Curtly Ambrose catapulting a rock-hard object at you from a great height. If he didn't get you with his first ball, the reward was the slow death of watching him walk back to his mark, before he turned and thundered in again.

'Oh God, it's coming . . . it's coming . . . it's coming . . . Aaaaarrrgggh.'

I just couldn't see the ball. The tension plus all those years of neglecting practice meant I never accustomed myself to the ball bowled at a faster pace. I'd watch David Gower move back and across and hook a 90mph bouncer for four as if the ball had been lobbed to him. When I was out there it was whoosh, whoosh, whoosh – balls flying past my head before I realised they'd left the bowler's hand. It was pure survival for me.

TOP SCORER TUFNELL (NO, REALLY)

It was only in the last few years of my career that I managed to get my pre-innings nervousness under control. By then, I'd been hit a few times, and while that hurts, I was still alive. I started going out to bat thinking, 'What's the worst that can happen?'

I'd spent my career just trying to hang around so the other batsman could add a few more runs to the total. I never got out because I wanted to and I did throw myself in front of the ball a few times. But looking back, I know I should have done better and developed myself into a useful number nine who chipped in with a fifty every now and then. As it was, I managed just one solitary half century in my entire first-class career. But what an innings it was.

August 1996. A beautiful sunny Saturday at Lord's, and a decent crowd of 2,000-odd in for the third day of a County Championship game against Worcestershire. We start the day in a rather precarious position: 167 for 6, chasing their first innings total of 369. We progress to 251 for 9 before I join John Carr at the crease.

Worcestershire have got a decent bowling attack including Richard Illingworth, Stuart Lampitt, Tom Moody and Vikram Solanki so I don't think they expect me to delay them unduly.

What follows is an hour of mayhem. From ball one, I play like I did when I was a kid, clearing the front leg and biffing the ball through the covers. For once, everything is hitting the middle of the bat. I pass my previous highest score of 37 in ten scoring shots – all boundaries.

With the prospect of my maiden fifty in sight, even the Worcester wicketkeeper Steve 'Bumpy' Rhodes is getting excited. He comes up to me and says: 'Tuffers, you're actually "in" now, mate. Make the most of it.'

And he's right. I'm in! For years I'd heard batsmen talk about batting becoming easier once you've got yourself in, but never actually experienced it. The ball is looking bigger and bigger to me.

One by one, all the Worcester players fielding on the legside are reassigned until they have an unprecedented eight-one offside split – two slips, a gully, a third man, point, a bloke on the cut boundary, cover, deep extra cover, mid-off.

So breaking the habit of a lifetime, I step inside the line of the ball and paddle the ball round to leg. The ball trickles down towards the long boundary and poor old Bumpy has to chase it down himself while we run four.

Bloody hell. I'm bossing the game!

But now I'm in the nervous forties, virgin territory for me, and the holy grail of a first-class fifty is within my grasp.

I go up to John and say, 'What am I going to do if I actually get to fifty? Do I take my helmet off? Do I jump in the air . . .'

'Don't worry about that, Tuffers. Just get there first!'

On 48, I smoke one through the covers, piercing Worcester's dense network of offside fielders. Seeing the ball crossing the rope, I stop in the middle of the pitch and regally wave my bat to the four corners as I've seen proper batsmen do over the years. It's an amazing feeling. The crowd go wild and even the Worcester boys seemed thrilled for me as they all come up and shake my hand.

I'm absolutely flying now. The ball looks like a beach ball travelling in slow motion to me and the Worcester bowlers are in bits having worked so hard to get us nine down only for Tufnell to thwart them.

Ramps is our previous top scorer of the innings with 64, and I ease past that. Blimey, I could get a hundred here . . .

But with my score on 67 (including 15 fours), and with John and my tenth-wicket partnership on 101 (only the second time since 1945 that Middlesex's last pair had enjoyed a century stand), Gatt declares!

So no century, but an innings that's still talked about by Middlesex members: 'Were you there when Tuffers got his fifty?'

Incidentally, Worcester set us a target of 251 in 49 overs in our second innings, and this time I came in at number 11 with Jamie Hewitt and blocked it out for a draw. Attack, defend – I could do it all!

WHAT IT FEELS LIKE TO BE A BATSMAN

In what proved to be my last County Championship game at Lord's, in August 2002, I signed off with another 'epic' innings, batting for almost an entire session.

When I join Ashley Noffke, our Australian fast-medium bowler and very handy batsman, after tea, we need to survive 30 overs to get a draw. Most of my teammates are resigned to defeat. But we get through five overs. Then another five. When I look up to the pavilion, I can see that none of the boys are moving from their positions on the balcony, a sure sign that they are starting to believe we might just be able to do it. Nobody dares move to break the spell.

I'm hardly scoring a run, just blocking. The Derbyshire bowlers are bouncing me, I'm surrounded by fielders, but I'm standing firm. Drawbridge up.

As we get into the last hour, I'm starting to think we can do this. Don't think about it, Phil. Just play.

With two overs to go and the crowd urging us on, I'm on strike facing medium-pacer Graeme Welch. Three dot balls. Yes, come on, we can do this. But fourth ball, with a famous draw in sight, I go forward and across and he nips one back at me, which raps my front pad. The whole Derbyshire team go up, two hours of frustration channelled into one massive appeal.

I've hardly ever been out lbw in my life – mainly because for most of my career my legs have usually been a couple of feet outside leg stump! But this is a new me, getting into line, and I'm pretty sure I'm plumb lbw.

I look up at umpire Ken Palmer. You always know when Ken's going to raise the dreaded finger because he leads with the shoulder first . . . there it goes. Oh no, I'm out.

Groans echo around Lord's. I drop to my knees and thrash at the pitch like Basil Fawlty. Ashley almost has to carry me off the pitch and upstairs to the dressing room.

Everyone is telling me 'Good effort', but I'm absolutely inconsolable. Usually, I'm philosophical about getting out – 'Oh well, I did my best' – but this time I just keep saying 'Sorry' over and over again.

And it takes me two or three days to get over it. In bed, eating my dinner, driving to work, during practice . . . wherever, the delivery that did for me keeps invading my thoughts: ball hitting the pad, the shouts of 'Howzat', Ken's face . . . don't give me out . . . the turn of the shoulder. Nooooo!

Just a couple of matches before the end of my career, I experience a new feeling; the feeling of what it is to be a batsman.

LIKE JOHN HURT GETTING READY FOR *THE ELEPHANT MAN* . . .

In the course of my twelve-year international career, I batted just twice in the nets, facing a grand total of four deliveries. I say 'batted' – I never managed to lay bat on ball.

My first net with England was in December 1990 on the eve of my first international appearance in a World Series match against New Zealand in Perth. The nets there are renowned for having the quickest, bounciest surfaces anywhere, and coach Micky Stewart has recruited some first-grade young Aussie bowlers from local clubs to bowl alongside Devon Malcolm and co. and put our batsmen through their paces. They are eager to impress and absolute greased lightning. Having watched David Gower and Robin Smith, two of the best batsmen in the world, ducking and diving merely to avoid decapitation, I decide it wouldn't be wise for me to risk injury before my big day.

I start packing up my gear.

'Where are you going?' says Micky. 'You haven't batted yet.'

'It's all right, coach. I'm feeling in good enough nick. I think I'll pass, thanks all the same.'

'Get your ****ing pads on and get in there.'

I'm not a happy bunny and make no attempt to hide my displeasure as I get padded up. Tomorrow I'm due to play the biggest match of my life and I'm being forced to go in and face dangerously hostile bowling on a lightning-fast surface. What's the point? It's definitely not going to turn me into Don Bradman and, even if I don't get killed, one of these bastards might hit me on the fingers or elbow and I'll be out of the game.

'I think this is crazy,' I mutter as I stalk into the net. 'I shouldn't be doing this.'

Fortunately, Devon understands the situation and bowls a nice sighter, which I can let go outside off stump. The Aussie boy up next, whom I'd seen rock up to the ground on a Harley Davidson earlier, is less charitable. He runs in and bowls a genuinely quick ball on a full length that cuts back sharply and hits me straight in the nuts.

I'm rolling around on the deck, tears welling in my eyes, while the audience of Aussie spectators behind me laugh uproariously.

'I ****ing knew I shouldn't have had this net,' I shout. 'I ****ing knew it. What am I doing in here?'

'Get up, Tuffers, you ****ing coward,' says Easy Rider who has followed through down the pitch and is now leaning over me. 'There's another one coming.'

That's it. I've had enough and hobble out of the net before another Pommie-hating speed demon can direct a missile at me. I'm not going to get maimed for the amusement of some Aussie kids the day before my international debut.

Graham Gooch, who has seen everything, intercepts me.

'Where are you going?'

I outline my position and Goochy couldn't be more under-standing. 'Get back in the nets,' he says.

That makes me really lose it. I chuck my bat down and tell him and everyone in the vicinity that they can go **** themselves. I cop a fine for that, my second in the first six weeks of my first England tour, and I haven't even played yet.

It's eight-and-a-half years before I'm coerced into having another net at the New Wanderers Stadium in Johannesburg, November 1999, during my last international tour.

Of course, I try to get out of it, but coach Duncan Fletcher is having none of it: 'You can't just say you don't really want one – you've got to have a proper net.'

Righto, you want me to have a proper net, Fletch, I'm going to make sure I'm protected. It takes me ages to get all the gear on. Five hours in make-up, darling. Like John Hurt getting ready for *The Elephant Man*. With every inch of my body clad and cushioned, finally I waddle into the net to face Alex Tudor.

Now, the sightline for batsmen behind the bowler's arm in the nets at the New Wanderers Stadium is terrible. It's just trees. So the first ball Tudes bowls, I lose it as soon as it fizzes out of his hand. A couple of hundredths of a second later, the poles are scattered everywhere.

'Okay, okay,' I say to myself. 'Game situation. I'm out. First ball. Try again.'

So I pick the stumps up and Tudes runs in again. This time

he bowls a yorker, bless him (I told him beforehand, 'Don't bowl it short'.)

Same result. Stumps flying.

What am I doing here? What is this achieving? This is really hopeless.

'I think that's enough, Duncan, don't you?' I say and toddle off.

I've done my net. I need to get back to the hotel and have a nice dry Martini by the pool.

Now can someone just help me out of this gear . . . ?

TUFFERS' TEN: QUICKS WHO SCARED THE BEJEEZUS OUT OF ME

Wasim Akram
Waqar Younis
Glenn McGrath
Merv Hughes
Craig McDermott
Allan Donald
Curtly Ambrose
Courtney Walsh
Patrick Patterson
Sylvester Clarke

Wasim Akram

I faced Wasim in the second innings of the Fifth Test of the 1992 summer series against Pakistan. The score was 1–1, and we were sliding to defeat in the decider at The Oval.

I'm batting up the order at number 10 (Devon Malcolm is in the team . . .), and as I walk out to join the Judge, who's 80-odd not out, the scores are dead level with just two wickets remaining.

Wasim is bowling at one end, Waqar is tearing in at the other. Consequently, I am crapping it. On arrival at the crease, I wander around and prod at the pitch a bit, because I've seen batsmen do that, before taking my guard. I want to ask for a yard outside leg stump, but I do my usual and ask umpire Dickie Bird for 'Two, please' – don't really know what that means, but it sounds good.

'That way a little bit, bit more, back the other way . . . yes, that's two, Tuffers,' he tweets in his broad Yorkshire accent, adding: 'It's left-arm round the wicket, there's five balls to come . . . And he's bowling *really* fast.'

Thanks, Dickie.

Wasim always used to wear Reeboks with no spikes. Little sandshoes. He seemed just to glide in to the wicket – schhhh, schhhh, schhhh – and all the speed came from his lightning-fast arm action.

He's bowling round the wicket, he's running up behind Dickie. I can't hear him because he's so light on his feet, then suddenly I just see this blur as his arm goes over. Whoosh. A couple of milliseconds later, I hear the clatter of timber and look back to see my stumps cartwheeling out of the ground.

Waqar Younis

Waqar Younis — he of the 90mph reverse-swinging, toe-breaking yorker. Oh yes, I loved batting against him.

In the first innings of that game at The Oval in 1992 he got me with his speciality delivery. I had come in with eight wickets down, and constructed a wonderful eight-ball innings of 0 not out, building partnerships of two runs with Neil Mallender and two with Devon Malcolm.

At the other end Wasim, who ends up with six wickets, is ripping through the tail, so I'm taking care of the 'weak link' Waqar who is making the ball swing sideways.

One time, he comes in to bowl, and in trademark Tufnell style, I, ahem, make room for myself. The ball just follows me like a heat-seeking missile, pitching bang on my toes. Yeeearrrggghhh.

Someone took a great photo of me yelping in agony as the ball strikes me on the foot – there's no wicketkeeper or stumps in the frame, because I'd retreated so far outside leg stump!

Glenn McGrath

McGrath's bowling was not quite as scary as some of the others, but he was just brilliant. I don't really have a specific memory of facing him, because a similar thing seemed to happen every time. He'd pitch the ball just short of a length on off stump, you'd play at it, the ball would deviate about half a bat's width, you'd nick it, get caught in the slips. Out. Or he'd bowl a straight one, you'd think you had it covered. Oh, it's hit my pads. Lbw. Out. Time and time again. Groundhog Day Glenn.

Merv Hughes & Craig McDermott

Batting against Merv Hughes and Craig McDermott on a fast, bouncy wicket was not my idea of fun. Standing at the non-striker's end in the first innings of the Fifth Ashes Test at Perth in 1991 watching David Gower, who's got just about the quickest eye for hitting fast bowling in cricket history, hopping about trying to avoid chin music from Craig McDermott does nothing to raise my confidence either.

After directing yet another ball at Lord Gower's bonce, Craig turns to me on his way back to his mark: 'That's ****ing David Gower, mate. What are you going to do?'

I don't endear myself to Craig any further when I bowl him with a peach of an arm ball in their first innings and bid him a joyful farewell.

'You've got to bat on this in a minute,' he says icily. 'Hospital food suit you?'

By the time I bat in the second innings, we are sliding towards a heavy defeat. Craig's words are still dancing around in my head as his mate Merv, who got me out for a duck in the first, charges in down the hill towards me, the Fremantle Doctor at his backside. Big, hairy creature, gut hanging out, eyes burning with pure hatred for Poms and batsmen in general.

First ball whistles past my chin. Pheeughh, that was close. I follow the flight of the ball all the way back to the wicketkeeper Ian Healy who is standing a country mile back.

What seems like two seconds later, thud, I hear the ball hit the gloves. Crikey, what the hell is going on here?

Once the shock has started to pass, I turn my head back round, only to be confronted by the frankly distressing sight of Merv Hughes' face, sweat pouring from his brow, snot tangled up in his mighty tache, staring down at me, his nose almost touching my forehead.

'AAAH!' I jump back in shock.

'Ya ****ing Pommie bastard.'

All right, well done, Merv. This is bloody terrifying.

He rumbles in again, digs it in again short of a length and the ball rears up at me again and this time in my effort to fend it off, it just flicks off my thumb. Despite a big appeal, the umpire does not seem inclined to give me out. With defeat inevitable, I decide to oil the wheels of justice a little.

'Ow, me thumb,' I wail. 'I think you've broken me thumb,' and head towards the pavilion. This doesn't leave too much to the umpire's imagination who belatedly raises his finger.

When I walk back into the dressing room, I'm waving my injured digit around like a five-year-old, calling for our physio, Laurie Brown: 'Ooh Laurie, I've hurt me thumb . . .'

Goochy, a veteran of so many battles with fast bowlers, is sitting watching the television monitor nearby. Hearing my pitiful whining, he turns and looks me up and down: 'You ****ing . . .'

He can't even bring himself to finish the sentence.

THE CAT WITH A BAT

Allan Donald

Facing him was scary as anything. The moment I remember most about Allan came in a match for Middlesex against Warwickshire at Edgbaston in the early nineties. And, thankfully, in this case I wasn't on the receiving end.

It's near the end of the game. They need just one more wicket to win and I'm batting with Chas Taylor. Donald is generating some serious revs. There are no fielders in front of square – just me at the non-striker's end, the umpire and Allan Donald. And all I'm thinking is, 'Oh God, just don't get me down there.'

Donald steams in again and bowls Chas a shin-high full toss. He's gone back and across to play it – textbook stuff – but the ball is so fast he's hardly finished his backlift before it raps him on the back pad. Plumb lbw.

Everyone's gone 'Howzat!', the umpire's raised his finger and the Warwickshire boys all start high-fiving and heading for the pavilion.

Meanwhile, Chas has toppled over in agony. The impact of the ball from Donald has just gone straight through his pad. He's lying on the floor, but amid the celebrations no one's paying him any attention except for me.

'Chas, you all right, mate?'

He's lying there going, 'Me leg, me ****ing leg.'

After a couple minutes, he's still hasn't got up and there's no sign of the Middlesex physio, so I pick him up and he hobbles off the pitch hanging on to my shoulder. We're the last people in the bloody ground!

Poor old Chas took one for the team there.

Curtly Ambrose

Curtly never used to say too much – he famously used to refuse interview requests by saying simply, 'Curtly talk to no man.' And on the pitch, he was the opposite of a sledger, one of the quietest fast bowlers you'd ever come across.

But he didn't need to chirp, his stare was enough to intimidate you, and his silence only added to the air of menace. Then the sight of this six-foot-seven-inch-tall giant running in, arms pumping, knees coming up to his chin, before unleashing the ball from about ten foot in the air – well, it was terrifying to say the least. Not that I ever tried to get forward to him, but I don't know how you did, because he could make it bounce up at you from a good length. You had to play everything with your elbow above your head, trying to keep the ball down. Pace, accuracy, bounce, lateral movement – an amazing, amazing bowler.

Courtney Walsh

Funnily enough, I played my best shot ever in Test match cricket against Courtney Walsh. Well, when I say shot, it was actually a 'leave'.

I come in to partner Jack Russell in a Test in Barbados in 1998. Jack's batting well, and I think to myself, I've got to hang in for him. So first ball from Courtney, he whips it down on a goodish length just outside off stump. I break the habit of a lifetime by pressing forward (rather than back and away to the leg side), before realising I shouldn't play at it, and pulling my arms up and away. A proper, authentic leave. Very proud of that one, and against one of the greatest bowlers of all time too.

Patrick Patterson

He was a sizeable unit, bit of a lunatic. Very attacking bowler. You always knew when Patto was bowling his fastest, because you used to see the full sole of his left boot as he got into his delivery stride before crashing it down as he was about to release the ball. That's all I can remember about facing him. I used to be transfixed by his boot, spikes gleaming. Watch the ball, Phil, don't watch his boot. The next thing I knew, the poles were out of the ground.

Sylvester Clarke

As a bowler he could generate pace and spiteful bounce, and he used to scare the wits out of me playing in London derby matches for Surrey against Middlesex. In fact, he intimidated me at the bar, let alone on the pitch.

After one of my first games against him, I'm in the Surrey Tavern having a beer. Sylvester walks in, his big, powerful chest preceding him, and goes to the bar. We've all looked across, and I'm whispering to my mates, 'Sylvester Clarke, Sylvester Clarke, it's Sylvester Clarke . . .'

He orders a pint of Guinness and a brandy. He drops two raw eggs in the Guinness, downs it, then downs the brandy and walks out.

There's me, aged nineteen, twenty, thinking, 'Shit!'

I only faced a couple of balls from Sylvester in my career thankfully. He didn't have the smoothest of run-ups, but then there was this flurry of arms and he had the strength to really bang the ball in at 85–90mph. If he thought you were scared, backing away to the legside, he used to follow you, too. And I was very scared.

BUNNIED BY SHANE

Amazingly, just three bowlers got me out more than once during my Test career. Such carthorses as Glenn McGrath, Wasim Akram, Muttiah Muralitharan and Courtney Walsh managed to breach the watertight Tufnell defence on just one occasion each. Yes, it took a very special type of bowler to earn the right to call me their bunny.

The élite club of three consists of two terrifying quicks – Merv Hughes and Curtly Ambrose, with three dismissals apiece – and the, frankly, baffling Shane Warne, top of the list with four.

Against Warney, I was clueless about what the ball was going to do. I remember one occasion when I went out to bat against him. First ball is a googly, which I don't pick and hits me on the thigh pad as I play forward. Then he bowls me a top-spinner, which I miss trying to cut it. By my third ball, the last of the over, I've given up on the niceties. The ball pitches middle and leg, I put my foot down the wicket and have a huge hack across the line. It's a massive leg-spinner, which grips and spins viciously towards first slip and, needless to say, I miss.

With over called, my batting partner comes down the wicket and says, 'Phil, I think that's the biggest margin I've ever seen someone miss a cricket ball by.' The middle of my bat was not within two feet of the ball!

THE CURIOUS CASE OF THE 'BAT SPONSOR', THE MARKER PEN AND A PLASTIC BAG FULL OF RUPEES

As you can imagine, over the years, bat manufacturers were queuing up to pay me big bucks to use their blades. With my ability to occupy the crease for long periods, investing in me was guaranteed logo airtime, which could persuade literally tens of potential customers that using the same bat would allow them to emulate my swashbuckling style. It's all about aspiration.

Shocking, then, that when I flew out to India for a three-match Test series in January 1993, I found myself to be the only England player without a sponsor. Clearly, this was an oversight by all the major bat companies of the world, and it wasn't long before this was rectified.

During net practice in Delhi in the early days of the tour, a guy who says he's from the Indian batmaking firm BDM comes over to me and asks if I want to use their bats for the duration of the tour. What with me being a spinner on turning Indian wickets, I guess he fancies I'll play in all three Tests (so do I). And maybe someone has told him that I'm unsponsored . . . although it is also possible that he spotted me ostentatiously waving my logo-less bat around as I walked out to bat in a warm-up game the day before (if you can imagine a batsman waving his bat to acknowledge all parts of the ground on making a century, that was me on my way to the wicket – not that I was desperate or anything).

He shows me the bat, and I, being a discerning connoisseur of batsmanship, give it a cursory once-over. Yep, looks like a bat-shaped piece of wood. Excellent, I would love to endorse your brand.

Only one problem, he says. They can't provide me with whites with their logo on. Could you just draw it on the leg of your trousers? Um, okay, if that's all right for you.

We shake hands on a fee of £500 and off he goes.

The next day I'm sitting in the dressing room at the ground, and this chap walks in again carrying a briefcase and a soft BDM-branded bag. Open up the bag and inside there's three BDM bats, couple of pairs of gloves, couple of pairs of pads. He clicks open the briefcase, which is stuffed full of £500-worth of rupees. It's a bit like a scene from a James Bond film. Less James Bond-like, he helpfully dispenses the cash into a plastic bag. Could use it as a thigh pad.

So far, so professional.

With the First Test approaching, I still haven't got any whites with the BDM logo. Obviously, I want to represent the brand properly, so I ask my teammate Robin Smith for help: 'Judgey, what shall I do?'

'Don't worry, Tuffers. I'll get me marker pen . . .'

We lay my Gray-Nicolls trousers on a table in the dressing room, prop the bat up in front of us, and very carefully take turns to replicate the logo at the top of the left leg of each pair. B . . . D . . . M. Beautiful.

As it turns out, the ready-cash stash proves very handy. I do about two hundred quid's worth of it in the first week, due to a slight misunderstanding of the tariffs for making phone calls from the hotel. The rest helps to pay off fines from team management for various misdemeanours.

'That's a fine, Tuffers.'

'May I pay in cash?' I say, pulling out my thigh pad of rupees.

As for the BDM bats themselves, I become the envy of the rest of the England team. All the other boys are using bats made by English manufacturers. But this BDM bat is a bit revolutionary. It's got a big bow in it, a meaty sweet spot and thick edges, the like of which none of us have seen before (and will soon, of course, become the trend). There's major bat envy going on in the England camp throughout the series, but I won't let anyone near my precious bats (even though I don't do any net practice – saving myself). I'm the BDM man.

And despite us getting thrashed in each of the three Tests, I give them value for money, and then some. Check out the squad's end-of-series batting averages (don't bother looking at the bowling ones). There riding high in seventh place, perched above such duffers as Robin Smith, Alec Stewart, Mike Atherton and Graham Gooch, you'll see the name P.C.R. Tufnell, boasting a fine average of 28. Three not outs and a classy innings of 22 not out in Madras, which included BDMing Anil Kumble straight back over his head for one of three boundaries. Bosh.

The way I was striking it, if I hadn't been left out of the First Test in Calcutta (that's a whole other story), Graeme Hick, who topped the averages with 52.50, would have been in trouble.

To this day, I still don't really know if BDM actually sponsored me, though. Years later I found out that this sort of approach is one of the ways in which match fixers 'groom' players to give them information. First, they give you some equipment and some money, next thing they are asking you who's going to be opening the bowling, and soon they've got you hooked.

I never saw any more of, or heard from, the guy who approached me and made the deal, though, so I have to assume it was all completely innocent. And if he really was from BDM, I hope he was delighted with my efforts in the middle (and with the marker pen).

THE BATTLE FOR JACK

I'm sure it's a lot more regimented now, but I can remember occasions playing for England when the toss had been made, we were batting and we were still negotiating the batting order. Allan Lamb habitually batted four (with occasional outings at three if required) but when his international career came to an end, the batting order from four downwards could be quite fluid.

The openers would be getting ready to go out and little huddles of players would form to negotiate who should bat where.

'Ramps where are you batting today?'

'I think I'm four. Or six? Nasser, where are you batting?'

'I'll go five. Thorpey, what about you?'

I suspect club cricket teams are more organised, but that's how we did it.

At the other end of the order, my concern was to secure my slot at number 11.

'Skip, who's number 11?'

'Oh, I dunno. It's between you and Devon.'

Devon Malcolm and I used to battle furiously for that highly coveted role. Sometimes the prospective number nine, and even eight, used to try and get in on the action.

My attitude was that I hadn't made all that effort not to practise batting for years for some chancer to take it over. I fought tooth and nail for jack, until I made it my own. The only reason Dev backed off and accepted the number ten spot was that he got it into his head that his West Indian heritage meant he could bat. He couldn't.

NAMED AND SHAMED: PEOPLE WHO'VE BATTED BELOW ME IN THE ORDER

Despite my best efforts to maintain my élite number 11 status, a few players occasionally usurped me during my first-class career. It's a very exclusive club, and few will openly admit to being a member of it for some reason . . .

Devon Malcolm
Ed Giddins
Neil Williams
Mike Gatting
Mike Roseberry
Keith Brown
Paul Downton
John Emburey
Simon Hughes
Angus Fraser
Norman Cowans
Wayne Daniel
Peter Such
Nasser Hussein*
Andrew Flintoff*

*Nasser and Freddie never actually batted below me but each was absent hurt once (in the second innings of the Second Test v New Zealand at Lord's, 1991, and Fourth Test v South Africa, Cape Town, 2000, respectively) and their names were thus listed below mine on the scorecard so I'll let them join the club. I'm sure they'll be delighted.

THE CAT WITH A BAT

BATTING AT THREE

I have to admit the above list would be a lot shorter if it wasn't for a match against Sussex in Hastings, 1989, when I batted at a career-high number three for Middlesex.

Gus is normally our nightwatchman, but he's had a long and frustrating day. He's bowled well, 26 overs, just 52 runs conceded, but has only one wicket to show for his efforts – that of Sussex's number 11, Andy Babington. After bowling them out on the first day, we're left with one over to bat.

In the dressing room Gatt turns to Gus and says, 'You're nightwatchman.'

'No, I'm not doing it. Why have I always got to do it?'

Gatt's not happy because he's our number three and doesn't want to go out and bat tonight. But after a heated debate he realises he's not going to win with Frase in this mood, so he looks round for a replacement.

'Right, Tuffers, you're nightwatchman.'

'What?!' We have a row, but this time Gatt's not budging, so I have to get padded up.

Sod's Law, our opener John Carr is out second or third ball, bowled Tony Pigott.

Never fancy facing Tony at the best of times, because he's quite aggressive – steams in, arms everywhere – and I'm not happy to be out there anyway.

First ball he bowls me is a length ball just outside off stump. I throw the kitchen sink at it. I get a thick edge, the slips duck out of the way because the ball's travelling so quick and it slams into the advertising boards for four.

Next ball, play the same shot, miss it. Bowled for four. So poor old Neil Williams has to come in as a second nightwatchman.

On the plus side, Gatt never asked me to do the nightwatchman's job again.

TUFFERS' BATTING MASTERCLASS

I finished my first-class playing career with a batting average of 9.69, just failing to break the magic ten barrier. I did manage 136 not outs in 349 games, though. Compare that to Sir Donald Bradman, who managed a mere 43 not outs in 338 innings. Okay, he batted a little further up the order, and he did average 99.94 in Tests against my 5.10, but mine are undeniably impressive stats. I guess that's why over the years so many people have said to me, 'How the **** can you bat like that, Phil?'

So now, for the first time, by popular demand, here's my step-by-step guide to batting the Tufnell way . . .

- Make a will. I made one for the first time before the 1998 West Indies tour and the lawyer taking my details immediately clocked my reasons for doing so: 'Tell me, Phil. You're making a will because you think Curtly and Courtney are going to kill you, right?'

- Avoid net practice at all costs. It will only highlight your weaknesses and make you even less confident. Two nets per decade will suffice.

- Suck up to the opposition's fast bowler. If you see him in the bar the night before, buy him a drink. Buy him two. And when you're bowling to him, never ever sledge him. You can always abuse their batsmen and weedy spinners instead.

- When you're waiting in the dressing room for your turn to bat, do not under any circumstances watch the game. Seeing your openers getting peppered with the new ball will only upset you.

- Find a quiet corner of the dressing room and have a 'Catnap' to kill time and save agonising over the hell that awaits you. Hopefully, when you drift into sleep, you won't have nightmares featuring red-faced Merv Hughes demons, but this is not guaranteed.

- Cricket balls hurt, especially if they hit you at 90mph, so ensure all areas of the body are well padded. Rip up sofas if necessary. Most importantly, protect the crown jewels. Never forget the box. Your gonads will still turn black and blue if you get hit flush in the box, but you'll be unlucky to suffer the same fate as David Lloyd when the force of a missile delivery from Jeff Thomson turned his box inside out and the Bumbleballs ended up squeezing through the airholes.

- Secure the number 11 spot. Middlesex tried to push me up the order a couple of times, but I soon realised that if I got out straight away to an awful shot, the trudge back to the pavilion on my own with spectators laughing at me was highly embarrassing. At 11, even if you get a golden duck, you can hide among the fielding side as you all walk off. You'll never walk alone.

- Play the fool on the walk to the wicket. Mess about, hold the wrong end of the bat, have a joke with the fielders. And leave your helmet off as long as possible to make absolutely sure the quick bowlers know it's you and don't mistake you for a batsman. With any luck, they'll feel sorry for you.

- Remember to take your bat with you. During an Ashes Test in 1981 at Edgbaston, legendary bowler (and number 11) Bob Willis was preparing to take his guard when he realised he'd forgotten this quite important bit of kit. Easily done.

- On arrival at the wicket (hopefully with bat) ask the umpire for 'Two, please'. It sounds like you know what you're doing and taking this guard means you are standing slightly to the legside already, which saves unnecessary movement later.

- Use your arse to the spinners. I invented this revolutionary technique (accidentally) to neutralise the threat of the great Shane Warne during the 1994/95 Ashes series. In trying to pad away a ball he pitched outside leg stump, I got my bat and feet tangled up, toppled over backwards and 'bummed' the ball. As Aussie wicketkeeper Ian Healy noted at the time: 'That's a new approach, Phil. I've never seen anyone try to play Warney with his arse.' As I said, revolutionary.

- Use your feet to the quick bowlers. Step back to the legside and out of harm's way as soon as you can. Timing is crucial, though – go too early, and the more sadistic bowlers will follow you, the bastards.

- Clear the left leg and give the ball a clout through the covers. With the advent of Twenty20 cricket, it's a common shot nowadays, but I was playing it decades ago. In many ways I was a pioneer, but at the time people seemed to think it was just a cowardly way of getting my body out of the line of fire. Pah, the very idea . . .

CHAPTER 7

HANDS OF A PIANIST

MARMALISED AT THE MCG

Fielding off your own bowling is an important part of being a spinner, but it's a dangerous business against the best batsmen in the world who are capable of drilling the ball back at you twice as fast as you bowl it. My first over in Test cricket made me painfully aware of that fact.

It was 28 December 1990. Second Ashes Test at the MCG. Sixty thousand people watching, an atmosphere unlike anything I've experienced before. Dean Jones standing at the other end, staring me down.

My plan is to bowl tight early on, get some rhythm. Jones has other plans. As I get to the hop in my run-up, I look up and see him running down the pitch, bat cocked like a hunter about to club a baby seal to death. Christ, what do I do now?

I can't bowl the ball on the length I'd planned to. What about over his head? Er, no, that might not go down too well. It's as much as I can do to get the thing down the other end of the wicket whereupon Jones fizzes it past my ear like a shell.

'Hard luck, Cat,' says my skipper Graham Gooch. 'Keep going.'

Keep going? That's the sort of thing you usually hear after a few overs' graft without a wicket. I've only bowled one ball! Visions of the worst Test career analysis in history flicker in my mind: P.C.R. Tufnell: one over, no maidens, none for millions.

Okay, come on. Pull yourself together. Just bowl it. The question is where, though?

I run in again, Jones runs at me again, perhaps even earlier this time. I fire it in so he hasn't got room to swing his arms. Hurray, a dot ball!

Morale boosted by this minor victory, my expectations lurch towards the possibility of actually taking a wicket. I decide to give the next ball a fraction more air and hold it back a bit. If Jones gives me the charge again but doesn't get to the pitch, I shall be waiting to pouch the catch.

I hold it back all right, but rather than throw his timing off, it just gives him more time to get into position to marmalise it even harder than he hit ball one. Before I have completed my follow-through, the ball hits me full on the right ankle.

'Aaarrrggghhh!'

I hit the deck and writhe around in pain for a while but no one seems to be rushing to my aid so I struggle to my feet unaided. I look around and realise no one has moved an inch in my direction and there doesn't seem to be much sympathy forthcoming.

Welcome to Test match cricket, Philip.

THE PHIL TUFNELL FIELDING ACADEMY

It is well known that I was neither the best nor the bravest fielder who ever walked a cricket pitch. Rather the opposite. I think Mike Gatting puts it best when he said I had the 'hands of a pianist and protected them like a pianist!' and it's true that I didn't really enjoy risking my delicate digits trying to stop/catch a cricket ball smashed at me.

By the end of my career, I'd turned myself into a workmanlike third man/mid-on, but I was pretty awful in the beginning. And if you are going to get your weaknesses exposed, I wouldn't recommend that it happens in front of 37,000 Australians.

On New Year's Day, 1991, we're up against the Aussies in a day-night ODI at the SCG. I actually bowl rather well, taking 3 for 40 off my ten overs, but my overall contribution is overshadowed by one cringeworthy incident.

The Waugh brothers are building a crucial partnership, when Mark knocks down a delivery from me, and Steve hares off for a quick single. Seeing that the fielder Eddie Hemmings is getting to the ball much quicker than expected, Mark stays in his crease, but Steve keeps running, arriving at the striker's end just as Eddie lobs the ball gently back to me. Seeing that the run-out is a formality, Steve begins taking off his gloves . . . except it isn't.

Somehow, I drop Eddie's dolly-drop throw and the ball rebounds off my Teflon hands ten or fifteen feet away. There's still plenty of time to retrieve the ball, jog back and knock off the bails, but in a blind panic, I sprint after it, pick it up and hurl it at the stumps, missing by miles. With no one backing up, Steve is able to jog back to the crease.

Well, Dame Edna's never got a bigger laugh in Sydney. The whole crowd are hooting as the sadists operating the giant screen replay the entire misadventure over and over again in slow motion from every conceivable angle.

I look to my captain Goochy for reassurance. 'You ****,' he says, which I think reflects the general feeling among my teammates at that moment.

My bottom lip starts to quiver. The only time I've nearly cried on a cricket pitch. Thankfully, a couple of balls later, I get Steve to nick one to Alec Stewart, but my fielding woes are not so easily exorcised.

The moment is replayed endlessly on Australia's Channel 9.

A few days later, as I'm walking out in Adelaide, a huge banner is unfurled in the stand. I turn round and follow its progress: Phil ... Tuf ... nell's ... Fi ... eld ... ing ... Academy. As the final 'Y' is exposed, it's the cue for hundreds of people, young and old, who've come to the match armed with tennis balls painted red, to start deliberately haplessly juggling the balls, dropping them, heading them and singing the Billy Smart circus theme tune.

In the match, Goochy, not showing the greatest amount of sensitivity, tells me to field at deep point right in front of my newly formed Academy.

At that point, I have three options.

Option one: cry, walk off the field during the match, never to be seen again.

Option two: ask Goochy not to put me there, in which case I might just as well take option one.

Or option three: take my fielding position and give them some back.

I choose the latter, walking towards them pretending to juggle and making stupid faces.

Despite my bravado, any confidence I had in my fielding evaporates, and I spend most of my time in the field on that tour praying the ball won't come near me. But the Australian players ruthlessly target me for the rest of the tour. In one match, fielding at midwicket, my nemesis Dean Jones plays cat and mouse with me (guess who's the mouse), hitting the ball to me and taking a single anyway. And when I move in closer in an attempt to stop them, he dabs it past me. On one such occasion, I chase down the ball, throw it in and am pleased to see that Jones is no longer on strike. I think I've restricted him to a single, before a teammate breaks the news that he's run three!

We ended up losing that series 3–0, and Goochy memorably summarised the experience as 'like farting against thunder', bemoaning our players' lack of competitiveness and describing our fielding as the 'worst I've ever seen in any team'. I couldn't help thinking that last comment was directed at me.

Without wishing to make excuses, I'd just like to, er, make an excuse. As Gus Fraser now says in his after-dinner speech, 'In Australia, Tuffers had trouble with grass . . . no not that kind of grass, the grass you play on.' And it's true. The grass out there is pretty coarse, and with the outfields cut and rolled in pretty patterns, the ball snakes all over the place as it travels across the surface. Down on the boundary, as the ball wobbled towards me like a Cristiano Ronaldo free-kick, I often started to question what I'd had to drink the night before.

I did mention this issue to Goochy at the time. His observation on the matter was not dissimilar to his comment on the Steve Waugh run-out fiasco.

OIK CAUGHT LARA

I did pluck the odd important catch out of the sky in my time, though. None more so than a sprinting, over-the-shoulder effort in Bridgetown, Barbados, to dismiss the great Brian Lara in the Fourth Test of the 1994 West Indies–England series. Aside from being rather spectacular, if I do say so myself, it proved to be a pivotal moment in West Indies' second innings as we went on to win the game.

However, a previous piece of fielding in their first innings had earned me the scorn of a West Indies legend. Chasing a ball to the boundary, I try to cut it off with my boot before it hits the wall, but when I turn round to pick it up and throw it in, I don't know whether the ball touched the wall or not. The batsmen, thinking the ball has gone for four, have stopped running, but when the ball arrives at the bowler's end, Jack Russell nicks the bails off and appeals for a run-out.

The umpires call to ask me whether the ball hit the wall. I say I don't know, they give the batter not out and, confusingly, give three runs instead of four.

Anyway, everyone gets rather hot and bothered about the incident, but no one more so than Everton Weekes, the legendary ex-West Indian player, who describes me in commentary as 'an oik of the worst sort'. Thanks, Mr Weekes.

DROPPING HOOPS

I used to go mental if someone dropped a catch off my bowling, but it has been said I was not equally apologetic if I dropped one off someone else's. Sometimes I paid a personal price for my mistakes, though, like the time Gus Fraser was bowling to West Indian all-rounder Carl Hooper in Antigua, 1998.

I drop what Frase thinks is an absolute dolly at mid-off (to my recollection, it was a full-length diving effort). Frase is livid, but I'm obviously not looking apologetic enough. As he walks past me on the way back to his mark, he spits at me:

'Well, you can ****ing bowl at him for the rest of the day.'

Suddenly it clicks with me. I hate bowling to Hoops – he's a totally brilliant player of spin. And when it's my turn to bowl, he duly makes me suffer for my fielding sin, on his way to 108 in three-and-a-half painful hours.

CHAPTER 8

THE ESTABLISHMENT VERSUS P.C.R. TUFNELL

NEVER MIND THE BOLLOCKS, HERE'S PHILIP CLIVE RODERICK TUFNELL

My brother Greg says that I've had a defiant streak for as long as he can remember. Even as a little boy, whatever I was told/expected to do, I'd do the opposite. Like the time I was selected to swim the freestyle event for my school.

I inform my teacher that I will be swimming butterfly – which I'd never attempted before – instead of my normal front crawl. Instead of winning the event as expected, I nearly drown.

When my dad comes to pick me up and I tell him what I did, he gets very angry, we have a massive row, and I won't back down. He stops the car and marches me into East Finchley tube station, buys me a ticket to High Barnet a couple of stops along the Northern Line and says he'll meet me there to give us both a chance to calm down.

By the time I get to High Barnet, I've mangled my ticket so

badly, I get done for not having a valid ticket. It goes to court and I get a fine.

I was eight years old.

By the age of thirteen, I was a punk without a clue. Five rings in one ear, Mohican haircut, booze and fags. I was expelled from Highgate, the private school that my dad worked long and hard to pay for me and my brother to attend (incidentally, the oft-repeated story that I burnt the gym down is an urban myth – I was just unteachable), and headed to Southgate Comprehensive instead. Much more my speed.

I was also developing an impressively deep chip on my shoulder for someone so young when it came to sport. What I hated as a kid was when I scored a hat-trick at football, I'd come off the pitch and they'd give man of the match to a boy who'd scored one. They'd say, 'Yeah, Phil, but you should have scored five.'

I always felt this sense of injustice, of being underappreciated, and that stayed with me through most of my cricket career. Not that I looked like having one back then.

My ability as a batsman and bowler had got me into playing for Middlesex Youth Colts, but by the age of fifteen I had given up cricket to focus on, well, nothing really. Just messing about with my mates, riding motorbikes, getting drunk and trying to pull girls. And it doesn't take a professional psychiatrist to pinpoint exactly why and when my rebel tendencies spiralled into full-on anarchy. The death of my beloved mum from leukaemia around that time was a shattering blow. I watched this strong woman, the rock of our family, waste away before my eyes, and when she died, so did any concept of fairness or unfairness in my mind. Nothing mattered to me for a couple of years after that. And I wouldn't listen to anybody. Why should I do what you want me to? Why's it so important? I've lost my mum.

THE ESTABLISHMENT VERSUS P.C.R. TUFNELL

A TALE OF TWO PHILS (AND TWO PLASTIC BAGS)

A lot of talented sportsmen fall by the wayside in their mid-teens. I could easily have become one of them. My dad was forever asking me, 'Are you going to training?' but at the time I couldn't see any future. I just lived for the day, and gave it all away.

Having left school with one O-level (art), I was just doing a bit of work at my dad's silversmith's workshop to earn a few quid to spend on arseing around. Dad loves his sport and he couldn't bear to watch me waste my talent.

One day at the workshop, as I joylessly hammer away at some precious metal, he comes over to me:

'Son, your eyes have gone dark. You're a good silversmith, but why don't you give your cricket another go? You loved it and you don't love this. You could be a professional sportsman, see the world.'

Me being me, I still take some cajoling and I have to thank my dad for persevering. He gets me back into training a bit with our local team and then to sign up for some coaching at MCC indoor nets at Lord's. Then he gives me a day off work, paid, to attend a trial for the MCC groundstaff when a vacancy emerges for a left-arm spinner (Keith Medlycott, their first choice, had got himself a full-time contract with Surrey instead).

One problem. Gordon Jenkins, someone my dad and I know well from my days with Middlesex Under-11s and Under-13s and now on the MCC coaching staff, tells Dad, 'Make sure Phil gets his mop trimmed and looks smart. Don hates scruffy buggers.' (The Don is Don Wilson, the former Yorkshire and England left-arm spinner and now MCC Young Cricketers head coach.)

My dad does his best, accompanying me to the barber's and forcing me to lose the Adam Ant look in favour of a short back and sides. He even stands over me as I get dressed in my school uniform on the day of the trial, but as soon as he leaves for work, I change into an old shirt, jumper, ripped jeans and winkle-pickers.

The first person my age I see when I arrive at Lord's is a lad with a massive afro, in jeans and a T-shirt. He looks like Jimi Hendrix, except instead of a guitar case he's carrying his cricket boots in a Tesco plastic bag over his shoulder. He'll do for me.

His name is Phil, too. Phillip DeFreitas. Or 'Daffy' as he'd come to be known.

We're wandering around the ground, a couple of wide-eyed kids. We see someone and ask where we're supposed to go: 'We're here for the MCC YCs.'

'They're meeting in the away dressing room,' he says and gives us directions.

We arrive about twenty minutes late. Open the door to see rows of boys, all immaculately dressed in blazers – London Schools, Hampshire, etc.

The coach Don Wilson looks us up and down: 'Fookin' 'ell. You're fookin' 'alf an hour late. Now sit down. And next time, put a fookin' tie on, and get yerself a fookin' blazer.'

Me and Phil sit in the corner, stunned, thinking this is a different world.

I played Second XI cricket for Middlesex and did well at that. Then I got put into the First XI. Did well at that. Whatever level I got thrown into I managed to cope. Even then, though, there was still no real plan in my head. It just sort of happened.

Daffy was always accelerating ahead of me. When he got his first full contract with Leicestershire, I got mine with Middlesex a couple of weeks later. He did so well, he made his first-team debut in July 1985, a year earlier than I did. At the end of the following season, he was selected for England's 1986/87 Ashes tour.

I was down in Oz that winter myself, having been sent there by Middlesex to get some experience playing club cricket.

THE ESTABLISHMENT VERSUS P.C.R. TUFNELL

Daffy's picked for the First Test in Brisbane and I go down to cheer him on. I walk into the Gabba in my tatty old jeans, carrying a plastic bag. And there's my old mate from Harlesden, the lad I used to get pissed with and try to pick up women with, rubbing shoulders with Ian Botham and David Gower, helping them to win the match. As I'm jumping around with all the England fans in the crowd, for the first time it occurs to me that maybe there is a career path here. If I do well for Middlesex, I can play for England.

It took me another four years to get there, but eventually I made it, too. Of all those boys in the dressing room with Don Wilson that day at Lord's, only the two scruffs who turned up late ended up representing England.

PONY-TALE

Hard to believe now in the post-Ashes-2005-Pietersen-skunk-haircut era, but my hairstyle delayed my own entry on to the England international scene. By 1990, word was getting back to the Middlesex dressing room that my name was being talked about by the England captain Graham Gooch. His best mate John Emburey says as much: 'You're bowling as well as any left-armer in the country, and they are definitely looking . . . but you've got to smarten yourself up and buck your ideas up. That means lose the ponytail.'

Yes, the lustrous Tufnell locks are tied back into a ponytail and, apparently, that look does not fit in with Goochy's military vision for his team.

I know I probably need a haircut anyway – the nickname 'Scrufnell' has been getting an airing – but I'm not going to be told to have one by anyone: 'I like the ponytail. If they don't want to pick me, that's their problem.'

A fortnight later – mid-July – we're playing Yorkshire at

Uxbridge. In the morning, Embers tells me he's pretty sure a couple of selectors are coming to watch me play.

'That thing has to go,' he says, pointing to the ponytail. 'I'm serious.'

'Bollocks,' I reply with the usual Tufnell sense of diplomacy. 'Why does everyone seem more bothered about my hair than my bowling?'

At lunchtime, Gatt taps me on the shoulder: 'Tuffers, can you come with me for a minute?'

I'm thinking he wants to talk tactics away from prying ears on how he wants me to bowl in the afternoon session, and I follow him out of the pavilion. But Gatt's in a hurry, and I have to break into a jog to catch up. By the time I do, he's in the car park.

'Hold up, Gatt . . . what? What are you . . .'

He grabs me, frogmarches me to his car, bundles me in, drives to Uxbridge High Street and stops at the barber's shop.

Once inside, he deposits me in the chair like he's my dad and tells the barber that I want a short back and sides. I sit there and sulk as I'm de-tailed, while Gatt reads the paper and makes sure I don't bolt for the door.

My bowling form remains the same as pre-chop over the next month or so. Then in early September, the England squad to tour Australia and New Zealand is announced. I'm in it.

Surely, I can't have been picked just because I had a haircut? That would be a load of pony.

WINGNUT AND ME: A LOVE STORY

In the pre-DRS era, a left-arm spinner with attitude was never likely to get on that well with umpires. So it was I spent a fair portion of my bowling spells, squatting down on my haunches, arms aloft, face screwed up, pleading unsuccessfully for lbw decisions that nowadays would be referred and have a good chance of being given out. And most umps didn't take kindly to the tirade of abuse that I had a tendency to dish out when such decisions went against me, as they usually did. There was one glorious exception to the rule – an Aussie ump whose first name was Neville, I think, although he'll always be 'Wingnut' to me.

I encountered Wingnut during my winter Down Under with Queensland University when I was twenty. All Australian umps, as I soon learned, had an aversion to giving anyone out hit on the front pad by a spin bowler. If my teammates had warned me in advance, I could have saved myself a lot of stressful appealing, but I think they rather enjoyed watching their temperamental Pom teammate self-combust.

The first time I came up against Wingnut, I finally cracked after he'd turned down my tenth lbw shout.

'Not out? Not ****ing out? Who the **** are you anyway?'

He replies drily: 'I'm the bloke who decides if it's out or not. Not out, you Pommie bastard.'

Well, at least I know where I stand and I can't help but laugh.

After that we develop a strangely affectionate piss-taking relationship built on the absolute certainty he'll never give me an lbw. He's a good bloke and doesn't even mind me calling him Wingnut for his red hair and sticky-out ears. As the season progresses, all my teammates want to field close to the wicket when Wingnut is umpiring and I'm bowling to listen in on the banter.

Eventually, I give up appealing. I just turn round and say: 'That's not out, is it, Wingnut?'

''Fraid not, ya pommie w***er.'

It was love.

GETTING THE UMP WITH McCONNELL

I don't remember all umps with such affection, though, most notably Peter McConnell who denied me my first Test wicket on my international debut, in Melbourne, December 1990.

I realise all's not well after a couple of overs, when on my way back to my mark I happen to ask him how many balls are left in the over. It's probably the first thing I've said to him all match.

'Count 'em yourself, you Pommie bastard.'

'Sorry? You what?'

No reply.

'Look mate, all I did was ask you how many balls were to go in the over. I'm not having that.'

The sight of England's *enfant terrible* arguing with the umpire must have the boys in the press box twitching at a potential story. Then my captain Graham Gooch comes over. I'm expecting a ticking off.

'Excuse me, umpire,' says Goochy. 'I heard what you said and you can't talk to my players like that.'

Phew. Relief for me to have the skip's backing and McConnell looks suitably embarrassed at being rumbled. It's not long before he gets his own back, though.

A few overs later, David Boon attempts to cut a short ball and gets an edge through to our stumper Jack Russell who takes the catch. I run down the pitch, celebrating. Yes, I'm off the mark.

It's only when I realise Boon isn't walking, that I look back to McConnell for confirmation of the bleeding obvious.

'Not out,' he says.

Daylight robbery.

'You ****ing bastard,' I spit.

'Now you can't talk to me like that, Phil.'

I never manage to get Boon or anyone else after that, and we lose the Test to go 2–0 down in the series.

THE ESTABLISHMENT VERSUS P.C.R. TUFNELL

Before the next Test, I keep having visions of my gravestone: 'Here lies Philip Clive Roderick Tufnell. Never got a Test wicket . . . but he should have had one.'

This nagging feeling is only made worse when I find out McConnell is standing again in Sydney. Sure enough, he turns down every lbw shout as does the other umpire, Tony Crafter. My only chance is to clean bowl someone or have them caught so blatantly there's no room for doubt.

Thankfully, Greg Matthews, their off-spinning all-rounder, eventually obliges after scoring a century, spooning a catch to Eddie Hemmings at deep mid-on.

As I sprint past Crafter on my way to hug big Eddie, I can't resist a dig, which is directed at his mate McConnell more than him: 'I suppose that's not ****ing out either.'

HOW MY SILLY SODNESS HELPED ME

For all my shortcomings in discipline and dedication to training, I always was a fierce competitor. I think my anti-authoritarian streak gave me my edge. Looking back, I don't necessarily think people were against me – they were probably just trying to make me conform to normal acceptable behaviour in society – but I chose to use their criticism to motivate me. The more people said I couldn't do it, or people had a go at me for wearing an earring or having a ponytail, the more I was fired up to think, '**** you, I'll prove you wrong.' Sometimes, I think I almost created aggro myself to give me something to bite on.

Whereas Geoff Boycott might stand in front of a mirror in his hotel room practising his forward defensive shot for hours, I wasn't conventionally dedicated, but when I got a ball in my hand I was ultra-competitive.

I saw the batsman as the enemy, someone who could send me back to 6 a.m. alarm calls and knocking up plaster on a building site.

I saw him as someone who was trying to ruin my career. Their presence at the crease was almost like a personal affront to me.

It was more of a boxer's attitude – kill or be killed. I must have had that more than most players who reached international level, because, God knows, apart from some natural talent for bowling, I didn't have much else going for me.

I always played on the edge. For instance, when I went into a day's play knowing that I'd been out drinking the night before, on the one hand it gave me a reason to deliver, and on the other an excuse for failure. If the coaches knew about my night out, I knew I had to perform or they'd be on my case. It could help to focus my mind. Equally, I was scared to be properly prepared, because if I'd done my training, eaten my muesli and still got 0 for 100, then, well, I was just shit!

My dad, who had problems with authority figures himself, always advised me to 'be your own man'. But being myself appeared to involve me getting overly aggressive, swearing at umpires and being fined a lot, which couldn't be right!

Before I toured India in 1993 with England, everyone was saying I had to change my attitude on the pitch and I thought maybe they were right. But I just ended up going through the motions on the pitch and lost the fire in my bowling, and without that, I became a bit run of the mill. I couldn't find any middle ground.

While I was a competitive, in-yer-face little sod during the game, once it was over that was it. I could never understand people locking themselves away after a bad performance. My attitude was forget about it, have a drink (or a dozen) and move on.

FRONTING UP TO THE BLOCK

I did feel that I was tagged as a troublemaker before I'd done anything wrong sometimes. One instance was when Middlesex brought in SAS soldiers to give us a bootcamp-style training session near the end of my career. With my dislike of authority and fitness training, it was never likely to end well.

The square block of muscle taking the session splits us into four groups and each one has to sprint up and down between cones.

As we're doing it, he's shouting encouragement – 'Good work', 'Go, go, go', 'Well done' – to everyone. Everyone except me. And I'm not doing anything wrong.

Then I can see 'The Block' staring at me. Call me paranoid but I feel like I'm being singled out. Is my reputation preceding me again?

When we do the next exercise, it's the same again. Well done everyone else, but not me. It's starting to piss me off. I'm thinking he's having a go at me now.

And he's looking at me again. 'Stop looking at me,' I think to myself. 'If you're not going to say well done, why are you looking at me all the time?'

So next time I run out, I kick every cone down, turn round and say, 'What's your ****ing problem?'

Everyone stops doing the drill.

'You what?' he says.

'I said what is your ****ing problem?'

'Right you, come here.'

I march up to The Block. It's a physical mismatch, but I'm fuming.

'Don't talk to me like that. I'm not one of your squaddies. I'm a professional cricketer. Have you ever played cricket?'

'No.'

'Well, don't ever talk to me like that.'

Our coach, Mike Gatting, intervenes: 'What's going on, Tuffers?'

'He's talking to me like a ****ing twelve-year-old.'

'I wasn't.'

Training comes to a halt and Gatt hauls me and The Block away to the bar area to sort it out.

'You say well done to everyone else but me. What's going on?'

'Well, what do you want? A thank you every time you do something?'

'No, but you give it to them every time . . .'

'No, no . . .'

'You were.' I'm on my feet and right in his face again.

'Sit down, sit down,' pleads Gatt.

After a bit more posturing, we both settle down and agree that perhaps we've got off on the wrong foot. He admits that maybe he has come into the job with some preconceptions from what he's read about me and felt that he had to make a point early doors. Equally, he says it's his first day, so I could cut him some slack.

I explain to him that I'm never going to be Carl Lewis, and he says he doesn't expect me to be, but points out that it doesn't do any harm to try and get a bit fitter and stronger.

Air cleared, The Block and I actually became friendly after that. I found out he was a great trainer, and for a fleeting time in my career I actually enjoyed going to the gym.

LUNATICS XI

David Smith
Robin Smith
Allan Lamb
Ian Botham
Peter Willey
Darren Gough
John Morris
Merv Hughes
Ray East
Carlisle Best
Clayton Lambert

David Smith

A six-foot-four opening batsman who liked nothing better than facing fast bowlers pinging bouncers at his head. He had a few fights at Surrey, who sacked and re-employed him three times. Once, when he played for Worcestershire, he marched into the Middlesex dressing room, picked up our bowler Simon 'Yosser' Hughes, who'd given him a bit of chirp when he was batting, and put him on a coat peg, saying, 'Don't **** around with me, Yosser, you little ****.' Yosser was hanging there like a rag doll and a couple of the boys had to get him down.

Robin Smith & Allan Lamb

The Judge and Lamby were a double act. Our two big South African/English middle-order boys would go out and sort everything out for us. They also liked to have a giggle.

In one warm-up game, they gave the twelfth man their own specially prepared refreshments to bring out at the drinks interval.

Judgey holds out his Gatorade bottle: 'Eh, Tuffers, do you want a bit of this?'

'No, I'm all right, I've got my own.'

'Go on . . .'

Lamby is grinning, so I think okay, I'll have a sip.

It's a bloody vodka and tonic on the rocks! And Lamby's got a lager-shandy on the go.

Funny boys.

Ian Botham

A lunatic to the extent that he had the most extraordinary capacity to burn the candle at both ends and still be brilliant and energetic in whatever he did. For Beefy, sleep was wasted life. He'd go out for a big dinner, a good old drink, but then be up at half six to go fishing or play golf on his day off.

It was the same after he retired, doing his John O'Groats to

Land's End walks for charity. He'd walk 25 miles, get on it with his mates in the pub, then be up bright and early the next morning as if he'd been tucked up early in bed. When I did a big charity walk, I had the odd night out drinking, but I really suffered the next day for it. How Beefy managed it, I don't know.

Peter Willey

He seemed almost to sneer at you when you bowled at him, and no one one messed with Pete. Legend has it he once picked up Ian Botham when he was a youngster and hung him on a coat peg. Anyone brave enough to do that to Beefy has to have a screw loose.

Darren Gough

Goughie is just a bit of a lunatic from Barnsley. Ask him why his nickname's 'Rhino': 'Because I'm as strong as an ox.' And I think he gave himself his other nickname – 'Dazzler'. No one calls himself Dazzler, do they, Darren? 'I do because I'm a real Bobby Dazzler! I'll give 100 per cent, me. I'll try all day and then I'll have a drink. Nothing wrong with a drink.'

Like Beefy, he wanted to live life to the full, throw himself at everything and do it with a smile on his face. He used to make faces and stick his tongue out at the batsman as he was bowling, and mess around when he was batting. His enthusiasm was infectious, and he was a brilliant, bubbly character to have with you on tour.

John Morris

'Animal', as he was called after the legendary *Animal Magic* presenter, was another larger-than-life character. Liked his grub, didn't particularly like training. He earns a place in the eleven for agreeing to co-pilot a plane with David Gower during a game in Australia, a stunt that meant he never played for England again. Oops.

THE ESTABLISHMENT VERSUS P.C.R. TUFNELL

Merv Hughes

A big, scary bloke on the pitch and, weirdly, a bit childish when he got pissed – massive bloke + juvenile tendencies when drunk = a bit of a worry. It'd be good to have him on my team for once, though. Also, the crowd always used to enjoy joining in with Merv's stretching routine, so he could lead our warm-up.

Ray East

A fine spinner for Essex, Ray was coaching their Second XI when I was playing for Middlesex. He was a funny fella and I love the story about him fielding at fine third man to a left- and right-handed partnership at Colchester. They kept on pushing singles, so he was constantly running across. In the end, he asked a spectator if he could borrow his bike so he could cycle instead.

Carlisle Best

He played for the West Indies a bit before my time, and memorably, his first scoring shot in Test cricket was a six off Ian Botham. But the maddest thing about Carlisle was that he used to do a running commentary on himself when he was batting.

'And here's Carlisle Best coming to the crease. He's asking the umpire for middle stump – can I have middle stump please, umpire – that's middle. Lovely. He's under a bit of pressure here. First Test match. Who's bowling? It's the legendary Ian Botham' . . . 'And Botham running in to bowl his third ball to the debutant. It's short. Oh, and that's a wonderful hook shot. It's over the fence. Six runs. Magnificent shot by young Best.'

He only played eight Tests, but he'd get a hundred caps for my Lunatics XI.

Clayton Lambert

Big-hitting opening bat, Clayton liked to sing reggae songs when he batted. When we were on tour, he was singing away as the bowler ran in. After the first over, our short leg came up to the slips: 'I think he's singing'.

'Nah, can't be . . .'

Next over, all the slips are listening intently.

'Underneath the coconut tree, me hon-ey' (hitting the ball on the first syllable of honey).

'****in' hell, he is bloody singing!'

Imagine him and Carlisle together at the crease? It would mess with people's minds.

CHAPTER 9

'YOU WILL *TRY* NOT TO GET INTO ANY TROUBLE, WON'T YOU?': TUFFERS ON TOUR

TWO BOBS AND MICKEY'S BUDGIE-SMUGGLERS

I went on my first-ever overseas cricket tour at the age of eighteen, with England Young Cricketers to the West Indies, taking in visits to Barbados, Jamaica and St Lucia. Me, my mates Jamie Sykes, Phil 'Daffy' DeFreitas, Mike Roseberry, Steve Andrew and the rest of the boys let loose on an all-expenses paid trip to the Caribbean? Dear oh dear.

Bob Cottam, who co-managed the tour with Bob Willis, told me years later: 'From the point of view of discipline, you and a few others were the worst group of layabouts I have ever had the misfortune to work with. Bloody headbangers. You could bowl all right, but we should have sent you home within the first week. If we had done, maybe you wouldn't have had all those problems later on.'

He might be right. Through my career, I did seem to have more difficulty than most understanding the difference between a holiday in the sun and a professional cricket tour in a hot country. So what happened on that fateful trip? These are the bits I can remember . . .

First day, we land in Barbados and are driven in a minibus to a very posh B&B on Accra Beach. All very exciting. We dump our bags in our rooms and head out. Chance upon a bar called the Carlisle Club (now known as Harbour Lights). Seven Bajan dollars for as much rum as you can drink. It all goes downhill from there.

We roll back in to the B&B about 5 a.m., absolutely plastered. Two Bobs are waiting in the hall to count us back in. Not happy.

The next (same) day, Two Bobs impose a curfew and warn us that we'll be fined if we're not back before midnight. We decide among ourselves to levy a fine on anyone who is in by then. For the next two nights, I don't see the right side of 7 a.m.

I'm not interested in practice, or nets, or fielding, or batting, just bowling in the middle. Bob W hauls me in and tells me I'm not concentrating enough. He cites an incident of me sunbathing when we were batting. Can't really argue with that.

Even if I actually go to bed, I'm sharing with a chap called John Addison who's a right lunatic. He goes running along the beach at three in the morning and leaves the hotel-room door open. It's the first time I've ever experienced having a room that opens on to the beach. There's a beach bar nearby and a nightclub up the road. The boys are just going mental.

Things don't improve in St Lucia where I get really bad sunstroke. It's a practice day and I forget to put my hat on. Everyone says go back and get it. Oh no, don't worry about that. I spend the next two days honking and hallucinating in my room at our hotel, the Green Parrot. If you've ever stayed at the Green Parrot you'll know it's not a great place to be hallucinating.

Another day, on the coach coming back from practice, Mickey Roseberry asks the driver to pull over at the bank in Castries. He's been wired some money and needs to collect it. It's baking hot, so we're all in shorts, but Mickey is wearing Speedos and a T-shirt instead for some reason. Real pair of budgie-smugglers they are.

The coach pulls over and Mickey wanders off to the bank. Five minutes later, we see Mickey haring towards us with the men and women of Castries in hot pursuit and passing old ladies trying to bash him on the head with their shopping bags, amid shouts of 'Put some clothes on, you pervert!'

He jumps aboard: 'Drive! Drive!'

Unsurprisingly, Two Bobs only selected me to play in one of the 'Test' matches on the tour. That did give me my first sight of future Windies stars Jimmy Adams and Carl Hooper, though. Carl seemed to follow me around for the rest of my career after that . . . just in case I might be bowling so he could give me a whack.

A report on the tour in *Wisden* later claimed that despite losing most of our matches, 'the English players returned wiser cricketers'. I'm not sure Bob C would agree with that. But I did return home with a suitcase full of fine local rums from the islands we visited.

THE WONDER OF NED

Just as Bob Cottam regrets not sending me home from that youth tour, I suspect that, with hindsight, the England management team might rue their decision to have me share a room with Northamptonshire opening batsman Wayne 'Ned' Larkins on my first senior tour, to Australia. For me, he was the best and worst of roommates.

An aggressive strokeplayer, there was no doubting Ned's batting ability, but he did seem a peculiar selection for the squad by captain Graham Gooch and coach Micky Stewart. He was knocking on a bit at 37 and on his last tour of Oz in 1979, he'd played in just one of the three Tests, scoring 25 and 3 (on the plus side – and this was a big plus for Ned – a Northampton brewery still saw fit to award him and fellow tourist Peter Willey seven barrels of beer for their efforts). More to the point, though, there was no one less likely to conform with the new health and fitness regime Goochy was trying to impose on the squad.

In theory, the idea of putting a senior player with the new boy is sound, but as I discover sitting next to Ned on the flight to Australia, this senior player is a law unto himself. He plies me with so much alcohol during the 24-hour journey (not that I need much persuading) that I'm smashed to pieces by the time we land.

After checking in at our hotel in Perth, we wobble down to our bedroom and Ned goes straight past the door.

'I think this is the one . . .'

'Come with me, young man.'

'Where are we going?'

'To the team room?'

'Why?'

'Follow me.'

He opens the door and it's like a beer cavern inside. Cases and cases of Castlemaine XXXX.

We take a case each back to the room. Ned hands me a can, cracks open his own and drains it. Down in one. Then he cracks open another and another, and I do my best to keep up. The pile of empties grows rapidly under plumes of fag smoke.

So this is the life of a Test match cricketer? I think I'm going to like this job . . .

After an hour or so, there's a knock at the door. It's Graham Gooch.

'Come on, boys, we're going for a little run to loosen out.'

'Why's that, skip?' I reply. 'There's always a steward to throw the ball back.'

It's my first real conversation with my captain, and he doesn't really appreciate my joke.

'Twenty minutes. Downstairs.'

'YOU WILL *TRY* NOT TO GET INTO ANY TROUBLE, WON'T YOU?'

Aware that I am the new boy and I have not made the best first impression, I decide I better drag myself out to join the joggers. Ned declines the opportunity in favour of watching telly and working his way through the beers.

After staggering around with Goochy and co., a few of us decide to go for lunch together. I pop back to the room to get cleaned up. Ned's propped up on his bed, smoking and chugging on another XXXX.

'Going for a spot of lunch, Ned. Do you want to come?'

'Nah, mate, I'll be right as rain here,' he replies.

After lunch, I go into town with a few of the boys to have a look around, so I don't get back to the room till eight in the evening.

I open the door to find Ned still sitting up in bed, television still on, bags still unpacked and an impressive pyramid of empty cans against the wall.

'Hello, mate,' he says. 'Fancy a beer?'

SABRAGE WITH LORD GOWER

My visit to Geoff Merrill's wine estate in Adelaide during that tour was something of a social breakthrough in my England career. Beefy, Lamby and David Gower were friends with Geoff, and the newer players weren't usually invited along with the old boys on their jaunts. But this time we were all taken for a tour of the winery.

The place is magnificent. Acres of vines, a huge house with a beautifully manicured lawn where we all enjoy a sumptuous barbecue and quaff the finest vintage wines. This is a lifestyle I've never experienced before, a feeling confirmed by the sight of 'Lord' Gower opening a bottle of champagne with a swish of a big sabre.

There is a sprinkling of very attractive ladies present, too, which adds to my enjoyment of the occasion. I'm fast discovering that by hanging onto the coat tails of English cricket legends I seem to become more attractive, even if I'm just the little fella at the back picking up the crumbs.

'Who's he?'

'Oh, I'm in the team too . . .'

To round off a lavish day, Geoff says: 'Boys, take some booze with you for the rest of the tour.' Thereafter, we can barely squeeze into the team room where our seating for meetings consists of boxes of vintage wine.

I think this was the first time the penny dropped with me that it's not *what* you know, it's *who* you know. Before then, as a scruffy boy with anarchic tendencies, going to say hello to corporate sponsors after the game wasn't something that came naturally, but I soon became very savvy to the fact that it might be in my interests to do so.

Back in those days, there were no lucrative central contracts or big endorsement deals for England internationals, and yet by doing a bit of networking the door opened up to a lavish lifestyle way beyond our incomes.

PALATIAL LUXURY IN JAIPUR AND PLATEFULS IN MADRAS

Probably the most ostentatious example of the perks of being an England player I experienced was in India in 1993 when the team were invited to stay at Rambagh Palace hotel in Jaipur, by the son of the Maharaja of Jaipur. The world's most expensive wedding ever was held at this beautifully restored nineteenth-century palace and previous illustrious guests range from Jackie Kennedy to Prince Charles. There were peacocks strutting around the grounds, our rooms were massive, complete with four-poster beds, walk-in-wardrobes, etc., and we each had personal servants who couldn't do enough for us. Best of all it had an incredibly grand bar and we were allowed complimentary drinks for the duration of our stay.

'YOU WILL *TRY* NOT TO GET INTO ANY TROUBLE, WON'T YOU?'

I felt very David Niven as I joined my teammates for six o'clock cocktails.

The service at top hotels in India is fantastic, but on one occasion it went spectacularly awry for my mate John Emburey.

Staying at a hotel in Madras, one evening before retiring, he orders room service for the following morning: tea for two at eight o'clock.

At 2 a.m. Embers is awoken by a knock on the door. Half asleep he opens it and a line of twenty-odd servants wheel in trolleys bedecked with tea urns, cups and saucers, and three-storey cake stands of sandwiches and cakes.

'Wha . . . what's this?' says my bemused mate as the servants set out this elaborate tea.

'Your tea, sir.'

His order has somehow been mangled from tea for two at eight to tea for eight at two, and now Embers is looking at the world's biggest night-time Scooby snack.

Ordering room-service breakfast was always a precarious business on tour. I soon learned that filling out the card and hanging it on your door was not a good idea, because while you might tick the boxes next to scrambled egg on toast and a pot of tea, the boys who passed your room later after a night out would tick everything, and you could end up with breakfast for six.

'DOROTHY' ROBBERY

Some of the cities we stayed in on tour were a bit tasty. Take East London, South Africa. During the 1999/2000 tour we have plain-clothes policemen assigned to us the whole time we're there. They all carry guns, which isn't a big deal over there, but somewhat unnerving for us. At a briefing on our arrival they tell us about 'The Savannah' area between our hotel and the local shops, restaurants and bars. It's notorious for muggings and we're told to go in groups if we walk through there. So we take the advice and make sure that whatever time of day or night we pass that way, we go in threes and fours.

One day, a couple of us are sitting in the hotel bar having a drink and one of the security guards – a huge unit – says he's going to get some takeaway food.

'Oh great, can you get us some KFC?'

'Sure.'

'Are you all right going on your own?'

'No worries, I've got "Dorothy" with me,' he says with a smile, patting the gun in his holster.

So off he goes.

An hour or two passes and there's no sign of him and we're thinking it's a bit strange.

'He's been a long time, I'm starving . . .'

Finally, he turns up looking very dishevelled and sporting a fat lip.

'What's happened?'

'I've just been mugged on the Savannah. They took my gun!'

This guy is huge, and he's sitting there, his lower lip wobbling with emotion, bless him. He's really embarrassed. Suddenly, we're all having flashbacks to our own little daytime sorties across the Savannah, cameras round our necks, watches and jewellery glinting in the sunlight, and sometimes late at night in a state of some tipsiness. If this can happen to him, what chance would we have had?

We are all very sorry for our gunless giant, and he must feel the depth of our sympathy when he hears my next question:

'Er, where's my KFC . . . ?'

BRAND MULLALLY

During our downtime, we used to do a few group activities. And, naturally, us being sportsmen and all, we liked doing something competitive. Great for team-bonding, not necessarily safe. For instance, the day before the First Test in New Zealand in 1997, we all went go-karting in Auckland.

It's carnage. People cutting each other up, banging into each other and careering off the track. At the end of the race, we all hobble away from our karts battered and bruised, but no one suffers more than our fast bowler Alan Mullally. Somehow the inside of his arm makes contact with the hot engine as he gets out of the kart. Flesh sizzles, he jumps away in agony.

Any Honda executives watching the Test the next day must be pleased, though, when they see our opening bowler running in with the company's logo branded on his arm!

FLYING ZIMBABWE AIR

One aspect of being an international cricketer I loved was the chance to visit fantastic places I might not otherwise have got to see. The air travel to get there was a different matter, though. I've never been the happiest of fliers. I always have to touch the door of the plane and say a Hail Mary before I can go anywhere. Then it's down to drinking copious amounts of alcohol to take my mind off being thousands of feet in the air. All things considered, then, it's quite remarkable that I ever got to see Victoria Falls during England's tour of Zimbabwe in 1996.

It was a trying tour in every respect. On the pitch, we were robbed of victory, and the press reportage of our behaviour off the pitch was downright nasty. We were unfairly depicted as surly and rude to our hosts, and criticised for not making an effort to enjoy ourselves socially (now that was a first!) and take in the sights of Zimbabwe. It was also falsely claimed that none of us could be bothered to go and see Victoria Falls – in fact, our trip had been postponed a couple of times due to bad weather.

When a suitable day finally comes, we go to the local airfield and find two little planes there. One crop-spreader, one Cessna. An old guy comes over wearing a dirty shirt, pair of shorts and DMs. It turns out he'll be piloting the crop-spreader.

He tells us that the regulations state that each plane can take no more than four passengers. There are ten of us.

'We can fit you all in though, really, if you want to.'

We are all keen to see the Falls. Okay, let's go.

I'm thinking the Cessna looks the safer bet, but Athers and three of the other lads get there first. So I join the group with our man.

Touch the door. Hail Mary.

There are four seats dotted around and the rest of us just have to find a space on the floor.

As we're all settling in, our pilot turns round: 'One thing I need you to do – when I take off I want you all to run to the front of the plane, and when we land, run to the back.'

Hmm, this sounds like it could possibly be breaching a number of aviation laws. But we're aboard now.

So he fires up the engine and starts bombing down the runway. 'RIGHT, EVERYONE TO THE FRONT!'

And we all leap up and cram together by the cockpit like a pen of sheep.

A beautiful take-off.

As we approach our destination at the Zambia/Zimbabwe border, it's the same procedure in reverse: 'TO THE BACK, BOYS! TO THE BACK!'

Hearts descend from mouths as our intrepid captain makes a safe landing.

All a bit stressful, but it turns out we got off lightly. When the other plane finally arrives, Athers tells us that their pilot got completely lost in the cloud. In the end, they had to descend to 50-odd feet above ground level and Athers stuck his head out the window to try and locate the Falls!

At least we've got the reward of seeing the magnificent Victoria Falls . . . except it turns out that drought has reduced the largest waterfall in the world to a pissy dribble.

We're all standing there a little nonplussed: 'That's it, is it? Oh, right, lovely . . .'

Can't wait for the ride home.

TUFFERS' TEN: MY FAVOURITE INTERNATIONAL WATERING HOLES

Millers Beach Bar, Antigua

I discovered this brilliant bar when I toured the West Indies for the first time in 1994. We arrived at Antigua airport around midday, and were driven to the resort in minibuses. Halcyon Cove, it was called.

Rum punch, garlands round the neck, there's a band playing steel drums, people all wandering round in bikinis and shorts . . . Wahey, I'm on holiday! Oh shit, no, I'm here to play cricket.

I say to Matty Maynard and a couple of the other guys, 'Right, I'll see you by the pool in five minutes.' Get my kit, lob it in the room and head down.

We're all wearing our official England uniform – blazer with the Three Lions, white shirt, egg and bacon ties, grey flannel trousers, brown Church's brogues just out of the box, stiff as you like. Very much the Englishmen abroad.

The hotel is right on a beautiful white sandy beach with the turquoise waters of the Caribbean lapping gently, so we decide to go for a wander. Soon we come across Millers. Half a dozen tables. On the menu is a choice of fried fish or chicken with rice and peas. Behind the horseshoe bar area, there's a TV, a fridge full of beer and hundreds of bottles of rum stacked up – no order whatsoever. Just get all the booze, and put it over there.

We each sit on a bar stool, which are lined up on a plank of wood on the sand. The sea is lapping at our tootsies, so we take off our shoes and socks and roll up our trousers.

We're all sitting there drinking rum punch, reggae music playing, beautiful bikini-clad women occasionally sashaying to the bar and saying hello.

Matty turns to me and says, 'Well this, Tuffers, has to be the best bar in the world.'

'Matty, I think you're right . . . Barman, another rum punch, please.'

Time drifts away, the sun goes down, fried fish, rice and peas are eaten, many more rum punches are consumed. Around about midnight, we all wobble back along the beach to our rooms, and get our heads down, oblivious to the fact that we've all lost our shoes on the first day (it's the first of five pairs I lose during the tour, a habit that becomes a rum-assisted tradition every time I go to the Windies).

From now on, Millers becomes our team room. Usually, we'll use a room in the hotel for meetings, but why stay indoors when fifty yards away there's probably the best bar in the world? Every night, we meet there. And if you're ever bored or sitting in your room feeling lonely, you just take a stroll down to Millers. After a couple of days, it's like Cheers, the bar where everyone knows your name.

And in Millers one night, I witness the greatest rendition of 'Alouette' I've ever seen.

In the evening, as well as the hotel guests, a lot of boats park up, and the sailors are all big boozers. A lot of English visitors are in there among the locals, all having a chat. Then around midnight, Robin Smith hoists Matty (they are wearing matching Hawaiian shirts they bought together earlier) on to his shoulders, and from his lofty perch Matty launches into 'Alouette'.

Everyone gets involved, from the ladies in bikini tops to sea captains. People are stamping on the floor, singing along. The place is almost literally jumping, the banks of rum bottles behind the bar bouncing up and down to the rhythm. And Matty just keeps going and going, adding new lines to verse after verse, with poor old Judgey grimacing beneath him as he gamely holds him aloft. Just a brilliant night out.

Now I'm not quite sure how this happened, but the England management must have got the itinerary a bit wrong, because we stayed in the resort for two whole weeks. We only had one warm-up game during that time ... which I didn't play in! In effect, I had two weeks' holiday. It was paradise. Ideal preparation for a Test series.

Little bar in Auckland (can't remember the name)

After a controversial mini-series in Zimbabwe in winter 1996/97, we flew to New Zealand. The time in Auckland is eleven hours ahead of Harare where we started our journey, and when we land there after a day-long journey, including a few hours' stop-off in Johannesburg, we're totally disoriented. Body clocks all over the place.

Get to the hotel about one in the morning, which feels like early afternoon to us, so a good number of the team, the coaches, including Bumble, and the support staff decide to head out for a drink.

So we trawl around the centre of Auckland looking for some-where still open, without much success. It is only when we venture off the main drag that we stumble across this cosy little bar.

Despite an exhausting journey, the excitement of being in a new country and the new series of games ahead seem to energise us. We all get on a buzz and the drink flows freely. We've got three or four days off to acclimatise and everyone's enjoying themselves.

As the sun comes up, most of us are still there, including the coaching staff. All getting stuck in, having a great time.

Athers pipes up: 'Bumble and I have got to go. Got a press conference in an hour!'

To show a bit of solidarity, we all stumble out with them into the light. No one's paralytically drunk, just very happy. Absolutely flying.

Of course, by now Auckland is going to work, and we're weaving along the main street among the commuters.

Out of the blue, our physio Wayne Morton turns to me and says: 'Tuffers, have you ever done body surfing?'

'No, Wayne.'

So he lies face down on the pavement, arms extended, in the shape of a surfboard.

'Get on my back. Let's go surfing.'

So I've hopped aboard, side on, balancing on his back, Wayne humming the *Hawaii-Five-O* theme tune beneath me.

I'm waving to cars which are slowing down nearby, I'm chatting to passing commuters. They are all very friendly and seemingly oblivious to the surreal nature of the scene at around 7.30 on a weekday morning.

'Hello, Tuffers. Nice to see you. Welcome to New Zealand.'

'Hello, mate.'

'Hello Phil. How are you bowling?'

'Oh, it's coming out all right, thanks.'

I go along with the rest of the boys to Bumble's and Athers' press conference. Mints are sucked to ward off the booze breath, and a few of us are propping ourselves up on an elbow trying to keep our eyes open, but they do remarkably well.

Xenon, Johannesburg

A fantastic place in which I spent a couple of happy Happy Hours. My favourite tale from Xenon doesn't actually involve me, though, but my great old captain Mike Atherton.

November 1995. Athers has just made 185 to salvage a draw in the Second Test, one of the greatest innings ever by an England batsman. A few England players, South African players, pundits and members of the press head to Xenon to toast his magnificent achievement.

During the evening, Athers gets chatting with Ian Botham and makes the controversial claim that once you reach the age of forty, you can't drink any more. Bristling at the inference that his legendary capacity for alcohol has been diminished by the passing years, Beefy challenges Athers to a Cane Rum & Coke contest. And showing all the dogged resilience he'd displayed for the past two days on the pitch against the Saffers, Athers defies the odds to drink Beefy to a standstill.

(A slightly bizarre aside: according to eye-witnesses one of the South African players spent most of that evening walking around with his flies undone, happily waving his willy about. No one remembers why.)

Pelican Bar, Trinidad

The Pelican Bar was at the bottom of the hill near the Trinidad Hilton hotel where we stayed. It was a great meeting place for all the boys. After the games, West Indian and English players would be there, and plenty of fans. The steel-pan band would be playing. There was a bloke who stood outside selling delicious corn soup with little dumplings and bits of sliced corn in it. And we soon discovered that this soup gave you remarkable powers of recuperation. Whenever you felt a bit lashed, you'd just pop outside for a bowl of soup and return to the bar for another drink revitalised. Fantastic, and as the Pelican was open all hours, rather dangerous.

When we gather there after a Test match in 1998, Athers and Brian Lara spend a couple of hours standing by the bar, deep in conversation. Engrossed, they are. Two legends of the game chatting, having a few drinks along the way.

In the early hours, I happen to look over as Brian says good-bye. As he heads out on to the street, I look back just in time to see Athers keel over. I don't know whether Brian has been propping him up, but he just timbers like Del Boy in that famous wine bar scene.

We rush over to help him.

'You all right, Athers?'

In this situation, there's only one thing for it – we carefully administer corn soup and take him home.

Another drinking story involving Mike Atherton, cricket's answer to Oliver Reed (only joking, Athers!).

Saloon Bar, Melbourne

Love this place. It's like a saloon from the Wild West. The bar is made from barrels and you sit on stools topped by proper cowboy saddles. Put your feet in the stirrups, get the beers in and ride into the evening. Great fun.

There are also pool tables in there, and in a rather merry state I once took on the boss on the top table up on a stage. I broke off and he potted all his balls in one visit.

'Go on then, Tuffers,' he says. 'You've had a "Learner".'

'What's a Learner?'

'A "Seven Ball Learner". You didn't pot a ball, mate – that's trousers down and once round the table.'

So I have to drop my keks and have a jog round in front of a cheering mob who've gathered to watch the game.

Pisces, Kingston, Jamaica

I experienced the unique delights of Pisces in 1994, courtesy of a local Kingstonian calling himself 'Don King'. As per the infamous boxing promoter, the Kingston Don has electric shock hair, black streaked with a white flash, and he claims to be the main man: anything I want, go through him; anywhere I want to go, just ask.

The team has got armed guards and we've been told a few stories about Kingston being a bit scary at night, so while I always like to get out and about and sample the local nightlife, I'm not so sure.

'YOU WILL *TRY* NOT TO GET INTO ANY TROUBLE, WON'T YOU?'

'Nah, don't worry, man. You're with The Don. Don King.'

And true to his word, during my stay, he takes me to some of the dodgiest clubs in the heart of the most dangerous city in the world without my coming to any harm . . . just about.

The night before the First Test I'm sitting in the Pegasus Hotel bar when Don wanders in.

'Where you goin' tonight?' he says.

I've been left out of the team for tomorrow, but it probably isn't advisable . . .

'All right, then, where are we going?'

'I'll take you to Pisces.'

So I head out into the car park with him. Unlike the American version of Don King, he travels in a diddy white van rather than a chauffeur-driven limousine. Undeterred, I squish into this little sardine can on wheels and off we go.

Driving through the notorious district of Trenchtown, I am starting to think this might not have been the greatest idea, but Don is chilled to his boots as he drives us out into the hills.

When we arrive, we walk through a doorway down a dimly lit passage that opens into a courtyard. Even through the thick fog of cannabis smoke, I can see clearly that Pisces has the essentials of all good West Indian bars – a couple of banks of speakers the size of sightscreens and sufficient stocks of local rum and beer to sink a flotilla. However, I can't help noticing through the dense fug of cannabis smoke that a number of punters are sporting deep facial scars. Hmm, maybe this wasn't such a great idea.

I start tugging on Don's sleeve, and seeing the look of alarm on my face, he sits me down and offers reassurance: 'Don't worry, man. You're with me.'

The booming bass and the spectacle of some very attractive Jamaican girls dancing on a makeshift stage helps to take my mind off the somewhat menacing ambience. And when some of the girls start removing items of clothing – it is a very warm evening – I really start to relax and enjoy this slice of local culture.

The night continues agreeably, and it is only an interminable set by a rap act that persuades me that it might be a good time to leave. But just as the rappers wrap up, five blokes seated in the row in front of me pull out handguns and start shooting into the night air. I'm not sure whether this is their way of showing appreciation for the live entertainment, but Don and I are too busy legging it to the exit to ask.

Blues Restaurant, Cape Town

A fantastic restaurant overlooking the beach in the Camps Bay suburb of Cape Town, set against the dramatic backdrop of the Twelve Apostles mountain range. The food and drink there were amazing.

It's one of the poshest places in town, but when we were in South Africa for the 1999/2000 tour, the pound was especially strong against the rand, so we found it *very* hard to spend our *per diem* expenses allowance.

For lunch, we'd go down there and order four giant seafood platters and bottles of the finest, crisp, South African white wine. Usually, we'd be worrying about the cost, but we could sit there gnawing on crab claws and lobster, necking oysters and admiring the view all afternoon, and it would come to about a tenner per head. Wonderful.

A rum shack, Barbados

Among the many joys of Barbados are the tiny little rum shacks dotted around the roadsides. I stopped off for a quick one once, and imagine my surprise when a policeman rode in on a horse. Not bothering to dismount, he ordered a rum and sipped it casually while his horse patiently propped up the bar. Surreal.

'YOU WILL *TRY* NOT TO GET INTO ANY TROUBLE, WON'T YOU?'

Aussie Fish Café, Melbourne or Adelaide

On my first Australian tour, this was another of my first nights out with the stars of the team.

The whole squad is there and I'm sitting on the top table getting spangled on fine wines with David Gower and Lamby and taking delivery of platters of great seafood.

There's a jukebox, and when 'I Can't Get No Satisfaction' comes on I get up and do my Mick Jagger impersonation, clucking around like a mother hen on Red Bull, to the cheers of the lads.

As part of the evening's entertainment, the restaurant's waiters pull the ladies from their tables and dance with them. I'm feeling a bit left out, so I jump up and grab the life-sized bust off the bar and start dancing around with that instead, which has everyone in hysterics.

Strawberry Hill, Jamaica

'Good luck, Athers . . . Good luck, Angus. Take plenty of wickets . . . Ah, Tufnell. You will try not to get in trouble, won't you?' Thus Lord MacLaurin, Chairman of the England and Wales Cricket Board, bade the England party farewell as we headed off to play the West Indies in January 1998. As it happens, I was rather well behaved on that tour (by my standards). However, the same day as the Sabina Park pitch exploded causing the First Test to be called off on the first morning, I did accidentally cause some damage at the luxurious Strawberry Hill resort.

My journalist pal Peter Hayter, my then wife Lisa and her friend Claire take a taxi up there. The driver is tearful because he's so embarrassed at the game being called off. The whole island is in mourning at the shame of it.

The mood is lightened by a great meal, a few glasses of wine and a fantastic view as the sun goes down and Kingston lights up beneath us.

Near the end of our meal, I'm deep in conversation with Peter when a bloke whose face rings a bell approaches our table.

'All right, lads.'

Oh, it's Robbie Williams. Lisa and Claire look like they might faint on the spot. It turns out he's staying at the resort, he's into his cricket and says he's always wanted to meet me (which impresses Lisa no end). He seems like a nice enough bloke – says 'fantastic' a lot and seems almost deferential. Maybe he's a bit overawed finally to meet his idol!

I was in the middle of a conversation when he came over, though, and without wishing to be rude, I quite want to get back to that.

'Well, nice to meet you . . .'

Robbie takes the hint. He says something about going to watch football on telly in his room and shuffles away.

I accept Peter's offer of a glass of port (which unbeknown to us is going to set him back £60 when the bill arrives later) and we retire to a lounge beautifully furnished with nineteenth-century Caribbean furniture and illuminated by the flames of an open log fire.

I'm leaning back on my chair, savouring the ambience, when I lose my balance and fall backwards. All heads turn as I tumble, twisted wrought-iron legs of my chair loudly carving deep gouges in the previously pristine wooden floor.

I jump to my feet, almost shouting my apologies to all present: 'I AM TERRIBLY SORRY. I AM TERRIBLY SORRY.'

Sitting at the adjacent table is a well-to-do English lady who leans over, eyebrows arched, and says: 'Oh, it's you, Philip.'

Time to go.

On the drive back down to our hotel, it suddenly hits me.

'Bloody hell – did I give Robbie Williams the flick back there?'

PART TWO

JUST NOT CRICKET . . .
THE (JUNGLE) TRIALS AND TANGOS
OF A SPINNER TURNED TV 'CELEB'

CHAPTER 10

LOSING IT

They say there is a definite moment in every cricketer's career when deep down you realise you haven't got what it takes any more. Like a veteran boxer, you may try to deny it at the time, try to ignore it, but from that point on you're on the slide. You've lost the edge which made you a professional player. You've lost *it*. For me that moment came in an ill-tempered County Championship Division Two match against local rivals Essex at Southgate in July 2002.

It's a slow, flat wicket; nothing whatsoever in the pitch for me. During the afternoon session, Essex captain Ronnie Irani and their opening batsman Darren Robinson are cruising along to a century partnership. I can't buy a wicket. It's a day for doing the hard yards, trying to outwit the batsman, because it could easily take 20 overs to get your man in these conditions. In the past I would have stuck in there, but today, to be brutally honest, I simply can't be arsed.

Adding to my frustration at my inability even to look like getting anyone out is the stick I'm getting from the Essex boys. Ronnie and his crew know how to wind me up at the best of times and today I'm just not in the mood.

Then, after wheeling away fruitlessly for over after over, I'm bowling to Darren who clips me off his legs for two easy runs. Suddenly, something inside me just snaps. As he's running to my end, I go up to him:

'You ****ing ****'

Then as he turns for a second, I kick him in the leg. A really big kick. 'You ****.'

He goes: 'Oh, oh . . .' like that.

'What's happened there?' says the umpire, who must have been looking elsewhere.

'Nothing, nothing,' I reply, thinking, 'my God, what have I done?'

'Go on, carry on . . .' I say, feigning innocence.

'What?'

'I said play on, play on. What are you getting worried about?'

All the while, Darren is going, 'Oh, my ****ing leg! My leg!'

By some miracle, the umpire hasn't quite understood what's happened and the square-leg umpire hasn't seen it either, so we just play on.

Two overs later, it's teatime. Ronnie, all padded up, and their coach Goochy march into our dressing room.

Our coach Gatt comes over, too: 'Phil, Phil, you can't do that.'

'I know, I know,' I say. 'I'm really sorry.'

And I really am. I feel like a total mug. Totally ashamed. I've had more than my share of onfield tantrums with batsmen and umpires, but it's always been down to my will to win. This is different. Instead of using my years of experience and fighting hard to earn a wicket, I've just given up and kicked someone.

I sit there for ages, shaking my head in disbelief at what I've done.

'Well, I've been forever waiting for this time,' I say to myself. 'This is the time.'

Maybe it was the embarrassment and disappointment that made me say it aloud. But it showed that deep down I knew my number was up as a professional. Of course, I kept on playing until the end of the season, by which time I was thinking I could maybe play a few more for Middlesex. However, in truth, that petulant kick marked the moment I lost the desire and competitive edge you need.

Retirement beckoned, and it came a lot sooner than I expected.

I'M A CRICKETER . . . GET ME OUT OF HERE! HOW NOT TO NEGOTIATE YOUR FINAL CONTRACT

All through my career at Middlesex, I was on a rolling three-year contract, and at the end of each season another year was added, almost automatically. It gave me some security, and I think it was good for the club to have their top wicket-taker on a long contract, too.

By the end of the 2001 season, aged 35, it was clear my England days were over – perhaps the face didn't fit any more, if it ever really had. I wasn't playing much one-day cricket for Middlesex either, which wasn't my decision, but I was still Middlesex's main wicket-taker in the County Championship as I had been for the past decade. With no more international cricket to play, I could focus solely on doing my best for Middlesex, play till the age of 40, then say thank you and goodnight. So when I went in for contract talks in autumn 2001, I expected to be offered my usual one-year extension.

I go to see the captain Angus Fraser and club secretary Vinny Coddrington in the Middlesex Room at Lord's. They are sitting behind a circular table, a freshly minted contract in front of them. Say hello, then the conversation goes something like this:

'Everything's good,' I begin. 'The England stuff's gone, you know, but I love Middlesex, still love playing cricket and I'm still taking wickets . . . so I'm looking for my usual extra year.'

'Well, Phil, things have slightly changed,' replies Gus.

'Okay. What's new?'

'We're only giving out one-year contracts now.'

'Oh, right. Why's that?'

'Well, you know, we want to keep people on their toes and if you give people long contracts . . .'

'Well, yeah, but I've been here for sixteen years so you know what I'm about.'

'It's just to keep people on their toes. And I don't think you've done enough to earn that extra year.'

'What do you mean?'

The big problem here is that Gus and me are mates. We've sat together in the dressing room for years, and I confide in him. And in the recent past, I've seen my second marriage go up in smoke and had a pretty horrible time off the field. He alludes to that, claiming my behaviour is affecting the team, which I think is out of order.

'I told you that in confidence. Judge me on my performance, and I'm your best ****ing bowler.'

I have a rant, but when I've calmed down (a bit), I accept that I'm not going to get an extra year. They're not finished, though.

'And it will be reviewed after three months . . .'

'What?'

'Well, we're going to review everyone's contract after three months.'

This revelation I don't take quite so well.

'Wha . . . what am I? ****ing hell! You're treating me like a triallist.'

'You're no different from anyone else, Tuffers.'

'I ****ing am!' I said. 'I've been here for sixteen years. I've trained next to your spotty arse.'

This is Angus Fraser, my partner on the Bench of Knowledge.

'I didn't mind the one-year contracts. Look, if you want everyone to prove themselves that's fine, I've got nothing to worry about. I'll earn a contract every ****ing year. The little boys that are rubbish and getting paid, they're the ones that are going to be worried, not me. But to say it's going to be reviewed . . .'

Seeing they are not going to budge, I completely lose it. I start shouting at Gus again. He decides he's had enough of me, too, and stands up, giving as good as he gets. Vinny, meanwhile, is just sitting there looking as shocked as Bishop Brennan after being kicked up the arse by Father Ted.

I grab the contract and throw it: 'There's your ****ing contract!'

It's only held together by a paper clip. As we scream at each other, the sheets float down gently between us.

I stride out of the room, cursing and slamming the door behind me.

When I leave the room (as Gus tells me later), Vinny and him sit there in stunned silence for about half a minute, before Vinny pipes up:

'What the bloody hell has gone on there? He can't behave like that. We've got to discipline him.'

'No, he's all right. Don't worry about it.'

'He can't talk to us like that.'

'Vinny, it's like that in the dressing room most bloody days! If I'd got in trouble for every time I had a raging argument with Gatt, I'd have been fined every week, too. We'll leave it . . .'

Just as he says that, I storm back into the room, unleash another volley of abuse, and then storm out again.

So, that all went well.

The following season I helped a young and inexperienced Middlesex team, captained by Gus's successor Andrew Strauss, to promotion to the First Division. Then out of the blue, during the off-season I received an offer from ITV to appear on the second series of *I'm a Celebrity . . . Get Me Out of Here!* where 'celebrities' are dropped in the Australian jungle for a couple of weeks and made to do various challenges to win their supper and viewers' votes. The first series, won by veteran DJ Tony Blackburn, was watched by millions. It looked like a fun little challenge, something different, and the money on offer would come in handy, too.

Nowadays, *I'm a Celebrity* is broadcast in winter, but this series was scheduled for spring and was going to cut into the pre-season training schedule. As my role in the team never depended on physical fitness and I had got all those years of experience behind me, I was confident I could do the show and still get my bowling match-sharp. But when I ask the powers-that-be at Middlesex, they refuse permission, which is fair enough.

Fast forward to pre-season training. Mid-March, 2003. We're down at Merchant Taylors' School, Northwood, doing a bit of middle practice. It's raining, everyone's freezing cold. No one wants to be there.

After a miserable morning, I'm lying on a table in the old school pavilion munching on a Sunblest ham sandwich I've just made, feeling sorry for myself. Then I turn to Nashy and say, 'What the **** am I doing here? This is the big thing I'm supposed to be here for? I could be going to the jungle and I've turned it down for this?'

I have to admit I cut a couple of practice sessions after that. Not surprisingly, Straussy is unimpressed and phones me up.

'Look, Tuffers, what the bloody hell is going on? We're back in the First Division, we're trying to prepare here. We can't have you doing what you're doing . . .'

After a few seconds pause, I reply: 'Why don't you all just **** off. That's me done,' and put the phone down.

Everything had caught up with me. Straussy was right, of course, but it was hard to take being told what to do by a bloke in his mid-twenties. And although I was still bowling well, I wasn't playing in a good team any more. Top players, and good mates, like Gatt,

Embers, Gus, John Carr, Neil Williams had gone, replaced by a bunch of kids. It could take years to get back to where we were and the truth was I wasn't enjoying the slog of county cricket any more, with all the training and travelling it involves.

That incident with Darren Robinson had been a warning sign that things weren't all they should be. And, looking back now, I actually think Straussy, Gus and Vinny proved to be the biggest allies in my career. They forced my hand and perhaps they were right to do it.

My Middlesex career was over. Time to do something else.

I call up my agent Mike Martin: 'Is that jungle thing still possible? Get me on it . . .'

JUNGLIST POSSE

So how did I become the King of the Jungle? Like all reality TV contestants, I got asked afterwards whether I went in with a 'strategy' and I didn't have a clue what they meant. I just turned up and got stuck in. In a game of cricket, you can outwit the batsmen, get a five-fer and help your team win the game, but on this show all you're doing is sitting in a camp in the Queensland rainforest, talking to people and occasionally having a bucket of mealworms chucked over your head. How can you have a plan when it all comes down to the votes of the public rather than any skill?

As well as the fee, my partner Dawn and I got an all-expenses paid trip to Australia – first-class flights, luxury hotel. The worst-case scenario was that I got chucked out first and spent a week in the Versace Hotel with Dawn drinking them out of Dom Perignon.

All I could do was be myself, try to get on with everyone and have a laugh. It turned out that quite a few of the 8.5 million viewers who watched on average each night enjoyed watching me do that, so I spent the full fifteen days of the show living in a tiny jungle camp while Dawnie lived the high life.

At first, there are ten of us in camp – an actress (Daniella Westbrook), an actor (Chris Bisson), a TV weather forecaster (Siân Lloyd), a model (Catalina Guirado), a TV chef (Antony 'Wozza' Worrall Thompson), an eighties pop star (Toyah Willcox), a ballet dancer (Wayne Sleep), a TV interior designer (Linda Barker), an ex-footballer (John 'Fash The Bash' Fashanu) and me. Each day of the first week, the public vote for the person they want to do a 'Bushtucker Trial' and in the second week, people got voted off daily.

Aside from the trials and the odd expedition to find the 'Celebrity Chest' (which gives us the chance to win treats) very little happens each day. In fact, the daily experience is not that dissimilar to spending a washed-out Wednesday in the pavilion at Headingley, only with a few more creepy-crawlies knocking about. I think this gives me an advantage over the non-sportsmen in the group. All those years sharing a dressing room with a group of guys, living in each other's pockets on tour, have taught me that you can't be selfish. Being a team member comes naturally to me. Whereas I can see one or two people claiming the best bed, the last bit of rice or whatever, I try to look out for other people and let them do their thing, whether it's Toyah meditating or Fash doing his martial arts exercises and saying 'Focus' a lot.

I really enjoy my time in camp. We have to get our own water and wood for the fire – it's just like being a Boy Scout again. And even when there isn't much going on, you can sit round the campfire, have a chat and listen to someone tell you their life story. It's a lovely thing to live without the mobile phone going off every five minutes, get some kip, and do something completely out of the ordinary.

My cricket career seems well and truly behind me, and the thought that I should be back in the nets at Lord's never enters my head. However, one day, they do send a Kwik Cricket set into camp so we have a little game. I'm sure my old Middlesex and England colleagues will have enjoyed seeing Fash run me out with a smart bit of fielding and 'It's a Mystery' singer/bowler Toyah take my prized scalp with a fine delivery that pitches on a crack and nips back through the gate.

Before going into camp, we've been briefed about the dangerous wildlife to look out for – black widow, funnel-web and redback spiders, snakes, bugs and the like. I see a few spiders and there are always loads of rats running about, but after a day or two, it doesn't really bother me. In fact, the discovery of a spider on one of the beds leads to one of the funniest moments. Thinking it might be a redback, Chris, me and couple of the other guys pick up sticks and surround it. We're all standing there looking, and the spider is standing stock still. Then – boo! – suddenly it makes a move. Chris takes such a fright that he jolts back, loses his balance, topples off the little ridge he was perched on and smashes his head really badly. Well, perhaps Chris doesn't find it so funny . . .

The lack of food and cigarettes is the only downer. Before the end of the first week, a lot of conversation around the campfire has degenerated into wistful Homer Simpsonesque food fantasies – 'Mmm, egg and bacon sandwich' – and by week two, people are feeling pretty undernourished. On the Bushtucker Trials you have to collect stars, each of which is supposed to equate to one meal, but when the food parcel arrives each evening, it seems as if half a carrot is regarded as a meal's worth. It's lucky we've got chef Wozza in there with us – lob him a few hundred grams of wallaby meat, a courgette and a couple of potatoes and he can do wonders. But even he gets upset one night at the meagre rations and stages a walkout in protest. Thankfully, he comes back and doesn't get voted off till a couple of days before the end, so the little we do get to eat is cooked by a pro.

Being a bit of a chain smoker, my limited ration of ten cigarettes per day is the hardest thing to deal with. Catalina has somehow managed to smuggle a few extra ones into camp in her hair, so I ponce a couple from her. However, one night I drink a couple of glasses of wine we've been given as reward for successfully completing a task. Having had very little to eat, the alcohol goes straight to my head. By the early hours of the morning I'm in high spirits, but out of ciggies and I really fancy one.

I can smell smoke coming from one of the little huts around the camp where cameramen are stationed at all hours to record proceedings. The guy's obviously having a crafty one while he's on shift.

'Psst. Gissa fag.'

No reply.

'Come on, gissa fag, please. I'll give you £500 for a cigarette.'

Still no reply. Then he pretends to bark like a dog. It's not very convincing.

On the following evening's highlights show, viewers are treated to nightcam footage of a nicotine-deprived ex-cricketer kicking a hut door in search of his cigarette fix.

Viewers never vote for me to do a Bushtucker Trial in week one, but I volunteer to do a couple in the final week when it's down to the campers to decide.

In 'Shooting Star', I have to swing around over a gorge, trying to hit stars with a stick. It's at least a hundred foot drop, but I'm harnessed up and don't mind heights so it's actually quite enjoyable and I get eight out of nine stars. The second one, 'Jungle Slide', involves being tied to a bungee rope and dragged through an eel-infested swamp and up a muddy slope where you stick your hand into a snake pit to grab a star before twanging back down again, which is less enjoyable. But I get four out of six stars, which isn't bad.

By the last day, it's down to just three contestants – Fash, Linda and me – and each of us is given a task. I get the now infamous 'Bushtucker Bonanza' eating trial. While the presenters Ant and Dec stand there giggling, I force down wichetty grubs, dung beetles, moth pupae, ants and worms. It's edited down to a five-minute segment on the show, but I sit there for about half an hour, swearing at the wichetty grubs and psyching myself up to do it.

I really do recommend eating things that are dead rather than live creatures you can feel wriggling about as you swallow them. Horrible. Again, though, I think my background as a professional sportsman helps, because (like Fash) I know how to focus and just get on with it.

Afterwards, I feel a peculiar sense of achievement at overcoming my fears and stomaching all five Bushtucker dishes (for a week afterwards, I do wonder whether I might fart a moth, though). More importantly, those among the ITV viewers who pick up the phone and vote seem to have been mightily impressed as I am later crowned 'King of the Jungle', with Fash and Linda finishing in second and third respectively.

And so it was that I joined a select band of cricketers who've won something in Australia, even if it was a crown of ferns rather than that little wooden urn.

THE PIED PIPER OF SUTTON

On coming out of the jungle, the main priorities are having a bath, a nice bit of grub and a few beers. Sadly, my shrunken stomach swiftly rejects the three milkshakes and a couple of Big Macs I shovel down, and after two beers back at the hotel I'm plastered. The following day, we fly home.

When we walk into the arrivals lounge at Heathrow, I'm bewildered to find hundreds of paparazzi waiting for me. I've had a few text messages from mates saying they've been watching, but no grasp of how big the show has become. My agent Mike rings and tells me that 12.73 million people watched the final show, and, because I won, my nominated charity, Leukaemia Research, will receive over £400,000 as a percentage of the phone vote. This means a lot to me and I'm very grateful to everyone who voted. Fantastic news.

'Oh, and you need to get your arse down to BBC Television Centre because you're on the Jonathan Ross show tonight.'

'What?'

When I see Mike later in my dressing room at the Beeb, he runs through the mountains of offers he's received for me, which has me dancing around the room with a mixture of joy and disbelief.

'What is going on? This is madness.'

I was earning reasonable money at Middlesex and the makers of *I'm a Celebrity* matched my annual salary. Very good money for sitting in a jungle for a fortnight, and I was told that I might get some work off the back of the show, but there was no grand plan after I decided to quit cricket. If I'd been voted off straight away, I might have been scrabbling around for employment.

A couple of days after getting back, I walk up the road from our house at the time to Sutton High Street to get a McDonald's and do some shopping. As I toddle along, I become aware of a presence behind me. I look back over my shoulder and realise there's a mass of people following me. I'm used to being recognised by young lads who like cricket, but this is boys, girls, mums, dads, grandparents. When I veer to the right, they do too. When I cross the road, they cross the road. By the time I get to MaccyDs, there's about 200 of them and they all follow me in.

I get as far as ordering myself a Big Mac, fries and strawberry milkshake. Everyone's being very nice, asking for autographs, but the crush is getting the manager worried and in the end he has to call the police to help usher me out.

A couple of weeks later, I pop down to Lord's to catch the First Test between England and Zimbabwe. As I'm walking through the Grace Gate with Peter Hayter, I hear a cry of 'IT'S PHIL!' Within seconds, I'm mobbed. I've walked through those gates a thousand times before and no one has paid a blind bit of notice. We have to run to the safety of one of the hospitality tents, before sneaking out the back way and sprinting around Lord's pursued by schoolchildren to get to our seats.

My life had changed.

At the back of my mind, I did still have a hankering to play cricket. I received a couple of offers to play four-day cricket in 2003, and I know I could still have done a job. But I've always been a Middlesex boy – I didn't want to play for anyone else – and I'd well and truly burnt my bridges there. No, my professional cricket days were over.

I needed to find something else I could focus on and develop into a lasting career. The world of television which I'd fallen into seemed to offer me the best opportunities.

CHAPTER 11

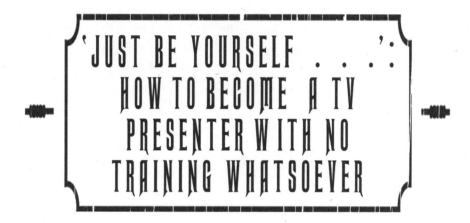

'JUST BE YOURSELF . . . .':
HOW TO BECOME A TV
PRESENTER WITH NO
TRAINING WHATSOEVER

BLOWERS FOR PLAYBOY TV!

The first year after I won *I'm a Celebrity* was just mental. A lot of cricketers really struggle to adapt to normal life after a career of playing in front of big crowds, and they can't find anything that gives them the same buzz. I was very lucky in that respect, because winning a reality show brought me lots of exciting opportunities that grabbed my interest straight away. I didn't really have time to be depressed or miss my old career.

I was often doing three jobs a day – opening a supermarket, recording some TV show and then going out and speaking at a dinner – every day, and that continued week after week.

I've always enjoyed meeting people, so that helped me, but it was a very strange time. An absolute life-changer. I became a so-called 'celebrity'/'celeb'/'sleb', which is a very odd thing to be, and I'm still very uncomfortable with that tag. I cringe when I'm asked about it, because I don't see myself as that.

Am I a celebrity? If I am, is that a good thing? Some celebrities seem to be famous without any obvious talent. At least I achieved something as a cricketer, and I'd represented my country before going on to do something else. But it was bumbling around in the jungle that made me famous to the wider public. The amount of times people have said to me, 'Aren't you the bloke who ate them bugs?'

'Actually, don't you remember when I bowled out Viv Richards?'

'Who's Viv Richards?'

Strange world.

It was a difficult time for me and Dawn, too, because we hardly ever saw each other. And because people had this image of me as a bad boy who loved the birds, a lot of people were trying to push me that way again, and it wasn't what I wanted any more.

I did have the feeling that I should make hay while the sun shines, but after a while I did start to flag. I was knackered by the time I turned up for the third job of the day, and couldn't remember what it was like to have a weekend off. I couldn't keep smashing into everything. And while I was interested in pursuing TV work, I wanted to find something with a bit more potential for longevity. I knew my jungle fame couldn't last for ever and, with only one O Level to fall back on, the captains of British industry were not exactly queuing up to offer me a place on the board.

I turned down £150k to become a presenter on Playboy TV for six months because I thought that it might cut off other opportunities. I don't think the BBC would have fancied having a soft-porn presenter on the *Test Match Special* team. Although, thinking about it, Blowers would be a mind-blowing Playboy TV presenter. Just imagine . . .

No, presenting porn was not for me, but being a TV presenter was an option. As a cricketer, I'd never been particularly frightened of being in front of a camera, which some people are. Rather than being shy, my attitude, if anything, had always been to go out and have a bit of a laugh with it. My perception of working on TV was that it would be another buzz. It might not replace the thrill of playing big-match cricket, but I could see similarities in the demands of it. Just like when you're thrown the ball to bowl against the Aussies in an Ashes match, when the director calls 'Action' you have to get on with it. You have to do it now.

'DON'T FALL IN THE POOL!' THE SHORT LIFE AND DEATH OF A CATCHPHRASE

My first proper presenter's job after *I'm a Celebrity* was a year later, co-presenting a primetime Saturday night show on ITV1 with Kirsty Gallacher called *Simply the Best*. A revamped version of *It's a Knockout* (for younger readers, think *Total Wipeout*), it featured obstacle courses, physical and mental games, quizzes, and lots of dressing up in fat suits. There was also live music from pop stars in between the games.

Each episode was designed to be 'a clash of the titans' between teams representing the United Kingdom's biggest cities, from London to Glasgow, Belfast to Newcastle. Two teams of six gym-fit contestants, who'd auditioned for the privilege of taking part, were supported by four celebrities per side who had ties to each city, competing for a place in the finals.

Making the series has the familiar feel of a cricket tour because they send us off to Jersey for the whole of July 2004, recording episode after episode, one day on, three days off, so there's plenty of opportunity for 'refuelling' and high jinx in between times.

Two teams of contestants and celebrities arrive, say, on the Thursday. You greet them all, have a drink in the bar with them, do the rehearsal on the Friday, then the show in front of a live audience of 1,500 spectators on the Saturday. On the Saturday night everyone's buzzing about the show, so you all go out and have a few more drinks. Sunday off to nurse the hangover and then Monday the next mob arrives. And so it goes on.

The social element is not a problem, but I'm absolutely terrified about presenting the programme. It's one of the biggest shows ITV have commissioned for Saturday night for years, so I could really do with a bit of training. I've never fronted a show before and I've had absolutely zero preparation. I'm forever saying to the producers, 'I haven't had any training.' They're all very nice, but the response is always the same:

'Don't worry about it, Phil. Just be yourself. Anyway, here come the guests now . . .'

'Oh, all right then . . . Hello. Do you want a drink?'

Be yourself? My dad's always offered me that advice, but it's not something I've heard too many captains, coaches and disciplinary committees say during my cricket career. And, for once, I actually want to practise.

Problem one for me is that I've never read an autocue in my life, and I'm a bit dyslexic. So I read my links beforehand and try to commit them to memory, because if you try to read them from scratch it goes horribly wrong. Of course, I drop a few clangers anyway, putting the punctuation in the wrong place and such like:

'And we've got Dave and Sheryl here from Parsons. Green Dave . . . er, so what do you do when your not wearing a sumo suit?'

It's also the first time I've ever had an earpiece. So while I'm trying to remember my lines and read the autocue, I've got the director barking instructions in my ear. 'Cue left.' 'Cue right.' 'Okay, coming to you, Phil . . .'

'Hi, it's Saturday night, and I'm here with Dave and Sheryl from Parsons. Green Dave . . .'

I'm really trying hard, but just wide-eyed with fear at times. Some of the cameramen and floor staff I get friendly with try to guide me, but, again, the advice is usually, 'Be yourself', 'Just do it', which doesn't seem any use at all to me.

One thing I'm very keen to sort out early doors is to get myself a catchphrase. I grew up watching the great gameshow hosts – Bruce Forsyth with his 'Nice to see you, to see you . . .', 'What do points mean?', etc. – and I fancy a little slice of the action.

I'm lying in bed one night thinking about it, just like when I was working out how to bowl people out. The old penguin on its back again.

Now, we've got a game where the contestants, dressed in fat suits, have to carry buckets of water across these revolving cylinders over a swimming pool. Ding! Light bulb moment: 'Don't fall in the pool!'

I'm convinced it's a winner.

When the time comes to play the game, I release my brainchild like a proud father dropping his daughter off for her first day at school.

Episode one – 'Don't fall in the poooool': none of the spectators seem to be shouting it along with me.

Episodes two, three, four – come on everyone. 'Don't fall in the poooool!' Am I the only one saying it? Hmm, I guess even Brucie's famous phrases took a while to catch on. Just a matter of time before viewers at home are shouting it at the telly . . .

Some contestants wish they'd followed my advice, though. They all arrived in Jersey brimming with health and fitness, but quite a few go home in bandages and slings from falling off obstacles and bashing their head or breaking an arm on their descent into the pool. The organisers must have suspected it could get messy, as they always bring out four standbys for each team.

After a couple of weeks, I think the pressure of presenting a high-profile show on the hoof, without any previous experience, is getting to me, and I have to admit the relief of finishing an episode does trigger some epic drinking sessions with the contestants.

By the end of the month's filming, I'm absolutely shattered, shot to pieces. I took the job thinking, 'Good money, a nice month away in Jersey – do it for a bit of fun and throw yourself into it,' which is what I did. I hadn't really thought about what I was taking on, but I just about got away with it. And looking back now, I can see that being thrown in at the deep end like that stood me in good stead as a TV presenter, because it taught me to think on my feet. I'm quite good at it now . . . not that I've discovered exactly what 'it' is. I guess I'm just better at 'being yourself'.

Simply the Best simply didn't prove popular enough with the viewers, though, and a second series never made the screen. Even more tragic, the much-loved (by me) patented Tufnell catchphrase 'Don't fall in the pool!' sank along with the show, consigned to the dustbin of catchphrase history.

POPTASTIC DJ TUFNELL

I was thrilled to be asked to co-present one of the last-ever episodes of *Top of the Pops*, an iconic show that I'd grown up watching. I was also very nervous.

It's recorded 'as live' and I really screw up the start of it. Rabbit-in-the-headlights stuff. As soon as the cameras start rolling, I find myself talking in a curious Smashie and Nicey, mid-Atlantic, DJ-mongous voice.

'Hellloooo, and welcome to Tahppovvvtha pahps . . .'

My co-presenter Fearne Cotton tries to get me to relax and 'be yourself', but whenever I look at the camera, I can't seem to open my mouth without channelling Kid Jensen crossed with a cruise ship bingo caller.

I can hear myself doing it and am cringing with embarrassment.

It's so bad that with the famous Top Ten rundown approaching, which I'm supposed to be reading out, I turn to Fearne and say (in my normal voice):

'Can you do the rundown for me? I can't do this.'

So I never get to announce the number one.

CHAPTER 12

THAT BLOKE OFF THE ONE SHOW . . .

WHY WETWANG?

If I hadn't gone into the jungle, I think any media work I might have been offered after my playing career would have been purely cricket-related, as a pundit or summariser. It is a very crowded market with lots of very knowledgeable ex-players competing for a limited amount of broadcasting work through the year. Thankfully, I have managed to maintain my links with the game I love through regular TV and radio work, but the wider recognition I gained from appearing on *I'm a Celebrity* has also given me opportunities to dip into life away from sport. And few programmes allow you to explore the charm and quirks of day-to-day British life more than *The One Show*.

I am a member of 'the family' as it's called. I was chosen to be one of the original set of reporters when the show first started in 2007, and I'm now one of the last family members left.

One of the earliest jobs I had was to go to a shopping centre and ask people for their opinions on the muzak that shops play. I'd take old ladies into trendy clothes shops where music was banging out and ask them for their reaction. Surprisingly, they didn't like it, and 'The One Show Complaints Choir' would compose and sing a complaint on the spot.

We had another little strand where I would go to towns and villages around Britain and meet people to try and investigate how the places got their names. For instance, the wonderfully named Wetwang, a village in East Yorkshire (where, incidentally, the late *Countdown* presenter Richard Whiteley was once honorary mayor). One theory was that Wetwang derives from the Old Norse *vaett-vangr* meaning 'field for the trial of legal action'. Another was that it was the 'Wet Field' as opposed to the nearby dry field at Driffield.

In Ramsbottom, in Greater Manchester, I met someone who said it came from the Old English words *ramm* and *botm* meaning 'valley of the ram', and another person who argued that the 'ram' was derived from *hramsu*, or wild garlic, which grew at the bottom of the hill, hence Ramsbottom.

Quite often we discovered that no one actually knew for sure where the name of the town or village originated, but the theories were very interesting nonetheless!

Duncan Fletcher may find it hard to believe, but the producers saw me primarily as their go-to man if there was any sort of physical challenge to be done.

For instance, they got me to climb up an aerial erector at RAF Stenigot radar station in Lincolnshire. Four of these 360-foot-tall transmitter masts were built to provide long-range warning of raids in the Second World War, but only one remains. It's a Grade II listed structure and used for climbing-aptitude training for RAF erectors (is that what they're called?) – one of the first things they have to do is see if they can stomach the heights. 'Up you go, Phil.' And I did get all the way to the top.

I also tend to get first dibs on the sporty features, which has led to some fascinating experiences, such as visiting Roger Bannister's old student digs in Oxford overlooking the track where he broke the four-minute mile. And I travelled to Musselburgh Old Links in Scotland, the oldest golf course in the world, with legendary commentator Peter Alliss. I played a couple of holes using old-style golf balls with hickory-shafted 1920s golf clubs against the club pro who was playing with modern clubs, while Peter walked round with us talking about golf. Peter has such a great voice and a lovely turn of phrase, I could have stayed out there and listened to him for hours despite the freezing weather.

Indeed, my assignments for *The One Show* often involve taking long early-morning train journeys to somewhere bitterly cold, standing out in it all day, stopping every now and then for a cup of tea and some shelter to warm up, and then coming home on the train frozen to the bone. Not unlike a day in the field at Headingley in April then.

THE TRAMP AND THE TALKING BIN

In 2011 I joined Keep Britain Tidy's 'Love Where You Live' campaign. Along with the likes of Kenny Logan and Amanda Holden, I recorded a message for 25 talking bins placed around London. So it was that Londoners who put their empty crisp packets in my bin might be greeted by my voice: 'That wasn't a googly, that was straight in!'

For *The One Show*, though, we decide to take it a step further, rigging up a microphone inside a bin in a park so I can interview pedestrians 'from the bin' from a van parked nearby.

My first passer-by is an elderly tramp, wheeling a shopping trolley full of his belongings. He seems pretty well oiled for so early in the day and doesn't take kindly to a bin telling him what to do.

'Put your rubbish in the bin,' I say as he passes by.

'Who thhhe **** iz in that bin? Ya ****in' bastard,' he replies as he gets a teapot out of his trolley and starts pouring tea (at least

I think it's tea) into the bin. Not quite suitable for the BBC1 7 p.m. audience.

PHILIP TUFNELL, ART CORRESPONDENT

I've always had an interest in art – it is my only O Level after all. However, I only got back into painting myself a few years back when Dawn and I were strolling along the Brighton seafront.

Underneath the arches there are a lot of little art galleries and we're keen to buy something. Dawn walks into the gallery owned by Julie-Ann Gilbert, and we get chatting to her.

'I've always wanted to have a go at that,' I say, looking at the large canvases.

'Why don't you, then? You can come and paint in here.'

So I do. Dawn and I make a weekend of it whenever we can. Stay in a nice little hotel, and each morning I put on some old clothes and get down to the studio at eight o'clock. Dawn heads off shopping and leaves me there.

Julie-Ann's studio has the canvases and all the paints and I can swish about without worrying about getting it on the kitchen table. And whereas in cricket you are always judged by five-fers and how you've bowled, all that matters is that I'm happy with the painting I make. It doesn't matter what anyone else thinks. I love the freedom of it – I can get completely lost in painting. The next thing I know, it's five o'clock when Dawn taps me on the shoulder. 'Come on, we've got to go to dinner.'

One day, a local resident comes in looking for a present for his wife. As I'm painting, he looks over my shoulder and says: 'That's nice, I'll have that one.'

His name is Norman Cook, aka Fatboy Slim.

When *The One Show* found out about my interest, they started sending me out to cover visual arts topics and I've since become their unofficial art correspondent. I think it has worked because while the world of art has always been seen as a bit snooty, everyone has pictures on their wall. Rather than a Melvyn Bragg-type whose highbrow style might be a bit inaccessible to the average punter, I think that the viewers can relate more easily to me, an art enthusiast on a bit of a learning curve myself.

I fell into it, but I'm genuinely interested in art and it's been a privilege to meet some great artists, such as Antony Gormley and Quentin Blake. I get a chance to go down into the archives of art galleries and museums where they store millions of rare items, some of which the public don't ever get to see, so it's very enjoyable.

In 2008 I did a piece on the Royal Academy summer exhibition. Anyone can enter their work and it has a chance of being hung in the show. I was so inspired that the following year I entered my own painting, an abstract based on the Union Jack. I was very pleased with it, but the judges didn't pick it, sadly. I was genuinely disappointed. When I went back to the Academy to do a follow-up on the artworks that had got in, I must admit the old competitive nature kicked in and I was walking round thinking, 'Mine was better than that!'

One of my favourite people I've met through the show is the art historian Sister Wendy Beckett. She's in her eighties now and quite frail, but a great lass.

For some reason, I have a habit of calling her 'Sister Mary'.

'Phil,' she says, in her wonderful whispery, lispy voice, 'Mary was the big one, I'm just Wendy!'

We are an unlikely pair, but we've built up a rapport, and always have a good laugh. It's fascinating spending time with her. The historical religious art that she is an expert in has so many hidden meanings, and she's taught me to look beyond the surface.

Once Sister Wendy was showing me a painting that depicts Jesus and Mary at a party and they've run out of wine. She's telling me how it's as if Mary is looking at Jesus, urging him to do his thing and fill the wine up.

'Cor, I'd like him at my party!' I say.

'Aw, Phil. You are a one.'

Another time we were talking about saints. I've always worn a Saint Christopher necklace, which my mum gave me, whenever I fly, because he was meant to be a giant who carried people on their travels. I've always thought he was a real saint, but Wendy tells me he never actually existed, that he was just made to give people faith when they were travelling.

I was bit crushed by that so I looked him up on Wikipedia and he's got dates and now I'm just confused. I'll keep wearing the necklace just in case.

BRIAN SEWELL'S W.G. GRACE REVELATION

In 2007, my second year on *The One Show*, I was invited to appear on an ITV programme called *Don't Call Me Stupid*, which was another chance to indulge my interest in art. I was paired with art critic Brian Sewell, and the idea was that we'd teach each other a bit about our specialist subjects.

Brian took me to the Queen's Gallery, next door to Buckingham Palace. There he showed me a painting by Caravaggio – one of the greatest painters in history. Brilliant at hands.

'Now, Phil, this is how you look at a painting. You see how the hand is in the middle of the painting, drawing the eye . . . Chiaroscuro – light and shade.'

He gives a wonderfully detailed description in that magnificently posh voice of his.

Then I chip in with a question. Make it a good one, Phil. Don't want him to call me stupid.

'Who's this woman?' I say, pointing at a striking, long-haired brunette.

'Woman? That's Jesus!'

Oh my God. I've called Jesus a woman on camera. To Brian Sewell.

'Actually, that's quite observant of you,' says Brian, 'because this is one of very few paintings you will see of Jesus without a beard.'

So there is some insight in my ignorance after all. A tiny bit.

I was very nervous about meeting Brian, but he's very nice to me and gets things across so well. He takes me round a couple of galleries, teaches me about Renaissance and Baroque art and I drink it all in.

Unfortunately, Brian is not quite so interested in cricket. 'I don't care about silly mid-off,' he says.

To try and get him enthused I take him to a pub in Hambledon, Hampshire, where the first cricket matches were played in the eighteenth century. There's lots of great cricket memorabilia on the walls, and I start by showing him a painting of a cricket legend.

'This is W. G. Grace, Brian. One of the most famous cricketers of all time.'

He examines the painting carefully and I'm expecting him to do a critique on the quality of the artwork. Instead he picks up on a detail I've never heard mentioned before or since by cricket historians.

'He's got a very big cock!' says Brian.

At the end of the programme we're tested on what we've learned. Unsurprisingly, Brian can't explain what a silly mid-off is, but I can remember what the Italian painter's nickname Botticelli means – that's 'Little Barrel', art trivia fans.

THE STRANGE AFFAIR OF THE POLKA-DOT LADIES

There's a charming photo taken in 1951 called 'Blackpool Railings'. It shows two young women sitting chatting on the railings by Blackpool beach, one wearing a polka-dot dress billowing up in the breeze revealing a bit of leg.

I go to meet her for *The One Show*. She's in her late seventies now, and we take her for lunch and have a nice chat.

A couple of weeks later, I get a phone call: 'Phil, that wasn't the lady in the photo!'

A viewer has phoned up to say it's actually her in the photo and that she has the stills and polka-dot dress to prove it.

We don't go back to the other lady, bless her. I guess she's been going around for years claiming it was her in the picture and when the BBC came calling she couldn't go back on her story so she found herself on telly in front of millions!

The real polka-dot lady is sympathetic, too, but, equally, she wants it to be known that it's her in the picture, so I trundle back up to Blackpool to redo the item with her.

TUFFERS' TEN: RANDOM DISPATCHES FOR *THE ONE SHOW*

1. In winter 2008 I visited the post office in the village of Bethlehem in Wales. Visitors come from as far afield as Australia to send their Christmas cards franked with the Bethlehem stamp. They made up a stamp with my face on, especially for me.

2. There was a fella who showed me how he created scenes out of food and then photographed them. Looked absolutely realistic. There was a sea made from smoked salmon, a house made of sweets. I ate the roof.

3. I met Martin Elliot, the photographer who took the famous photo of the woman tennis player showing her bum that sold over two million copies as an Athena poster. I may well have owned one myself, back in the day . . .

4. I was allowed into the vaults to see the steel bar of exactly one metre in length on which all metric measurements

are based. It's kept under lock and key because if you pick it up there's a danger it will wear away and then where would we all be?

5. To mark the centenary of the commercial toaster, I went to see a lady, in Lincolnshire I think it was, who had a wonderful collection of old toasters, including the oldest in existence. Thank God for toast. I love toast.

6. At the Extreme Sports Festival on the Isle of Wight, I tried out aquaskipping with a bloke called Dave who holds the record for the fastest 100 metres on an aquaskip. I struggle to go 10 metres before sinking. It's a very silly sport.

7. I had a go at ice-sculpting with artist Duncan Hamilton. Duncan once made an incredible sculpture of the London skyline in Covent Garden. I made a snowflake.

8. I interviewed Jim Fitzpatrick, the Irish artist who created the iconic graphic image of Che Guevara that you see on merchandise all over the world. By chance, the teenaged Jim met Che in an Irish pub the Cuban Revolutionary was making a brief stop-off in the country. For many years Jim had no copyright over the image, which he told me he was fine about because if he had, it probably wouldn't have spread and become so famous around the world.

9. I did a piece on the revival of ventriloquism and got to meet Nookie Bear. When Nookie said, ''Allo, Phil,' I was so excited. Like a kid again.

10. I tried to get a 3D pavement artist I interviewed on the show to pitch up at Lord's. He makes these amazing scenes where if you sat in a certain spot, you looked like you were there. He could make a killing drawing Lord's there on a Test match day.

CHAPTER 13

'EVEN GOD DOESN'T DANCE ON A SUNDAY'

Of all the entertainment shows I've been invited to appear on since *I'm a Celebrity, Strictly Come Dancing* is undoubtedly the biggest. By 2009, when I pulled on my sequinned shirt and high-waisted trousers, the celebrity Ballroom/Latin dancing competition was pulling in 8 to 11 million viewers every week and giving ITV's *X Factor* a run for its money. And if the huge audiences weren't enough pressure, I was following in the twinkle-toed footsteps of my fellow cricketers Darren Gough (2005) and Mark Ramprakash (2006) who had both won it.

I actually only make it on to the show as a late substitute for Matthew Hoggard when Hoggy pulls out. I'm on holiday in Spain with Dawn, by now my wife, when I get a call from my agent to say that *Strictly* are interested in having me on.

I've already been asked to do ITV's *Dancing on Ice* and had a trial in front of Torvill and Dean. That wasn't pretty. I was hopeless. I mean *really* hopeless.

They said, 'Phil, on to the ice . . .' and it was splat. Straight down, holding my side in pain. Dangerous sport.

They still want me, though, but the two shows clash so I can't do both.

Dancing on Ice offers more money, but the prospect of ending up in traction after attempting a double axel doesn't greatly appeal. I'm a BBC boy now, too, with regular gigs on *The One Show* and *A Question of Sport* so that tips me towards *Strictly*.

On the other hand, I'm worried about how Dawn will feel about the close physical contact I'll have with my female partner on *Strictly*. But Dawnie just says, 'Go for it.' She loves the show and if I take part she'll get tickets every week – two seats in the audience and four tickets for the green room. Happy days. So I go for *Strictly*.

The only problem is they want us to cut short our holiday to start training. We say no, so I start after everyone else, a little bit on the back foot.

There are sixteen celebrity/professional couples competing in the series – on the celebrity side, sports personalities Joe Calzaghe, Jade Johnson, Richard Dunwoody and Martina Hingis, TV presenters Chris Hollins and Rav Wilding and actors Laila Rouass, Lynda Bellingham and *EastEnders* stars Ricky Groves and Natalie Cassidy.

Everyone seems to be making the connection that because Ramps and Goughie are cricketers and they won it I'll be good too. Well, hold on, my dancing can best be described as 'good wedding dancer' standard.

I speak to Ramps and Goughie and their advice is just to go and enjoy it for what it is. Don't take it too seriously. Nevertheless, I think they ended up taking it pretty seriously when they realised they were good at it. My attitude is to have a good laugh, treat it as a chance to learn a new skill, get fit and see what happens.

I'm paired with Katya Virshilas and before we get started on training she comes round to our house to break the ice. She's one of the new professionals on the show, so she's very keen to go far in the competition, and she seems nice.

By the time I pitch up at a dance studio in Wimbledon for our first training session I'm petrified. The series lasts thirteen weeks and you have to learn a different dance for each show. Our first session lasts six or seven hours and that sets the tone for the next eleven weeks. My intention to be relaxed about the whole thing soon goes out the window, too. Working so closely with Katya every day, we quickly form a friendship and I can see how important it is to her to do well so she will be invited back next year. I don't want to let her down.

I do draw the line at training on a Sunday, though, unless there's a group dance we have to rehearse, which happens occasionally. When Katya suggests it, I tell her, 'Even God doesn't dance on a Sunday.'

It isn't long before the show is just about taking over my life anyway. Every spare moment between filming on *The One Show* and *A Question of Sport* is spent training, and each week has a rhythm to it:

Monday – start learning a new dance routine. I can't get it. Shout. Scream. I don't want to do it. I'm never going to get it right.

Tuesday – a little bit better.

Wednesday – a bit better still.

Thursday – forgetting it a bit.

Friday – just about getting it, but thinking, 'Oh God, am I going to forget it?'

Saturday – the build-up to the live show. Scared of two main things: one, forgetting all of my steps; and two, controlling my overwhelming desire to break out into the David Brent (from *The Office*) dance on live TV for a laugh.

The beginning of every week is particularly painful because you start from scratch again. Each ballroom dance has different variations in footwork, the way you hold your partner, and then the Latin stuff is totally different again. From week to week, it's like switching from spin bowling to swing bowling to fast bowling and then being told to bowl with the other arm.

Then you have to learn the steps to an entire one-and-a-half minute routine. Considering I forgot my own ten-step run-up in the last season of my career, this is no easy task . . . or was it eleven steps?

And on the night of the show, everyone's so nervous – there are experienced actors and performers pulling whities, fainting backstage. I've got no spit, my heart's jumping out of my chest. It's like waiting to go out and face Merv Hughes in Perth, except with a spray tan and wearing a ruffled pink shirt with sparkly rhinestones all over it, a very tight pair of trousers and high heels. Then I have to skip down the steps on to the stage and perform a difficult dance I've only had a few days to learn in front of a packed audience and millions watching at home. The potential to make an absolute tit of myself is massive and I can never wholeheartedly enjoy my Saturday night.

Dawn enjoys herself, though. I wear tails for my first-ever dance, the waltz, and she tells me afterwards I looked lovely. The judges – Craig Revel-Horwood, Len Goodman, Alesha Dixon and Bruno Tonioli – seem pretty impressed with my performance, too. Comments like 'great footwork', 'could be the surprise of the show', and, wait for it, 'debonair' are bandied about.

When I get the timing slightly wrong, though, it's so difficult to get it back. In one dance, the quickstep I think it is, I push off into a step too late, which means by the time I'm rising up, Katya is already going down and we end up hopping about in a circle doing 'Ring a Ring o' Roses' in front of 10 million people.

Generally, I feel the judges are a bit harsh on me during the series; I'm a little bit underscored. The worst time is week four, after injuring my knee in training so badly I have to have an emergency cartilage operation. Usually, you'd have to rest up for six weeks, but I have to come out a few days later, dance a salsa wearing a big knee brace under my trousers and keep going, which they don't seem to take into account.

I make it to week nine before being eliminated in a dance-off with Ricky Groves. Some people seem to think I should have gone further (see below), but sadly the Goughie-Ramps-Tuffers glitterball trophy treble is not to be.

I learned how to dance, though, which was my aim, and got some sort of masochistic pleasure out of going through the mill every week. I also appeared on a show with the legendary Bruce Forsyth to whom it has been said I have an uncanny chin resemblance. Brucie never confirmed whether or not I am his long-lost love child, though. He was too busy looking for digestive biscuits. Loves a digestive, does the Brucemeister.

MY *STRICTLY* 'JOURNEY' . . . AS TOLD BY YOUTUBE VIEWERS [SPELLING/PUNCTUATION IS ALL THEIR OWN]

Week one: Waltz to 'Sam'
Brilliant. V. elegant and graceful. Tuffers all the way.
Silvergirl100

I love these two especially Katya she's awesome ! Xxx
RuthLorenzoFan4eva

Very nice
TheLemonLover

Week two: Cha-cha-cha to 'Hey Daddy'
Awwww. He's adorable. Granted, he's not much of a dancer, but he's adorable.
uclmu2008

Loved his face at the end :)
IndieLuva2

Tuffers is a fit cockey geezer
Iluvashsimpson1

why is he holding his stomach roll all the time ??
liatjetta

just tell me why all british men can't dance for shit ?? pls
barbarshater

Week three: Quickstep to 'Put On a Happy face'
Phil and kartya r my fav's i want him to win who would of though dareen gough would of won TEAM TOPKAT
CuteButCrazyChicky

He's just so cute and happy. I love watching him. Technically maybe he's not perfect but he's a joy to watch
EJNormanOfficial

Week four: Salsa to 'Long Train Runnin'
Considering he had a knee surgery this same week he did VERY well.
Barbie0676

for some reason i liked phil. he has this partcular charm and confidence.
SuperBailey2009

sick, he was terrible
anoukwakely

love this song & Tuffers is a great performer
nazmondo

Week five: Viennese Waltz to 'Mad About The Boy'
love this song! deserved 8's and 9's
katya <3
Tashyy034

Tuffers&Katya are very enjoyable to watch. He adds charm to his performances. He may not be the best, but he sure is competent.
Nazmondo

UNDER MARKED . . . Compared to the other male dances, Phil def. deserved 8's
Marcus Carcase

Week six: Samba to 'Daddy Cool'
Well done Tuffers! More of a ballroom boy than a Latin man though
gmfmusic85

phill is a fit cocknry geezer
Iluvashsimpson1

Woo Hoo I thought it was good . . . enjoyed it very much . . . . . BUT . . . yes agree with previous comment you excelled in the ballroom . . . BUT in saying that the Samba is a very tricky dance to master especially for the man . . . so well done again!!! :) . . . . . . in fact you looked much better than Anton!!! ;)
MarcusCarcase

Week seven: Tango to 'Back to Black'
as an aussie . . . tuffers is my favorite pommy player . . . total clod
63hezemans

oh tuffers, what are you doing
nathangonmad

Elegant but Sexy Dance by Katya – Phil's not bad either!
spinnerguy

Week eight: Rumba to 'Maybe I'm Amazed'
Pass the sick bag (another one please, used the first one watching Chris Hollins) . . .
geesabun

Week nine: American Smooth to 'Come Fly With Me'
Phil is a ballroom boy all the way!
Stroopwafel4

Tuffers could have won Strictly 2009. Ricky Groves winning the dance-off was a total fix, and beyond a joke. He is the best dancer of 09, beats Ricky W and Ali outright, great posture etc, etc . . . ah!
Futureframes

The Cat has gone and for me so has the buzz so will be watching x factor now. I wanted him to get in the finals he wouldnt have won but he was just great for the show. Len you old toad.
SAMJE123456http://www.youtube.com/user/SAMJE123456

'TORODE, YOU'RE JUST A BURGER CHEF!'

I was very disappointed not to fulfil my potential on *Celebrity Masterchef* in 2007. If I had felt my potential was to get trolleyed on wine that was supposed to be destined for a lovely sauce, insult one of the hosts, and be escorted from the building, then happy days, job done, but that wasn't really the plan.

I've always enjoyed cooking. In terms of my skills, I can do a thousand things with mince, but I mostly enjoy the therapeutic aspect of it. When the call came from *Masterchef*, however, the old competitive instincts kicked in so I called in reinforcements.

My mate Liam is a head chef, so the Sunday before the first round – where they give you a set of ingredients and you have to rustle something up off the top of your head – he came round to give me some tips.

He shows me how to cook chicken, then a piece of fish, but he says he reckons it'll be scallops because it's all seasonal ingredients. Lovely. I cooked scallops with Gordon Ramsay in his posh restaurant for his TV show a few years before and know how to do them.

Next day, I turn up at the studio. I'm up against my future *Strictly* nemesis Craig Revel-Horwood and children's TV presenter Rani Price. Sure enough, we get scallops in the invention test. Fantastic.

Knob of butter in the pan, place the scallops in the pan in a clock face – one, two, three, four, five, six – a couple of beats, then turn them in the order you put them in. Done.

Make a nice celeriac mash, wilted greens and a salsa verde sauce, plate it all up and present it to the hosts, John Torode, a chef famous for his carnivorous restaurant, Smiths, opposite Smithfield Market in London, and Gregg Wallace, a greengrocer with a big appetite.

The comments couldn't be better – 'The scallops are cooked perfectly, beautifully seasoned'; 'Phil, this is almost restaurant food.'

I'm feeling very full of myself as we go off to do our next task, a shift in a professional kitchen at the Aurora restaurant. Throw myself in and absolutely love it. All going well.

Next, we have to cook a two-course meal of our own choice. I hate desserts, so I decide to do a starter and a main course. But then, all of a sudden, I've gone blank. All I can think of is mash – cheddar mash, celeriac mash, garlic mash . . . I mean, think of something that's not potato, Phil.

I'm getting more and more nervous thinking about it, so to unlock my inner chef I open one of the bottles of white wine they've provided us with to make sauces.

I soon hit upon the rather uninspired combination of mushrooms and toast and olive oil for my starter, but I've got absolutely no idea for the main, so I pour another glass of wine and give Liam a call. He says just do a breast of chicken with a beurre blanc on some mash with chorizo or something. Sounds doable, so I ask for a chicken breast and all the other ingredients I need.

By the time we start the challenge, I've made excellent inroads into the bottle of wine, but I'm a bit shocked when I see the chicken breast they've given me. It's on the bone and it's the biggest breast of chicken I've ever seen in my life – like a pterodactyl breast. Massive.

I'm standing there thinking, what the hell do I do with this? So I heave it into the pan like Fred Flintstone, add a few aromatics and a slosh of white wine, brown it up, and jam it in the oven. This leaves me free to make my butter sauce and trademark mash.

When it's time to plate up, I drag the pterodactyl out of the oven and plonk it on the plate. Bosh. I add the mash and a butter sauce that looks rather thin, which I realise may be because I forgot to add the butter to it. Oh well, too late now, so I tart it up as best I can.

Actually, although the beurre blanc is a bit of a non-event, John and Gregg say the pterodactyl tastes all right – beautifully cooked – it's just the size of the bloody thing. Apparently, I should have taken the bone out.

Only one of the three contestants can go through to the next round, but as we line up to hear the judges' verdict, I'm still feeling reasonably confident because I'd done well in the other challenges and Revel-Horwood has just produced a spag bol which makes my pterodactyl look positively Michelin-star.

Not best pleased, then, when Revel-Horwood gets the nod, and Rani and I are eliminated.

I retire to the green room for a few more glasses of white wine, topping up the bottle I've drunk while cooking. By the time John and Gregg walk in, I'm absolutely lashed and the feeling that I've been robbed has intensified. John's explanation that my seasoning was a bit off is cutting no ice. I wouldn't usually say anything, but I feel like I've left a lot of love out there, I deserve to have got through. Perhaps I don't express this in the most tactful manner, though, because the next thing I know they're going, 'Can you get a taxi for Mr Tufnell?'

As two security guards are ushering me out of the room, I turn round and shout, 'Torode, you're just a burger chef! You know nothing about seasoning!'

I apologised to John next time I saw him and I've been down to his 'burger restaurant' Smiths a few times since because the food there is great. We actually get on. Still tell him I was robbed, though!

MR & MRS TUFNELL

Back in April 2008, Dawn and I agreed to appear in a new version of an old TV family favourite *Mr & Mrs*. Restyled as *All Star Mr & Mrs*, and presented by Phillip Schofield and Fern Britton, celebrities were invited on with their partners to try to win money for their chosen charity. We were booked in for the first show of the new season, up against Shane Lynch from Boyzone and his wife Sheena, and the late *EastEnders* star Wendy Richard and her partner John.

For those who have never seen *Mr & Mrs* (clearly, you haven't lived), it's a simple format where each of you takes turns to answer questions about your partner's likes, dislikes, habits, etc. while they sit in a box wearing ridiculous big earmuffs. Then they have to come out and try to match your answer.

We've got the board game at home, and we've always enjoyed playing it, and always seem to win when we play our friends. The game has caused some ructions among our opponents, though.

One Christmas, we're playing it with my dad and his second wife Val. The question comes up: what first attracted you to your partner? a) smile; b) great personality; c) bank balance.

Dad writes 'smile', but she's written down his 'bank balance'! My poor old dad.

Now, my dad is quite eccentric and he's been deliberately choosing funny answers during the game, and Val has been saying, 'Listen, we've got no chance of winning – stop showing off and answer properly.' So when she comes up with that, we're thinking now you're the one being comical. My dad's not easily shocked, but he's asking, 'You don't really mean that?' 'Of course not,' she says, but it all gets a bit testy chez Tufnell for a while.

Wanting to win as much money as possible for our charity the Children's Trust, of which I'm Honorary Vice-President, we decided to host a couple of *Mr & Mrs* nights at home to get some practice in before the TV show. We had one game with good friends of ours – no names, no pack drill – and it all got rather, um, emotional.

A question about what your partner wears in bed lights the touch paper.

He writes down 'boxer shorts'. She writes 'he sleeps on the sofa in his clothes.'

'What do you mean?' he says.

'Most nights you come back pissed and you don't actually come to bed.'

'What do you mean? Don't be ridiculous.'

'Anyone for more wine?' I interject, trying to lighten the mood.

'No, I don't,' he says.

'Yes, you bloody do. You're always pissed.'

It was all kicking off.

Despite the ructions we'd caused among our friends, by the time we appeared on the TV show our trivial knowledge about each other was finely tuned.

We have a couple of awkward questions along the way, but Dawn does really well on one about my favourite food (Italian over Chinese) and the only one I get wrong is an obvious one we should get right: 'What's the worst thing your partner has ever cooked?'

I've somehow forgotten the first time I ever went round to Dawn's when she cooked me dinner. She did beef stroganoff and I don't mean to be rude, but I could have used it to mortar the brick wall outside. I ended up vomiting in her back garden, which was partly due to the cement stroganoff, partly due to being extremely nervous on our first date . . . and possibly something to do with the copious amounts of wine I'd consumed.

Not a great first impression. As Dawn told me later, at the time she was thinking, 'I'm not sure about this chap.'

But tonight, under interrogation from Pip and Fern, her wisdom in hanging in there with old Tuffers is proven as we beat the other couples and arrow in on the £30,000 top prize.

For one round, we both have to sit in booths – side by side, but we aren't able to see one another. We each have a pink bat and blue bat. So for the question: 'Who brushes their hair most in the mornings?' the answer is Dawn and we both lift the pink bat. You have to match bats, see.

One thing we've agreed before the show is that we have to be honest in our answers, and not try to be polite and say what looks best. If you start doing that, you're going to mess up. This proves important when the following question comes up: 'Who washes the least?'

Now, Dawnie is no soap dodger, but I am a bit obsessive about washing – she'll have a shower a day and I'll have two. Of course, the audience might expect the opposite, but we've got an agreement. I go pink, she goes pink. Bing, bing, point!

For the final challenge, it's all down to Dawn and, fittingly, a cricket teaser: 'Who is Phil's cricketing hero?'

This time, there's no multiple choice, so she's on her own. As I sit there oblivious in a fetching pair of earmuffs, Dawn mulls over the options with Pip and Fern: 'Well, he's always said Shane Warne is the best bowler as in spin, so would he go for that? Or would he go for somebody old like W.G. Grace. Or more a great all-rounder and a great character like Ian Botham?'

She plumps for Beefy.

Get in there, Dawnie! She knows me so well. Thirty large ones for our charity, thank you very much.

'I HAVE A DREAM . . . THAT I'M A POTATO'

Hardly Martin Luther King, I know, but this was the claim I made during an appearance on BBC comedy panel show *Would I Lie To You?*, hosted by Rob Brydon, in October 2011. But was it true? The ensuing interrogation by the opposing team of David Mitchell, Greg Davies and Konnie Huq (with occasional interjections from one of my teammates, Lee Mack) went like this:

ME [reading from a card]: I am haunted by a recurring dream in which I am a potato.

ROB: David?

DAVID: How does the dreaming realisation that you are a potato manifest itself?

ME: I'm being chased.

DAVID: Oh right, yeah, of course, because potatoes get chased all the time!

ME: I am being chased by a pitchfork.

KONNIE: How do you know you're a potato?

DAVID: You can't move . . .

ME: No, no, I can. I'm like Mr Potato Head, wear a little trilby hat, little legs, and I'm running along in the garden with a pitchfork trying to poke me. And I'm sort of climbing up trees and things and the pitchfork's sort of going for me . . .

KONNIE: Has it ever caught you?

ME: No, it has never caught me. Well, just as it is going to catch me, I think I wake up.

DAVID: What do you think the pitchfork is trying to do? Is it trying to harvest you?

ME: It's a family show!

ROB: Heavy with symbolism, isn't it, David? The sturdy steel of the pitchfork; the soft, pliant flesh of the potato . . . I'm getting a bit worked up just thinking about it, to be honest.

LEE: He didn't say it was boiled, did he?

ME: I think it was baked.

DAVID: So you're a baked potato?!

ME: I think I'm a baked . . .

DAVID: What are you doing in the garden if you've already been cooked!

KONNIE: How long have you had this dream?

LEE: He only has it when he's mashed . . .

ME: I have it quite a bit, actually. It's quite at the forefront of my dreams.

ROB [mimicking my voice . . . I think]: I'm just sitting here listening to you. You could be related to Len Goodman from *Strictly Come Dancing* . . .

ME: Sev-errrrn.

ROB [still mimicking me/Len]: Could you just say for me, 'Your Paso Doble was lovely, I liked it. There was a bit over there, but you tried hard. Six . . . [reverting to his normal voice] I'm doing Len Goodman from *Strictly Come Dancing* . . . What do you think, David?

DAVID: Er, well, it's possible, isn't it. What do you think?

KONNIE: I'm not convinced.

GREG: I think it is without question a lie, because when he was asked how the potato was moving, I actually saw Phil's brain working to think of Mr Potato Head.

DAVID: It is true that lots of people have dreams where they are being, sort of, chased, don't they? That's quite an actual thing.

GREG: Yes, generally they haven't become a root vegetable.

KONNIE: You think it's true, don't you?

DAVID: Look, my brain is shot by this game, I think anything could be true.

GREG [staring at me]: I am so sure it's a lie.

DAVID: Well, we're going to say it's a lie, then.

ROB: You're saying it's a lie. Okay, Phil Tufnell, were you telling the truth or were you lying?

ME: I was telling . . . [I press a button and 'TRUE' appears on the big screen behind me].

GREG: No!!

ROB: It's true. Phil is haunted by a recurring dream that he's a potato. There's a technical term for Phil Tufnell turning into a potato: it's called evolution.

So, yes, it was all true. I'd never spoken to anyone apart from Dawn about the dream, so the show was a kind of therapy, albeit with a bunch of comedians. And if I'd told them the whole story, they might have believed me.

I'd been having this dream on and off since doing a piece for *The One Show* about the Ministry of Agriculture's 'Dig For Victory' campaign during the Second World War. I was focusing particularly on the posters and recipe books and I went to a museum and met a very old lady who wrote the recipes. She showed me all these fantastic posters and cartoon characters she'd created to encourage people to eat homegrown vegetables.

One character was 'Potato Pete'. There were Potato Pete recipe books to give women advice on different ways to serve spuds at mealtimes, and he even had his own hit song (incidentally, it was sung by Betty Driver who went on to play Betty Williams in *Coronation Street* for 42 years):

> *Here's the man who ploughs the fields.*
> *Here's the girl who lifts up the yield.*
> *Here's the man who deals with the clamp, so that millions of*
> *jaws can chew and champ.*
> *That's the story and here's the star,*
> *Potato Pete*
> *Eat up,*
> *Ta ta!*

Potato Pete had lovely little eyes and a lovely smile, and, as I told the WILTY mob, he had a trilby and little legs like Mr Potato Head. In the poster he was running along as if to say, 'Hello, I'm a little potato! Grow me'. For some reason, that image has stayed with me. I guess I must see something of Pete in myself. Thankfully, though, I'm yet to be forked.

MY OLD MAN, FUR COATS AND A FERRY TRIP TO FRANCE

The Tufnell family got what I believe still stands as the lowest score in the history of *All Star Family Fortunes*. I went on there in 2006 with my brother Greg, my dad, his wife Val and her daughter, up against Olympics golden girl Kelly Holmes and her family.

One of the questions is: 'What pet can you keep in your pocket?'

Now my brother's a bright guy and even he looks miffed, but we all have a guess, except for my dad, who isn't having it.

'But you don't keep animals in your pocket? Who does that?'

'It's a game, dad . . .'

'Well, it's a stupid game.'

You can almost hear the ITV executives groan at one of their iconic game shows being trashed.

Another question: 'If you saw someone you fancied across a crowded room, what would you do?'

I answer, 'Smile.' My brother says, 'Wink.' Then the presenter Vernon Kay gets to my dad, who says nonchalantly, 'Buy her a fur coat.'

When the laughter subsides, he just shrugs: 'Well, it always worked for me.'

I'm proud to have raised over two million quid for charity via various shows and challenges over the years, but this time we manage to win about £200 between us. Absolutely hopeless.

We win a couple of spot prizes along the way, though: a fridge and a day trip for two to France. My dad decides to take Val on the awayday. It doesn't go well as he reports on his return.

'****ing hell, we had to get up at six, drive three hours to the ferry, I threw up on the boat, and when we got there, it was raining, cold, and everything was shut. Got back home at half one in the morning with two bottles of wine which are bleedin' 'orrible.

'Was that a prize? Wish I'd gone for the bloody fridge!'

SHOULDERS OF LAM

Like anyone who agreed to appear on the BBC1 series *Hole in the Wall*, I hadn't left the dressing room before thinking 'What am I doing here?' For those of you who never saw it (or, please God, my particular episode in 2008), players dressed up in skin-tight silver all-in-one suits and had to get through cut-out shapes in a large polystyrene wall coming towards them. It was like a human version of Tetris, except if you didn't make it through the hole, you'd end up falling in the pool beneath the wall (note to self: should have lent the host Dale Winton my old 'Don't fall in the pool!' catchphrase).

Anyway, I'm in a team with cook Nancy Lam captained by *Strictly* ballroom dancer Anton Du Beke, up against a team captained by my old mate Darren Gough. Now Nancy is a generously proportioned lady, and during the game, she falls into the pool and can't get out. She starts flapping around like an abandoned seal, so Anton jumps in the pool, gets behind her and tries to push her up. He ends up with his head wedged up her arse while me and Goughie are pulling her up by each of her arms.

We finally get her out of the pool and everyone, including Nancy, is in hysterics.

It's only when she sits down and we're waiting for the next game that she realises something's wrong. She can't lift her arms. In our eagerness to help her up, it turns out Goughie and I have dislocated her arms from her shoulder sockets!

She's as brave as Adam Hollioake about it, though, and the show goes on while Nancy sits on the sidelines with her arms hanging off.

CHAPTER 14

CAPTAIN CAT

WOSSY AND 'WESTONIA'

With my reputation for reliability, diplomacy, even temperament and ability to lead by example, it is one of the great mysteries of cricket history that I was never invited to captain Middlesex or England. Seventeen years I waited for the call, but somehow I was overlooked. It's only since my playing career ended that my leadership potential has been uncorked.

My first experience of pulling on the armband comes on comedy quiz show *They Think It's All Over*, hosted by Nick Hancock. It's been going for fifteen series when I get called up in 2004 alongside ex-England goalkeeper David Seaman to take over the captaincy of the two teams from David Gower and Gary Lineker.

I've got Jonathan Ross on my side while David Seaman is paired with Rory McGrath, and every week a different sporting guest joins each side. For the first time I'm knocking around with non-sporting celebrities, doing the whole showbiz bit, and it's quite daunting. Making people laugh in a cricket dressing room is one thing, but trying to be funny in front of an audience and millions watching at home is another matter.

I've always been a bit cheeky and taken a fairly wry angle on life, but I'm not a comedian. Wossy, Rory and Nick just fire off the gags and at first I feel out of my depth. But you've got to start somewhere and, luckily, I've got Wossy with me, so I can just sit there while he rattles on.

Another plus point is that in the green room an hour or two before the start of recording we are all told the general subjects that will come up, so we can brainstorm a few ideas in advance.

One time, we're told there'll be a question about Estonia.

'Oh, that's just the other side of Westonia, isn't it?' I say.

Everyone says that's not bad, try and pop it in. Whoo-hoo – I've got a joke!

Later, during recording, I'm all psyched up to 'do my gag', and when the time comes, one of the other guys sets me up for it:

'Oh, where's Estonia?'

More wooden than an Ikea wardrobe, I reply: 'Oh. Isn't. That. Just. The. Other. Side. Of. Westonia?'

Absolute tumbleweed. I can feel my face redden and I just want to slip under the desk.

Afterwards, the producer tells me not to worry and reminds me that the show is recorded over an hour and half so any dross can be edited out from the final half hour that is aired.

'It doesn't matter. Just say something, because it might lead somewhere.' After that, I get a bit more confidence to pipe up and it becomes a lot easier.

I did three series before Boris Becker took my place as captain. It was a lot of fun to be part of it for a while and a great learning curve for me about showbusiness.

My favourite cricket-related memory of the show comes from when Tony Blair's former spin doctor Alastair Campbell was on my team. We were playing the quickfire 'Name Game' round with Wossy giving clues while Alastair and I guessed:

WOSSY: This is a cricket captain . . . [looking at Alastair] Same surname as you put out of work.

ME: Bush!

ALASTAIR: Blair!

WOSSY: That's good news, you heard it here first!

ALASTAIR [hanging his head]: I mean, Major, Major.

The name on the card was Saddam . . . I mean, Nasser Hussain.

SHANE WARNE RUINED MY LIFE

It was an absolute honour to get invited on to *A Question of Sport* as a guest. I'd watched it religiously as a kid. Being a sporty family, my mum, dad, brother and I all played along as we watched. The first time I was asked to go on the show, it was a massive buzz. I really felt it was a badge of honour. I remember saying to my dad: 'I've been invited on *A Question of Sport*; I must be good at cricket!'

I went on it six or seven times and always had a great time. I enjoyed meeting some great sportspeople and having a laugh with them. Being a competitive sod, I liked the quiz aspect of it, too – always wanted to get my questions right and win.

After Ally McCoist left the show, I was one of a few guest captains they tried out before they gave me the job permanently in 2008. Like *Test Match Special*, it's a British institution, so I do feel privileged to be part of it and doing the job ever since has been an absolute joy.

It is the best job in the world. There's a fantastic team working behind the scenes, I get to meet my sporting heroes – people like Michael Johnson – and I get on very well with Sue Barker and my opposing captain Matt Dawson.

With most of my television work, there are always a few nerves and stresses, but from the moment I walk into the *QoS* studio, I feel relaxed. There's no script. I just turn up and see what happens and I've got a licence to muck about. The only way they could make it better is if they held it in a pub.

There are some repeat guests who have turned up regularly over the years, and there's a few I always want on my side. I'm not the best on sports trivia, so I'm always very pleased when I'm given the team list and find the likes of Tim Henman, Will Greenwood and Laura Davies on my team.

Even if I lose, it doesn't matter, so there's no real pressure. Although if Daws's mob beat my team by one and it all hinged on one question which I should have known the answer to, I can spend an hour in the car on the way home cursing myself. It's like 'The Churn' all over again until I get a grip. For God's sake, Phil, it's only a quiz show.

The guests who come on the show are usually as delighted as I was to be invited, so being a *QoS* captain doesn't exactly require the motivational skills of a 'Bumble' Lloyd. Although Daws did tell me about one difficult guest he had on his team just before my time: boxing (and grilling) legend, George Foreman.

Big George arrives in a limo with four of his sons, who are all called George, and rather than come to the green room as is the norm for guests, he walks straight on to the set through the stage door and sits down.

With the show about to start, Daws is trying to break the ice, with little success. George isn't saying much and looks miserable.

Then Ally calls over: 'Oi, Daws. Ask him if he's got one of his grills in the boot of his car.'

The audience laugh. Not even a flicker from George, and Daws is getting more and more uneasy.

When the game gets under way, they start off with the 'Picture Board' round and a boxer comes up for Daws's team to identify. Great, a chance to get George involved.

'C'mon George. This is one for you, mate!' says Daws, patting him on the knee.

George turns round slowly to Daws, fixes him with a stare and says: 'Don't. Ever. Touch. Me. Again.'

Scary.

I've never had such personnel problems myself, but my Sherlock Holmes-like powers of deduction have let me down on occasion. One time on a celebrity edition, I'm playing the 'Guess Who' round. I have to put a series of caps on my head and pull off a sticker on the front to reveal the name of a sportsperson to my teammates, TV presenters Nick Knowles and Tim Lovejoy. I then have to work out who it is by asking questions, to which they are only allowed to answer yes or no. I get the first one okay – Michael Schumacher – but the next takes up the rest of the 90 seconds:

ME: Boy or girl? Boy?
THEM: Yes.
ME: Single sport?
THEM: No.
ME: Footballer?
THEM: No.
ME: Cricketer?
THEM: Yes.
ME: Er, still playing?
TIM: No . . . er . . . yeah, er, is he?
NICK: No.
ME: No, he's not still playing . . . erm, how old's he? Over fifty?
THEM: No.
ME: Under fifty?
NICK: Yes.
ME: Freddie Flintoff?
THEM: No.
ME [exasperated]: He's not playing . . . he's not playing. Erm . . . is he a big bloke?

NICK: Quite big.

ME [hands on my head]: Who's a big, fat cricketer? . . . Who's a big fat cricketer? . . . Who's a big fat cricketer?

TIM: Ask what country . . .

SUE BARKER: No! He has to ask the question!

ME: Does he play for West Indies?

THEM: No!

ME: England

THEM: No!

ME: Pakistan, India . . .

THEM: No!

ME [losing the plot, looking out to the audience]: Who else plays cricket?

NICK [in disbelief]: Who do we hate at cricket?!

ME: Oh, Aussie.

NICK: Yes!

ME: Gilchrist!

THEM: No!

ME: Taylor!

THEM: No!

ME: Who?

NICK: Come on!

ME: Warne!

THEM: Yes!

ME [drop-kicking the cap into the audience]: Shane Warne . . . he's been the pain in my arse all my life!

CHAPTER 15

THE PRIVILEGES OF 'CELEBRITY'

CHALLENGE TUFFERS

While I'm uncomfortable with the 'celebrity' tag, I soon discovered that I could take advantage of my new-found fame to raise a lot of money for causes that I believe in. No more so than when I got an offer to take part in the ITV show *With a Little Help From my Friends* soon after exiting the jungle.

The idea of the show was for celebrities to get the help of old schoolfriends and to use their fame to pull in favours in order to build facilities for charities in a week. It was a bit like the old *Challenge Anneka* programme.

When my agent receives the call from ITV, we immediately get in touch with London Community Cricket Association (LCCA) chief executive Andy Sellins to see if there is something we can do for them.

Andy and a bunch of cricket nuts set up the charity after the Brixton riots in 1981 and I became president back in 2000. Their idea was to develop projects aimed at getting unemployed, directionless young people to train as cricket coaches. Within twenty years they'd trained up over 500 inner city coaches and expanded to help other people with disabilities and special needs, staging hundreds of Special Needs School Festivals and going international to create England and West Indies Blind Cricket teams.

They'd already done some amazing work so I was delighted to get involved, but *With a Little Help From my Friends* gave me the chance to make a real impact.

Andy tells us that what he really wants to do is build a new cricket centre at their headquarters in Wallington, Surrey. Andy submits the plans to Granada and they agree to go for it.

My job is to get on the phone and get businesses to donate materials and labour to help us, and also to pitch in with my old schoolmates on building work. (Andy tells me later I was a lot better at the phoning round part – apparently, I could often be found sneaking off for fag when I should have been painting. Doesn't sound like me . . .)

I don't think any of us have any idea quite how big a project it is at the start. The foundations alone take about six weeks to put in, and in all it takes about six months to build. Not that you'd know it from the show. One minute, there's a shot of me helping to build a wall. Cut. A few minutes later, I'm seen putting in the last brick on a great big pavilion worth half a million quid, complete with dressing rooms, catering facilities, conference room and, naturally, 'Tuffers Bar'!

The grand opening is really emotional. All my old mates are there, a lot of the kids who will use the facility come down, and I get really choked up and start crying with happiness at what we've all achieved.

They get me to bowl the first over to the local cricket team. And guess what? First ball, I get the guy caught and bowled. Still got it.

The charity, now called Cricket for Change (C4C), has just got bigger and bigger over the last few years. The cricket centre has expanded to include a two-lane indoor training facility and they are planning to build accommodation to allow kids to stay there and play sport. They've developed 'Street 20', a fast-moving version of the game of cricket, which can be played anywhere (six players per side, 20 balls per team), and the C4C coaches are taking that into housing estates in the inner cities to provide sporting opportunities and role models for deprived kids around Britain. Working in association with Unicef, they've also set up successful programmes everywhere from Sri Lanka, where they trained up former child soldiers to become leaders in their community, to Afghanistan, Rwanda, Cuba, Tanzania, Uganda and Sierra Leone.

It's just a brilliant charity, and I'm very, very proud to be associated with it and do anything I can to raise awareness (the website is at cricketforchange.org.uk) and money for the cause. I say anything . . . the C4C boys are trying to persuade me to compete with them in a triathlon this year. Think I might just stick to cheering them on that day.

PRISONER OF THE WALK

I do sometimes take on physical challenges for charity, though, believe it or not. By far the toughest was my Npower 500 Walk in 2004 to raise £250,000 for the Macmillan Cancer Relief Fund. It's a cause very close to my heart because I lost my mum to leukaemia, so I said yes to it without really thinking about what I was taking on.

When I go to see a physio beforehand for a check-up, he asks me if I have any aches and pains from my cricketing days.

'Ooh, no, I'm all right,' I say, forgetting to mention that I always had trouble with my Achilles tendons through my career. A dodgy

Achilles – that won't be a problem on the longest walk of my life, will it? Nah.

The walk starts from Sussex's cricket ground in Hove to the sound of 'I'm Gonna Be (500 Miles)', which The Proclaimers have kindly agreed can be used as the theme tune of the walk, and one of my Olympic heroes Daley Thompson waves me off.

The plan is to walk about twenty-five miles per day, visiting twenty village cricket grounds and six Test match grounds along the way, finishing at Trent Bridge. Various celebrities, sportspeople and other charity walkers will join me along each leg, and at the end of each day I'll bowl the first over of a fundraising match at each village club.

It's all very exciting at the start. People cheer and clap as we walk past. Soon, though, we're hitting the A-roads and it's just our little group and a car in front and one behind to protect us.

Time passes. I'm starting to feel my Achilles.

I turn to Dawn who's walking with me and say, 'Have we nearly finished yet?'

'Er, no, Phil. We've only been going for two-and-a-half hours.'

We've got another five-and-a-half hours' walking to do today and then nineteen more days like this. I'm already starting to think I might have put my hand up for something I can't do. I haven't played cricket for a couple of years, and I'm not as fit as I was . . . and I wasn't very fit then.

Dawn's encouragement and talking to other walkers, including one brave bloke who is in recovery from cancer, gets me through that first day. And over the next few days I gradually get stronger. Despite the blisters and the nagging pain in my Achilles, I find I can keep going.

As Ian Botham, the original cricket charity walker, puts it, I become 'a prisoner of the walk'. He told me that on one of his walks from Land's End to John O'Groats, his mate Chris Lander, cricket correspondent of the *Daily Mirror*, came down to cover the start. Chris parked his car in Land's End car park and decided to walk the first few miles with Beefy. Sixty-odd days later he went back to collect his car – he walked the whole thing!

For the first three or four hours of every day, everyone's laughing and chatting and that takes your mind off the pain. And on the odd morning after the night before, I find that Beefy's recommended hangover cure of a shot of tequila and Tango orange works a treat.

A couple of weeks in, novelist and former Olympic athlete Jeffrey Archer joins us for the walk. Before the start he's doing all sorts of stretches and when we get under way he sets a cracking pace as we all stagger along behind. He seems very focused.

'Jeffrey, you all right up there?'

'Yes, fine!'

With a couple of miles to go, I decide I'm going to catch him up, and by the end of the route we're both throwing ourselves at the line like its *Chariots of Fire*. I think he just nicks it.

Another day, England rugby captain Martin Johnson turns up. Huge unit. The night before he played for Leicester Tigers and he's struggling with all sorts of injuries.

'Is it all right if I just start off?' he says. 'I haven't been home for two weeks.'

'Yeah, no problem, mate. It's amazing you're here just to raise the profile.'

Anyway, he spends the next eight hours at the front of the group urging us all on. They keep sending a car to take him home, but he keeps waving it away. Another prisoner of the walk.

'Martin, that's unbelievable. You didn't have to do that.'

'Tuffers,' he says, 'if you start something, you've always got to finish it.'

He just can't switch off that walk-through-brick-walls mentality, which helped him win the Rugby World Cup.

I'm going to be like Martin from now till the end of the 500 miles (actually, it's 584 miles with various police diversions). Nothing can stop me.

A couple of days later, coming down the hill into a village near Saddleworth Moor with the troops, The Proclaimers' tune blaring out, people clapping on either side of the road, I put my left foot down and bang! I feel like I've been shot in the ankle by a sniper. I go down like a sack of Jeffrey Archer novels, writhing in agony. A lady from the village comes rushing up, no doubt to offer medical assistance.

'Can I have your autograph, please?'

Not that she would care, but, luckily, I haven't ruptured my Achilles, and with a bit of strapping I'm able to make it all the way to Trent Bridge. I've done my mum proud, we've raised over £600,000, more than double our target, and I'm a free man again.

JUMP AROUND!

I've always enjoyed playing darts since those early cricket off-seasons when I should have been out driving a minicab but ended up spending most of the day in the pub with my mates. So when I was invited to compete in a pro-celebrity darts event at the famous Lakeside, Frimley Green, home of the BDO World Darts Championship, I jumped at the chance.

I'm put in a team captained by Bobby 'Dazzler' George with Holly Willoughby, Michael Le Vell and James Hewitt, against a team captained by Andy 'The Viking' Fordham.

Pre-match, we all go round to Bobby's home near Colchester, George Hall, an eighteen-roomed, self-built mansion designed in the shape of the flight of a dart. Naturally, he's got a pub inside, and we're all sitting there having a drink and a chat before throwing a few darts so Bobby can see what he's been landed with.

The TV cameras are there to record the practice session, which makes us all a little bit nervous, but Michael seems most confident.

I step up and manage to threaten the '20' bed, scoring 41 or something like that.

'Not bad,' says Bobby.

Next up is Holly, and she throws three half-decent darts, too.

'Yeah, good, good.'

Michael is next to go. He steps to the oche, throws his first dart.

It flies straight and true, diagonally downwards into the skirting board.

We're all in hysterics.

'Fackin' 'ell, mate,' says Bobby. 'You've fackin' put an 'ole in me skirtin' board!'

On the morning of the tournament proper, I turn up at Lakeside at about 8.30. I walk in to the bar where the practice boards are. The Viking is already there with Johnny Vegas and the rest of his team. They are already on the Guinness and pints of white wine soda.

Never one to turn down a challenge, I join them and manfully try to keep up.

By late afternoon, when the tournament starts, most of the competitors are well and truly mashed. Quite a few of the darts players are able to drink loads and still play brilliantly, but it doesn't seem to work for me.

I've got the plum draw of 'Skirting' Le Vell in the first round. Sadly, a combination of barely being able to see the board due to drunkenness, and losing my whooper under the pressure of playing on the famous stage, and Michael clearly having practised his nuts off since his 'yip' at Bobby's house, leads to my elimination.

In disgust, I go outside and lob the darts that Bobby had given me into Lakeside's lake. (Sorry, Bobby.)

Surprisingly, I'm invited to play in another pro-celebrity darts event, this time in Wolverhampton, partnering Dutch legend Raymond Van Barneveld. Phil 'The Power' Taylor, Wayne 'Hawaii 501' Mardle, Mark 'The Spider' Webster and James Wade are the other top pros, and ex-footballer Neil 'Razor' Ruddock, athlete

Steve Backley and rugby's Mike Tindall are among the celebs.

While we're sitting in the practice area getting prepared (i.e. having a drink), Wayne, an extrovert Essex man known for wearing his loud Hawaiian shirts on stage, demonstrates his party piece.

'Have a look at this.'

He goes to the oche, stands square-on to the board, places a dart in his mouth, tip first, and spits it. Phhhhtttttt. Straight into double 16! Unbelievable. We are falling on the floor in amazement.

I've chosen 'Jump Around' by House of Pain for my walk-on music. Good choice. The 2,000-strong audience go mental as I bounce down to the stage.

I play a lot better than I did at Lakeside. With a bit of luck, I even manage a score of 160 on one visit (treble 20, double 20, treble 20) in my first game with Barney, and we beat James Wade and Mike Tindall. The old magic is coming back.

We then have two hours to wait until our next match, which leaves plenty of time for refuelling, so by the time I go out to play again, I'm extremely merry. Consequently, my walk-on is even more extravagant than before. I pogo through the dry ice yelling 'Jump Around!', whipping the crowd into a frenzy, tripping up the stairs on to the stage, before the crowning glory of a Michael Jackson moonwalk. Promoter Barry Hearn later tells me it's the best walk-on he's ever seen.

Once everyone has calmed down, it's time to play. This time we're up against Mark Webster and Steve Backley. Game on.

I reach for my darts, which like a true pro I'd tucked in the chest pocket of my darts shirt. Oops. They must have flown out when I was leaping around. Thereupon play is held up for five minutes, punctuated by occasional cries of 'Got one!' as the audience scrabble around on their hands and knees looking for my darts.

Clearly, the delay upsets my finely tuned preparations and when the match finally gets going, my form dips alarmingly.

Calls of 'SEVENNN', 'EEE-LEVENNN', 'THREEEEE' from the

MC mark my visits to the oche as I slowly die onstage. Not even Barney can compensate and my dreams of pro-celebrity darting glory are ended.

AZHAR'S OLD BALL AND SIRALAN

Taking part in the 2006 Sport Relief cricket tour of India was one of the most humbling experiences I've ever had. I captained a Celebrity XI including Jack Russell, Chris Evans, Patrick Kielty, Nick Hancock, Dermot O'Leary and Nick Knowles and we went over and played a series of friendly matches.

It's horrific to see the conditions people are living in. The most shocking example is a rubbish dump in Chennai, a city I'd last visited touring with England fifteen years before. There's syringes, glass and even foetuses among this huge stinking heap of rubbish, and kids are scavenging in their bare feet to find anything they can sell. Around the edge of the dump, there's a green bubbling pit of liquid. We're told that American protestors recently sat in it to highlight the appalling living conditions and two weeks later they died.

There are some lighter moments, though, when we have a game with the kids, most notably when Nick Knowles appeals for lbw against a bloke with one leg. He gets the decision, too.

In contrast, we play a fundraising game against a Bollywood XI at the very posh Braeburn Stadium in Mumbai at the climax of the tour. I go out to the middle to do the toss with former Indian captain Mohammad Azharuddin. He wins and says to me: 'You don't mind using an old ball, do you?'

'Yeah, whatever. It's for charity.'

I realise we're a bit up against it when I ask Dermot O'Leary to go and field at mid-off.

'Twelve mid-offs could come and slap me round the face and I wouldn't know where that is,' he replies.

So we bowl through their innings with a bashed-up old ball, up-and-coming R&B star Jay Sean doing a decent job as my opening bowler, and Dermot not knowing where the hell he is, only to find that when it's Azhar's team's turn to bowl, they've got themselves a brand new cherry. Not only that, halfway through our innings we notice they've got thirteen fielders. Unsurprisingly in the circumstances, we lose, but the Sport Relief campaign ends up raising a total of £14.5 million that year so no one really cares.

A couple of years later, I took on a very different task – *Sport Relief Does The Apprentice*.

It's men v women. In our team, there's me, Kelvin MacKenzie, Lembit Opik, Hardeep Singh Kohli and Nick Hancock. The girls have got Lisa Snowdon, Jacqueline Gold, Louise Redknapp, Kirstie Allsopp and Clare Balding.

The challenge is for each of us to use our contacts to get hold of a lot of free gear, open a pop-up shop in a day's time, and sell as much as we can at the highest possible price.

Each team gets a penthouse suite in the Mayfair Hotel to plan strategy.

On the boys' team, we all want Kelvin to be project manager. He was the editor of a national newspaper after all. '**** off,' he replies cordially.

Okay. How about you, Hardeep? He says yes.

Forty minutes of arguing later, Kelvin accuses Hardeep of 'acting like Hitler annexing Poland' at which Hardeep takes umbrage and storms off into a bedroom. I'm dispatched to try and coax him back into the fold. Eventually, he agrees, but he's not prepared to be leader any more.

Lembit is our third nomination for project manager in less than an hour, and he reluctantly agrees to do it. His first job is to lead the negotiation with the girls over the choice of celebrity shop assistants to help us. As he's a professional politician, he should be the man for the job. I give him a pep talk before he goes in with

Hardeep just in case: 'If it's not going well, bamboozle them with a load of bollocks.'

Lembit returns a couple of minutes later having not negotiated because he wanted to clear the decision with us first, which is a bit pathetic as the whole point of him going was to make a decision.

I get quite angry and do a pretty good impression of 'Siralan' (this was the pre-Lord Sugar era), yelling, 'Let me get this straight, you've come back here with nothing! YOU'VE COME BACK WITH NOTHING!'

I then suggest to Kelvin that perhaps he should be the boss again: 'Stick your head above the parapet. You've been keeping your nut down.'

'No, shove it up your arse. I'm not doing it,' he replies. He then predicts we are likely to raise less money than was in his kid's piggy bank when he was six.

The next day as we're getting ready, we have a peek inside the girls' shop. It appears they have got a lot better celebrity contacts than we have. They've got diamond rings from Garrard, Chanel handbags and loads of Harrods gear. We've got some weights from Lonsdale, a set of golf clubs and forty T-shirts from Fruit of the Loom. Actually, as Hardeep points out as we're assessing our stock, we have also got a canteen of cutlery. 'And the funny thing is it's the only decent thing we've got and we've left it in the hotel,' he says, as he collapses on the floor in hysterics. 'We didn't even ****ing bring it!'

Unsurprisingly, the girls destroyed us, and Siralan was not impressed. Poor old Hardeep got fired, but the rest of us dodged a bullet because we were an absolute shambles.

SAVE THE RHINO

Another fantastic once-in-a-lifetime experience outside cricket that working on telly brought me was a trip to Assam as part of the

2007 *Saving Planet Earth* series. I was sent there to report on the endangered Indian rhino and learn more about conservation projects aiming to save the species from extinction.

Assam is a little finger up on the top right-hand side of India where they grow tea and no one goes except to see the rhinos. It takes about five hours by car from the airport along the worst roads I've ever seen in my life to get to the only hotel in Assam. We see lorries turned on their side, dead bodies, everything.

The first full day, we go out in the ranger's truck to look for rhinos. And when we find one, it's very exciting and we have to creep up on it like David Attenborough would do. Amazing to see this huge creature up close.

By the second day, we've seen loads, though. I joke to the cameraman: 'They don't need saving, there's hundreds of them.' But actually the numbers we see just show the good work the local rangers are doing in protecting them from poachers, who hunt the Indian rhino for its horn, which is supposed to be an aphrodisiac.

It's the monsoon season, but the rangers in these stations haven't even got proper boots. They earn two bob and go home to see their families just once a month. All they've got to fend off poachers is an old Lee-Enfield-type air rifle. Many of them end up getting shot by gangs of poachers because they bravely front them up despite having inadequate gear.

At the hotel, which is really just a concrete box, we're kept awake all night by monkeys on the roof. I start giving them names: 'Shut the **** up, Goochy!' 'Athers, get off the roof!' And there's a very well-groomed monkey I name 'Stewie'.

Things get really interesting when we're having breakfast one morning and the side of the hotel slips into the back garden due to all the rain. It's not exactly the Rambagh Palace, but the excursions make up for the discomfort.

One day, we ride out on elephants to see the rhinos with their babies. They would attack people to protect their kids, but rhinos can't see very well and they can only see and smell the elephants when they walk past, so we could sit on them and get a really close look. Amazing.

Another amazing thing – and this might not be the sort of thing David Attenborough would tell you – is the size of a rhino turd. It's a huge, bouldery pyramid almost as tall as me. When I get back to England, a friend of mine tells me about a cricket pitch at Everdon Hall, Northamptonshire, owned by someone he played for, the brilliantly named Captain Dick Hawkins. It was a country house cricket ground in the Victorian era, where the villagers played the toffs, before it got turned over to grazing cattle. Captain Dick reclaimed it for cricket and was told the best way to get the wicket right was to roll it in rhino shit. Ever since, he's had truckloads of the stuff brought in from Whipsnade Zoo and it works a treat apparently. Another good reason to save the rhino, then . . .

WEMBLEY CAT-ASTROPHE

I fulfilled a childhood dream of playing at Wembley when I got to play in the first-ever game before the new stadium officially opened in 2007. It was a charity match to test that everything worked in and around the stadium before they staged proper professional matches. And now Phil 'The Cat' Tufnell shall forever be remembered as the, ahem, 'goalkeeper' who let in the first goal there, scored by former Crystal Palace striker and football pundit Mark Bright.

Later, I'm at home watching *Match Of The Day* and they show my big moment. Very exciting.

Alan Shearer and Alan Hansen are in the pundits' chairs, and Shearer says: 'Brighty keeps on phoning me up going on about how he scored the first goal at the new Wembley.'

'Yes,' replies Hansen, 'but did you have a look who was in goal?'

WAR STORY

I was very fortunate to take part in a BBC1 documentary series called *My Family at War* in 2008, which allowed me to learn more about what my granddad did in the First World War. He was a coppersmith in No. 46 Squadron, Royal Flying Corps, making and repairing biplane engines. Part of his job was to go into No-Man's Land to find and bring back planes that had been shot down.

It wasn't many years since aeroplanes had been invented, and he was working at the cutting edge of their aerial combat capability. Previously, planes had just been used for reconnaissance, but No. 46 Squadron was one of the first to realise that they could also be used to drop bombs and shoot down enemy planes.

I've never really spoken in depth to my dad about his father before the programme. He tells me a nice story about when he was a boy growing up in a little two-up, two-down terraced house. On Sunday morning his mum used to say, 'Shh, don't wake your father,' the reason being that he'd been out with his surviving squadron mates the night before and got absolutely smashed. Dad had to creep out the house to go and play football.

We dig out a great picture of my granddad and his pet dog, a lovely big Great Dane. He had to give it away before he went off to war, so he gave it to the pub landlord who had a few quid and could afford to feed it. When hostilities were over, Granddad came back to find that his dog had finished third at Crufts!

The highlight of the programme is going up in the only operational Avro biplane from the RAF base in Hampshire where it's kept. Only forty-odd people have been up in it, including Bill Clinton, so, even though I'm a nervous flier, I feel very lucky to have the opportunity.

It's a lovely sunny day and sitting in the cockpit, I get very emotional thinking about the dangers my granddad and the pilots had to face. The life expectancy of a pilot in the First World War was just eleven days because a) there were very few experienced pilots so they often crashed in training, and b) you could throw stones at these planes and knock them out of the air.

We flutter up into the sky, do a couple of manoeuvres and then flutter back down, but pilots in the war used to take a pistol up with them, because the bastards didn't give them parachutes. They were sitting on a wicker chair above a fuel tank in a plane made of wood, so if something went wrong they'd shoot themselves rather than burn to death. It was only later the army generals realised that the pilots were, in fact, more important than the planes because they knew how to fly, so they gave them parachutes.

An unforgettable and moving experience.

CHAPTER 16

PHIL VERSUS LIFE (PART 2)

NEVER EVER GIVE ME A FIREWORK...

I love Bonfire Night, and a few years ago, Dawn and I decided to host a little party for family and friends round our house. I was put in charge of sorting the fireworks.

Luckily, I've got a mate who supplies public firework displays, so I give him a few quid and on November the Fifth he brings over a box full of absolute belters.

'Make sure you read all the instructions, Phil. These are bad boys.'

The centrepiece of the Tufnell fireworks extravaganza will be a 50-shot repeater. I read the instruction on the back and it says to dig a trench twice the depth of the packet.

So I go down the end of our garden, which is about a couple of cricket pitches long, and start digging. But it's a horrible, rainy day, and after a few prods at the earth, I decide to go inside, have a cup of tea and try to think of an alternative that requires less spadework.

Ah, the washing-up bowl! I can fill that up with sand. Perfect. One of my mates coming tonight is a fireman so it'll all be fine.

The evening comes. Music playing, we're all partying. Okay, time for the fireworks. Let's have a go.

It's still pouring with rain, so we all grab umbrellas. My fireman pal and I plod down to the end of the garden while the rest of the adults and kids gather on the patio outside the back door.

I take the baddest of the bad boys and wriggle it into the sand in the washing-up bowl. The bowl is about the same depth as the firework, but it seems to sit quite snugly in there. That'll do.

I light the fuse and run back halfway up the garden.

Whoosh! The first of the 50 shots zooms straight up, piercing the night sky. Eveyone's looking up ooh-ing and ah-ing.

I look back at the bowl.

The force of the blast has jolted the firework on it's side. It's now pointing directly at me, my pal and, beyond us, my nearest and dearest on the patio.

'OH NOOOOOOOOO, GET INSIDE!'

My mate and I jump for cover in the arbour, while everyone else dives inside the house as quickly as possible and shuts the door.

Tracers fizz overhead and explode against the side of the house. A corner of leafy Kingswood, Surrey, is transformed into the set of *Tropic Thunder*, only not so funny.

The shelling goes on for two minutes but it seems like hours as we're pinned down among the rose bushes. When it finally ends, we pull ourselves up out the mud and trudge shamefacedly inside to be greeted by shocked, scared guests. And that's just the adults.

No one is talking to me – well, apart from Dawn who is screaming at me for being an irresponsible bastard. She's right. I'm so sorry.

A year later, Dawn, me and the kids are in Koh Samui, Thailand, for Christmas. On New Year's Eve, we go for dinner in one of two lovely restaurants on the beach. As we're eating we watch the locals planting little fireworks in the sand setting them off into the sky.

After dinner, I say to a chap we've met, 'They're not very good, them rockets. Let's go and get some big ones.'

PHIL VERSUS LIFE (PART 2)

I go up to one of the Thai guys on the beach: 'Bit small, bit small – get some big ones?'

'Yes, yes. Okay. I get.'

I give him 500 baht, around a tenner, which goes a long way out there, and he trots off.

He comes back with a few little fireworks and what looks like an artillery shell. Absolutely massive, it is.

He gives us a couple of the little ones first, though, which we stick in the sand and let off. There's loads of families on the beach by now, fireworks and lanterns going up into the clear sky. It's a beautiful scene.

Then he hands me the big Bazooka Joe.

Now, acutely aware of my tarnished health and safety credentials with fireworks, this time I make sure I pack the firework down securely in the sand.

But as soon as I light it, I can see something's not right. What I haven't realised is that this is the kind of firework that is supposed to fly up into the air before exploding hundreds of metres in the air, but it hasn't moved an inch.

'OH ****, RUUUNNNN . . .'

It's Armageddon all over again, although this time, the tracers are flashing into the restaurants. Everyone within a 50-feet radius is in danger. It's really scary.

When the bangs stop and the smoke clears, for a few seconds it's silent except for the sound of children sobbing (including ours). Luckily, no one's been seriously injured.

But soon people have worked out who caused the carnage and are shouting and swearing at me. The missus is furious (she won't speak to me for two days). And the maitre d' who welcomed my family to the restaurant we were dining at earlier comes out wielding a big kitchen knife, shouting: 'Get off my island, you crazy man! You crazy man! You never come back!'

'RUUUNNNN!'

'DRIVE IT LIKE YOU STOLE IT'

As a chap who likes his beer, one of my most enjoyable gigs was 'working' as an Ambassador for Foster's for three years between 2004 and 2006. It involved going along and meeting people and having unlimited free beer thrust into my hand – not exactly a hardship.

One time, they hold a huge promotional event in Trafalgar Square where they create a West Indies beach scene – sand, dancing girls, steel pans band, the lot. My dad is down in London the same day, so he pops down to say hello while the event is in full swing.

'Phil, about ten yards to the left of where you are standing drinking a beer and playing cricket and having a laugh, is where I played the trumpet on VE Day!'

Here I am twatting about in a pair of Bermuda shorts, getting all the benefits of being an ex-England cricketer and being sponsored in the same place where my dad was part of one of our country's most historic occasions.

As part of my ambassadorial role, I also got the chance to drive a couple of supercars flat out around the Goodwood track.

In the morning, I do a few laps in a Ferrari 360 with the help of a test driver alongside me. I love cars and I've never been in a Ferrari before so it's great for me.

'Drive it like you stole it,' he urges.

So I absolutely moose it, driving down the straight foot flat to the floor. It just needs a touch on the brakes to take the corners smoothly. The more I drive, the later I find I need to brake and the car responds so well, remaining beautifully flat. It's point and shoot driving. I'm really enjoying myself, laughing my head off and driving pretty well if I say so myself.

After lunch, I get the chance to drive a Maserati, another beautiful car. It's very quick too, but handles a bit more like a canoe. I'm flooring it down the straight, and as we come to the corner, my instructor says: 'Okay, brake now . . .'

I'm in Ferrari mode and leave it a bit late.

'BRAAAAAKE!'

I dab the pedal expecting the anchors to drop, but I just plough straight off the circuit into the wasteland. Belatedly, I crunch on the brakes, the car rocks on to two wheels and down again as it donuts to a halt. Bang. Lights flashing, smoke billowing out of the engine.

The bloke looks at me: 'Well, Mr Tufnell. I'm afraid you've failed your driving test.'

We get out of the car and as I'm trudging away wondering whether the sponsor's insurance covers me, a crane is deployed to airlift the broken Mazza back to the pits.

HOW I WON THE (SAUSAGE) OSCAR

In 2007 I was invited to act as a judge in the prestigious 'Legendary British Bangers' competition. Come British Sausage Week, I join a panel of sausage connoisseurs and we set off on tour around the country, stopping off to taste the best sausages of each region. Great job because I do like a nice sausage, and I get to sample sausages that I never knew existed – tutti-frutti sausages, gold leaf sausages, jelly babies sausages.

On the last day, we're sitting in a Birmingham pub tasting entries from the Midlands region. In front of us is a roomful of press people and local sausage-making farmers who, naturally, take the competition very seriously, because winning the award can mean a lot for their business.

But I'm feeling a bit dicky. We're in the basement of the pub, which is packed with people, and it's rather hot and sticky, so at first I think it might be just that. But as I'm nibbling on a sausage, I suddenly realise I'm going to be sick. Maybe I've exceeded my maximum sausage units for a week?

'Excuse me one minute. I've just got to go to the . . .'

I stand up, put my hand to my mouth and make a dash for the toilet. But it's too late. Within a couple of strides, there's spew spraying from my nose and mouth and I crash through the door of the gents leaving a trail of meaty chunder behind me.

After cleaning myself up, I emerge red-faced (with a touch of green).

'I'm terribly sorry. I'm not feeling very well.'

Thankfully, the organisers are sympathetic to my untimely illness and don't let one untimely chunder spoil what has been a magnificent week for British sausages.

In fact, I am presented with the 'British Banger Award For Out-standing Service to the Great British Sausage', the Oscar of the sausage world. The trophy is a giant golden sausage mounted vertically on a plinth. My name has been misspelt 'Phil Tuffnell' but I'm not about to complain after my unfortunate barfing incident.

The golden banger award takes pride of place on the mantelpiece in our games room at home. Except now it's black. Dawn decided to paint it so it fits in better with the décor. And it does, although it has been said that it now resembles a rather frightening sex toy.

SHEPHERD UNDER PRESSURE

One of my earliest TV jobs after coming out of the jungle was appearing in the first series of an ITV show called *Celebrities Under Pressure*. In the first episode, Tara Palmer-Tomkinson had ended up in tears at failing the test, and by the end of my experience I can understand why.

My challenge is to learn how to be a shepherd, which is something completely new for me. The nearest I've ever got to herding sheep was trying to keep tabs on Allan Lamb on a night out (he might argue it was the other way round).

PHIL VERSUS LIFE (PART 2)

To immerse myself in the art of shepherding, I live with a family of four on a little farm in the middle of nowhere in North Wales for a few days. Every day, I'm working with their sheepdogs, practising herding sheep into a pen. At night, the dad and I go to the pub for a drink, so by the day of the test, I know the family really well.

I've gone into it thinking it's just a bit of fun, but the clue's in the name of the show. The prizes are incredible. A new 4x4 vehicle, a week at Disneyland for all the family, a quad bike, feed for the sheep for a year. About £30,000-worth all in all.

I come down for breakfast on the morning of the trial, and the atmosphere in the house has changed.

'Phil, we really need this.'

'All right, I'm going to do my best . . .'

'No, but Phil, the kids have never been to America. They've always wanted a quad bike. We need that jeep for the farm . . .'

The kids are hanging off my leg, going, 'Phil, Phil, you've got to win.'

All of a sudden, it's turned from a little bit of telly into something much bigger. This is people's lives and I don't want to let them down.

When the production team come to pick me up, they are waving me off ('Phil, you can do it'). And I can see them all there watching me on the hillside later as I'm about to start the test. I won't be able to look them in the eye if I don't do it now.

My challenge is to guide the sheep through a course and into a pen in less than three minutes.

Thankfully, the dog is amazing. I don't really have to do much. Just whistle a bit and say 'Come by' a lot, and the dog guides all the sheep round the course and into the pen. I shut the gate with about ten seconds to spare.

All the family and their friends come running on and joyfully bundle me to the floor: 'WE'RE GOING TO DISNEYLAND!'

Thank God. If I – well, the dog – hadn't done it, I would have been mortified. I think I'd have had to write the cheque myself.

IF I COULD SWAP LIVES . . .

. . . it would probably be with one of our cats, Oscar and Suki. They're Persians, great balls of fluff, and they live a life of luxury. Once a month, a pet groomer comes round to give them a shampoo, trim their hair and cut their nails. Oscar is a right diva – he sits there, holding his paw out like Mariah Carey having a manicure. Then the lady cleans their teeth with chicken toothpaste.

Most pampered and best turned out cats in Surrey, they are. Like feline Alec Stewarts.

PART THREE

INFILTRATING THE ESTABLISHMENT: CAT THE CRICKET PUNDIT

CHAPTER 17

'OH, HE'S TWATTED IT THROUGH THE OFFSIDE . . .'

DROPPING THE T BOMB

I started doing a little bit of TV and radio work in the last couple of years of my playing career. I did phone interviews for BBC Radio 5 Live before getting the occasional 'colour' commentary gig for Sky Sports, working with the likes of Bob Willis and Michael Holding. It took a while to adjust my normal dressing-room observations on the game to the requirements of a public broadcast.

During one England game at The Oval, I mark a very fine off-drive by saying: 'Oh, he's twatted that through the offside.'

The producer comes running in: 'Phil, you can't say that.'

'What're you talking about? It's a cricketing term.'

'No, you said he c-worded it through the offside.'

Oh.

It was a sharp learning curve, but from day one I loved the work. Getting paid to watch and talk about cricket? Fantastic.

THE SHEER JOY OF *TMS*

First and foremost, it's an absolute honour for me to be involved with the BBC's *Test Match Special*. One of my earliest memories of cricket is of sitting in the back of my dad's Ford Cortina estate with my mum and my brother, stuck in a traffic jam going down to Brighton. Sweating, windows down, the only relief coming from the voices of John Arlott and Johnners wafting through the summer haze. As a youngster, television ruled over radio. Radio wasn't cool, but as I've got older, I've become more and more appreciative of the pleasures of listening to *TMS*.

When they approached me to come on board as a summariser in 2003, I was actually quite nervous. But there's a great team, a great set-up there. From the people behind the scenes, like the producer Adam Mountford – all good cricket people and a good laugh – to the main men, Jonathan Agnew, Henry Blofeld and Christopher Martin-Jenkins, everyone made me feel so welcome. From day one, I just sat down and had a chat.

In the early days, I used to chuckle to myself that I was actually there. There's Blowers describing the action in his inimitable way, and then turning to me for my opinion.

And, at first, probably because of my image as something of a lunatic (for which I have to take some blame), I think he was bit surprised that I actually had some intelligent thoughts to contribute on the game.

'That's a great field position because he opens the face of the bat and he's tossing the ball up to tempt him into the drive.'

'By jove, Tuffers, my dear old thing. I think you're right!'

It must have been a bit of a punt for the BBC to take me on in the first place. I'd just retired from playing, been in the jungle, become a so-called 'celebrity', but one thing I had going for me is that I do know the game. As I hope I've shown in the years since, I have got a good cricketing brain. When he was England captain,

'OH, HE'S TWATTED IT THROUGH THE OFFSIDE . . .'

Nasser Hussain used to say so and he would come to ask me for my thoughts on strategies to get batsmen out. You can't be an international-level spin bowler without that, which is why I spent so many hours in bed 'penguining'.

I still love analysing the game, breaking it down. And doing this job has made me think I could be a good coach. My ex-teammate Gus Fraser, who's Managing Director of Cricket at Middlesex now, has got me in to chat to one of their up-and-coming spin bowlers, and I think I would enjoy being a specialist spin coach.

Working on *TMS* is something I couldn't have fully appreciated when I was younger and all I wanted to do was go out drinking in bars and clubs. Now, I'm happier to have a nice cup of tea, a slice of cake and a good chat with interesting people, and that's what they are in the *TMS* box – very knowledgeable, interesting characters.

It's a pleasure just listening to the guys, but I also like to surprise them occasionally by slipping the odd general knowledge fact into the conversation. That's where working on *The One Show* comes in really handy. On one occasion, I'd just done a report for them on the Battersea Power Station, which I discovered was constructed from 61 million bricks.

So there I was sitting in the box at The Oval with this little nugget of information in my head, and during a break in play, I say to Aggers:

'Where are you staying, Aggers?'

'Just down the road. Lovely hotel. Look out my window, there's Battersea Power Station.'

Oh, yes, couldn't have fallen any easier for me.

'Battersea Power Station? 61 million bricks.'

'What?'

'Sixty-one million bricks in Battersea Power Station. The second largest man-built brick structure in the world. The largest is a muslim temple in Sri Lanka.'

'No way!' he says, turning to our resident statto, Malcolm Ashton. 'Malc, get on that.'

Malc taps away on his laptop.

'Sixty-one million bricks. He's right!'

One bit of advice I was given when I joined the team was to say what you see. But I was surprised to find that sometimes it is better not to say anything. As it's radio, I thought you couldn't afford to have a second of 'dead air', but at a big Test match the listener can hear the roar of the crowd in the background (well, unless the game is in Dubai!). You can give it a beat or two. CMJ, Aggers and co. are so good at getting that balance. At first, I was diving in feeling the need to say something, but over time I've relaxed into it and realised it's not necessary.

That's what I particularly like about Test match cricket – you can let it breathe, whereas one-day cricket and Twenty20 is more frantic. Of course, when the bowler's running up, you have to focus back on the action – you can't be blathering on about power stations and cake when Jimmy Anderson is charging in – and you do have to mention the score regularly, and there's a summary of play every five overs, but you do also have these lovely passages of random conversation.

It's just a fabulous job. The BBC always get the best vantage point at each of the English grounds, so I've got the best seat in the house. I'm sitting with my mates, having a great laugh, and being paid to watch top-quality cricket and talk about a game I love. And I get to sample the best of British cakes sent in by listeners around the country. What's not to like?

One of the things that a lot of ex-sportsmen who've competed at the top level struggle with after retiring is how to replace the excitement of playing. And you can't, but I'm so lucky that *TMS* gives me the chance to feel part of the occasion. It's an absolute joy to walk into the ground for a big Test match. On the first day, I always wear a suit and my *Test Match Special* tie. At Lord's, I wear a suit in case I'm asked to go out to do the pitch report. A couple of times, early on in my career, I rolled up in my usual jeans and leather jacket, thinking I'd just be in the commentary box, and I felt a bit underdressed out there on the hallowed turf. Since then I always make sure I look smart.

The atmosphere is building, but you haven't got the pressure of actually playing. I'm out there among the players, getting the buzz I used to have as a player, thinking about how the game might unfold, but then I can leave them to do all the hard work. It might be a second-hand buzz, but it still gets the old goosebumps going.

CHAPTER 18

THE *TMS* ECOSYSTEM

Test Match Special has become a Great British institution because from the days of John Arlott through Brian 'Johnners' Johnston and Tony Lewis to Jonathan Agnew and co. today, the BBC have got the mix of characters in the commentary box just right. I think listeners are drawn in by the interaction between the chaps on the microphones as much as the game of cricket we're commenting on.

At the heart of the *TMS* ecosystem, we've got the big beasts, Aggers, CMJ and Blowers, sharing duties at the front of the box, leading the commentary and discussion. Alongside them, there's Malcolm 'Ashtray' Ashton, keeping score and feeding the team with statistics and trivia to back up the conversation. Then dropping in for stints in the front row, there's Geoff Boycott, Michael Vaughan, Vic Marks, myself and other occasional guest summarisers to splash a bit of extra colour on the scene. Producer Adam Mountford sits at the back, keeping an ear on proceedings and prompting new debates, while our brilliant production team work away next door to keep us on air. Listeners play their part too, feeding us with a constant stream of observations, opinions and extraordinary trivia via email, text and Twitter.

Yes, *TMS* is so much more than just a radio show. It's a community with tentacles that reach around the world, fuelled by a shared passion for cricket and, in the commentary box at least, the consumption of huge quantities of cake.

AGGERS

Aggers has a great voice for the job and paints a vivid picture of what's going on. He's brilliant at maintaining that balance between having a laugh and being serious. He has the title of BBC Cricket Correspondent for good reason, and he's the man that holds it all together.

His experience as a player means he really knows his stuff. He was a great bowler for Leicestershire, once taking over 100 first-class wickets in a season (101 in 1987), and was unlucky not to play more than three times for England. Middlesex batsmen always knew they were in for a tough time at Grace Road with Aggers and Les Taylor steaming in and cutting the ball all over the place.

He retired young to move into the media when he realised his international ambitions were not going to be fulfilled, and it's proved to be a brilliant decision. He might not have thought that when he interviewed me following England's First Test win over New Zealand in January 1992, though. We won by an innings and four runs on the final day in Christchurch, but only just. The Kiwis could have saved the game with their captain Martin Crowe still at the crease alongside their number 11 Chris Pringle, who was hanging in there gamely. Crowe knew that one meaty blow would be enough to save the game, because there would not be enough time for the teams to turn round and us to knock off the winning runs.

Anyway, happily, Crowe knocks one of my floaty 'ball on a string' deliveries up in the air and Derek Pringle clings on to the catch. I finish with 7 for 47 after notching 4 for 100 in the first innings to earn my first international man of the match award.

After meeting the written press, having a couple of gaspers and a tinny of the local brew, it's time to speak to Aggers for the Beeb.

He lobs me a gentle loosener to start: 'Well Phil, that was an extraordinary performance. The New Zealanders didn't know how to play you at all.'

'Yeah,' I reply, 'They was shittin' themselves.'

Not quite the response Aggers was expecting and some slick editing was required to make the interview suitable for transmission on the BBC sports news.

Mind you, Aggers himself has been responsible for turning the airwaves blue over the years himself (sort of).

There was the infamous 'Botham Legover' incident with Johnners in 1991, of course, and I was lucky enough to be present for another beauty at Lord's twenty years later during the England–India Test series.

Out in the middle, KP has just changed the rubber grip on his bat handle, causing Aggers to launch innocently into a monologue on the difficulties of such an operation:

'Welcome back to Radio 4 longwave. You haven't missed anything except the excitement of an impromptu drinks break, which we think was brought about because Kevin Pietersen needed a new bat rubber on his handle and, as all amateurs will know, it is not easy to do that. You've got to roll it on down the stick and make sure it is all in place, and no floppy stuff on the end of the handle, you can't have that. It's a bit of a procedure and I thought he did it very well.'

I'm sitting at the back of the box, quietly creasing up. Vaughanie, who's sitting next to Aggers, looks round shaking his head. We're all thinking, 'Where are you going with this?' but Aggers ploughs on oblivious to the innuendo:

'Michael Vaughan is beside me – It's not easy putting a rubber on, is it?'

Vaughanie, just about holding it together (despite me kicking his legs under the table) manages to reply drily, 'No, it's not. I was never good at that.'

Blowers, who's been quietly reading in the corner on his break, has twigged what's going on, too, and he is struggling to contain his giggles. Surveying the scene, Aggers himself finally realises why his references to KP's rubber-rolling technique are causing such mirth.

He shoots us a disapproving schoolmasterly look and says, 'You know what I meant,' which only makes us laugh more.

'Shall we move on,' splutters Vaughanie.

'You know what I meant,' repeats Aggers slowly.

Still laughing, Vaughanie trumpets in a posh voice, 'Hello, Henry . . . he's playing well, KP, isn't he?'

'He has played well,' agrees Aggers. 'Now he's got a new rubber on he might play even better!'

On another occasion, when I walk into the commentary box to do my shift, I'm rather thrown to find Aggers talking on air in similarly explicit terms about 'dampness in the beaver this morning'. It takes a minute for me to realise that he is referring to his home in the Vale of Belvoir in Leicestershire.

I thought Playboy TV missed a trick not getting Blowers on board as a presenter, but maybe I nominated the wrong man . . .

Aggers usually does the regular lunchtime 'View from the Boundary' interview with special guests at home Tests. He's had some amazing guests in the box from Russell Crowe to Lily Allen, and if there's room, I like to squeeze in and listen. One time he interviewed Queen guitarist and astrophysicist Brian May. He was talking about the difficulty of cleaning up waste particles floating in the atmosphere (or something – it went a bit over my head, to be honest).

After the lunch interval Aggers turns to me and says, 'So Tuffers, what do you make of this particle problem?'

'Simple. Get a brush with a very long handle.'

CMJ

CMJ is like a very nice public-school cricket master. Very posh, immaculately turned out in a blazer and tie and always enthusiastic and upbeat – come on boys, let's go and have a jolly good game of cricket!

He hasn't played at professional level, but his boy Robin played for Sussex, and he really understands the game himself.

I'd met CMJ a couple of times as a journalist in my playing days, and as I've got to know him better, I've found him to be a great laugh and, like all of the *TMS* lads, really generous in spirit. I would never have thought that he'd be someone I'd go out and have a beer with, but I love his company. When we are working away from home, all the boys often go out for dinner as a little team.

The gentle clash of cultures between us adds to the fun. For instance, one time, at Lord's, I grabbed my lunch around the back of the stand at the Nursery End, which was packed with people eating and drinking, live music blasting out.

When I come back to the commentary box, I say: 'Cor blimey, CMJ, it's like Glastonbury out there.'

He replies in his beautifully enunciated voice: 'Oh, yes, Glastonbury, yes.'

As the next ball's being bowled, images flash through my mind of CMJ dressed in multi-coloured hemp clothes, feather in his hair, sitting cross-legged outside a teepee in the Green Fields smoking a giant dooby.

'When was the last time you went to Glastonbury, CMJ?'

'Well, no, I haven't been to the festival, but I have been to the Abbey a couple of times!'

Then we end up chatting about Glastonbury Abbey, when it was built, its features, etc. And I love all that. The way the conversation can just meander off at tangents.

Another time I got CMJ to play the porn star game, except I changed it to 'rock star'.

'Rock star game, eh? What's this then, Tuffers?'

'Well, you take your mother's maiden name and the name of your first pet.'

'Right, well, I had a cocker spaniel called "Rambler" . . .'

I can't remember his mum's maiden name, mainly because me and the rest of guys were falling about . . .

BLOWERS

The one and only. From his dress sense (stripey jacket, bow tie, sky blue or canary yellow trousers with red socks and brown suede loafers) to his brilliantly plummy voice, you can't mistake him for anyone else. Blowers was a brilliant schoolboy cricketer and captained Eton back in the fifties. He might well have gone on to play at international level if it hadn't been for a near-fatal road accident. In fact, he nearly did anyway when he was covering England's 1963/64 tour of India as a reporter and was put on stand-by as an emergency batsman to replace the ill Micky Stewart in the Bombay Test. Micky dragged himself off his hospital bed to play, but not before Blowers had informed England's tour manager that he'd play, but if he scored 50-plus, he expected to be picked for the next Test!

So Blowers knows his stuff all right, but as much as his cricket knowledge, it's his eye for quirky details and his turn of phrase that makes him so entertaining, whether it's a parade of cement-mixing trucks 'with stripes round their bellies' trundling past the stadium in Dubai or a flock of pigeons flying overhead.

I like to check in with Blowers to find out what he ate for lunch, because it's often something rather grand.

'So, Blowers what did you have today?'

'Oh, a lovely lobster thermidor. Beautiful buttery dressing with parsley and tarragon. Dash of Tabasco, I believe, too. What about you, Tuffers?'

'Hamburger.'

ASHTRAY

Ashtray was the scorer for England and used to come on tours when I played and he's a good guy to have around.

His handwritten scorer's book is a work of art and it's amazing to see him in action. He keeps track of everything going on. He knows how many times a batsman's left the ball by the way he dots it.

And on top of that he has to deal with us asking daft questions about how many bricks there are in Battersea Power Station. He does it all seemingly without breaking sweat, no matter what we try to do to break him.

Ashtray is an absolutely crucial member of the team, because cricket is a stats game and many listeners really enjoy that aspect. He's forever unearthing some record that can be broken or a bizarre trivial fact that relates to the game situation (or what the rest of us have been wittering on about).

You might imagine he's a bit of a geek, but he just loves his sport, and he's a very humorous guy to have in the box. Even when he's busy doing his scoring, you can see him giggling along with the banter among the commentators.

Malcolm, of course, replaced the great Bill Frindall,

'The Bearded Wonder' who was in the box when I first started my *TMS* career. Bill was another lovely fella, witty and engaging, and with an extraordinary knowledge of the game. It was such a tragedy when he died in 2009. He was only 69, still very active. He contracted Legionnaires' disease during a charity cricket tour to Dubai with the Lord's Taverners and passed away soon afterwards. That was a very sad time, and it's a credit to Malc that he's come in and taken on Bill's mantle, because he was a very hard act to follow.

THE 'COLOUR' BOYS

Leading the charge for the 'colour' boys of course is the legendary Geoff Boycott. Always immaculately turned out in pastel colours and a panama hat, Boycs says it exactly as he sees it and he's not afraid to upset people. And you can tell from the moment Boycs walks into the box whether he's got something he needs to get off his chest.

'Oh, Geoffrey's off the long run today,' we'll say and duck for cover. When he gets up a head of steam he's unstoppable: 'You cannot do it like that, it's a disgrace . . .' 'You can't have medium-fast bowlers bowling short on this pitch. It's ridddiculous . . .'

A viewer sent in a prototype 'Boycott Bingo' card, a grid with twenty-four of his favourite sayings in each box. At the end of play one day, when we were about to do the summary, Aggers whispers, 'Let's wind up Geoffrey.'

So we're asking him questions purely so we can tick off the sayings on the card:

'How do you think Glenn McGrath bowled today? Did he get in the right areas?'

'Oh, yes, the thing about McGrath is he consistently gets the ball in the corridor of uncertainty . . .'

Ding!

'And that was a very lucky escape for Bell when he was dropped on 24 . . .'

'Well, my mother could have caught that in her pinny . . .'

Ding!

'So, Geoffrey, that was a poor shot by Prior. He could have easily hit that, don't you think?'

'It was rrrrrrubbish. I could have hit that with a stick of rooooobarb.'

Ding! Ding! House!

Great value is Geoff and, whether you agree with him or not, you can't question his knowledge and passion for the game.

I also enjoy working with Vic Marks, a journalist who played the game at the highest level for Somerset and England, and has been part of the *TMS* set-up for over twenty years. Very measured, but very funny as well, he's a fellow spinner, so if we're doing the colour together we always get into a good little conversation about spin bowling.

Former England skipper Michael Vaughan joined the regular colour team a couple of years ago and he's been a great addition. A very good analytical brain and a good laugh. He's a captain I wish I'd played under, actually, because I think he would have suited me. He's got the right balance between being one of the boys and thinking independently.

CAKE

I've always heard about people sending in cakes to *TMS*, but I had no idea of the scale of the cake mountain until I joined the team. We get thousands sent in during the summer. Piled high they are. Even with the production team gorging themselves, there's only so much we can eat, so we cut them all up and give them to people passing by in the corridor. The Sky boys often drop in. Bumble is always on the prowl for a slice – ''Ere, Tuffers, where's that chocolate caaake?'

Apart from getting some jolly nice cakes, I think the tradition, which was started by Johnners, sums up the warmth of the relation-ship and the bond between the *TMS* team and the listeners. It goes way beyond the cricket.

'This fruit cake has been sent in by Mary Swiddlehurst from Loughborough – she sends in a cake every year to Edgbaston. And this one is an absolute triumph, isn't it, Tuffers . . . oh, sorry Mary, Philip Tufnell can't speak at the moment because his mouth's full . . .'

The characters who send in cake, write letters (or email, text and tweet us, nowadays) all contribute to what makes it special.

The listeners' generosity doesn't end there. In summer 2011, at Trent Bridge for England v India, I was not feeling very well. Very bad throat, and feeling a bit sorry for myself. On air, I mentioned that I didn't know what to do for it. The next day: delivery for Tufnell. A huge pile of medicines, tablets and natural remedies, with letters from people saying what's worked for them. It just shows how much people engage with the programme. It's lovely.

AND FINALLY . . . THE BILL FRINDALL TRIBUTE BEARDED WONDERS XI

W. G. Grace
The Godfather of English beards (and cricket).

Monty Panesar
2006 Beard of the Year winner, back in the Test team and back among the beard honours, scooping the 2012 Beard of Winter award.

Saeed Anwar
Like a beard of bees. Magnificent.

AGGERS, BLOWERS, CMJ AND CO.

Hashim Amla
Top of the beard game. Got its own Facebook appreciation group.

Ishant Sharma
An act of faith to add this fine young Indian bowler to the side, but he is showing great beard potential.

Matt Prior
Named beard of the 2011 England–India series by the Beard Liberation Front.

Mike Brearley
Grew one for the 1979/80 England tour of Australia and earned the nickname 'Ayatollah'.

Greg Chappell
Matched Brearley beard for beard in that 1979/80 series, the first time since 1893 that the two opposing England–Australia Test captains had been fully bearded up.

Mohammad Yousuf
Battling with Hashim Amla for beard supremacy in the modern game.

Mushtaq Ahmed
Little Mushy, big beard. Now with a dashing Dickie Davies-esque streak of silver.

Fidel Castro
Captain of the team. Not sure about his cricketing skills, but he is a proven leader with an iconic beard.

CHAPTER 19

THE DAY THE LAUGHTER STOPPED

It's very rare to have a fun-free day in the *TMS* box, but the day the revelations of spot-fixing broke during the 2010 England–Pakistan series was one.

I had been commentating when Mohammad Amir bowled that massive no-ball on the first ball of the third over of the Fourth Test at Lord's, just as the fixer Mazhar Majeed had said he would to undercover *News of the World* reporters.

> AGGERS: Six for no wicket. Here's the third over and Amir rushes in, bowls outside the off stump. It's a no ball.
> ME: My . . .
> AGGERS: Ooh, I tell you what. Look at that. It's a big no-ball!
> ME: Ooh, it's a big no-ball!
> AGGERS: It's a *huge* no-ball. To go with that big wide, he's not very happy, Amir.

Although we were shocked by how far over the line he was, none of us were suspicious at the time. Partly because we've all made horrendous mistakes in our time as players, and also Pakistan have had a reputation for their erratic play over the years. Part of the excitement of watching them during the series was wondering which Pakistan would turn up.

On the Sunday the story is published, it's like a wake in the commentary box. We don't know what we are watching any more. Everyone is sitting there thinking, how do we commentate? I feel like the game I get excited about before the start of play each morning, and the job that I'm doing as a commentator has been completely mugged off. Cricket is like a religion to those of us who love the game, and you need to have faith in what you are seeing.

And I think back on my own career. I bowled a lot of no-balls. People might ask what was he doing bowling no-balls when he was a spinner? Every honest player is put under a cloud by these crooks.

In the time since, Amir, and the other two players involved, Salman Butt and Mohammad Asif, have been jailed for their crimes and been handed lengthy bans from the sport. It's very sad to see a great young talent like Amir out of the game for five years. His career may never recover from the suspension. Some say he should have been banned for life, but I think the punishment is about right.

Generally, I'm all for rehabilitation because I know myself that you can do stupid things when you're young that you later regret. But this is the integrity of the game that's at stake here, so players have to know they will be severely punished, otherwise it will just continue and the whole ethos of the sport goes out the window.

THE OTHER SIDE OF THE FENCE

As a player, you develop a siege mentality, particularly when things are going wrong. And things often went very wrong during my

England career. When I was playing, I sometimes felt that writers, commentators and/or pundits had it in for us.

Now I've crossed over to the dark side, I realise that you have a duty to say it how you see it. I think the trick is how you frame your criticism. For instance, one of my stock phrases is: 'He'll be disappointed with that.' But sometimes your instant response is to blurt out, 'Oh, that's a terrible shot,' because that's exactly what you'd be saying in the dressing room as a player, except in riper language. If a batsman comes down the wicket first ball to a spinner and heaves across the line, against the spin, when there's no urgent need to score runs, well, that is an absolute shocker and you have to call it.

We were confronted with that when Steve Harmison bowled that infamous first ball of England's disastrous Ashes tour of 2006/07, the five-niller.

We were all geared up for it in the commentary box. Come on England. And then he bowls.

'Oh my God, it's gone straight to second slip! What a horrible start . . . That is just about the worst delivery I've ever seen in Test cricket,' says Aggers.

In that case, what else could you say?

Bumble who was commentating for Sky had a brilliant line on it: 'What usually happens when the ball goes to second slip is it's usually followed by an appeal.' Classic.

It wasn't quite so spectacular, but a similar thing happened when I played at the start of the 1994/95 Ashes. My mate Phil DeFreitas bowled the first ball to Michael Slater at the Gabba, short and wide outside off stump, Slates cuts it over point, one bounce for four. Like Harmison's mega-wide, that moment kind of set the tone for the whole series and they ended up tonking us 3–1.

So I always try to keep in mind what it was like when I was out there, that it could be bloody hard work and that I made my share of dreadful errors.

Excellent players enduring a bad patch also have a habit of proving you very wrong. For instance, before India toured England in summer 2011, there was talk about dropping Stuart Broad. Broady had had injury problems, wasn't getting wickets, wasn't scoring runs, and calls for Tim Bresnan to take his place were growing. Then he came out at Lord's, scored a hundred and got a five-fer.

Alastair Cook was under pressure after some cheap dismissals against Pakistan back in 2010, and if he hadn't scored a century at The Oval he might not have gone to Australia for the Ashes series where he broke records left, right and centre.

The player himself will be aware that his place is under threat if he doesn't perform better, so it's okay to say so, and mention the other options selectors may be having a look at, but I personally try to avoid going as far as saying, 'I think he should be dropped,' because that isn't up to us.

In the time I was playing, every Test was like that. I never felt my place in the team was secure. I think some of the press who were following the team back then were almost enjoying the failure. I think it reached a tipping point when we started losing all the time, and it became easier just to slag us off.

When we were bowled out for 46 by the West Indies in 1994, the *Sun* sent us to the moon in a rocket with our little faces peering out of the portholes. Me, Devon Malcolm and Alan Mullally were photoshopped as bunny rabbits all sitting there – 'The worst tail there's ever been'. Looking back, it's hysterical, but at the time, I was thinking, 'Don't take the piss. We're trying our nuts off out here.'

When things were going badly for the team and I was shipping a lot of criticism for my own performances, I did think that the world was against me at times. But unlike tabloid newspapers, which tend to take an extreme position – it's either triumph or disaster – *TMS* gives a balanced view. That is essential to its remit.

EXTRAS

There's enough time in a Test match commentary to discuss issues from every angle, with lots of opinions thrown into the pot, and we're not looking to create headlines.

One of the golden rules of commentating on England for *TMS* is: 'Do not say "us" or "we".' As representatives of the BBC, we are supposed to be impartial, but the truth is that every English person in the *TMS* team wants England players to do well. No one wishes ill of anyone. And sometimes with me, impartiality goes out of the window.

When we regained the Ashes at The Oval in 2005, I couldn't stop myself singing, 'It's coming home, it's coming home, Ashes coming home,' and people around the ground listening to *TMS* on their headphones started standing up and singing it back, with me conducting them.

That's where Aggers, CMJ and Blowers come into their own, by staying very neutral, while I get away with it a little bit.

If I'm out in the middle before a day's play, I'll say hello to the players, especially the guys I know pretty well, such as Swanny and Jimmy Anderson, but I keep it brief: 'How're you doing, mate', 'Well bowled the other day – coming out well.' That's because I know they've got a job to do and need to concentrate, although the England players now seem far more relaxed and happy to talk than I was. When I was playing in a losing team, I felt under so much pressure I could hardly eat, let alone speak to anyone. Playing against Australia, with them 300-odd for one, when I was sitting at breakfast trying to get my scrambled egg down, my stomach churning at the prospect of another battering in the field, I'd look across and see the Waugh brothers sitting there seemingly without a care in the world. I guess the England boys today have that same calmness because of the great results they've achieved.

RADIO MAYHEM WITH MURRAY AND CHRIS

To add to my *TMS* work, I started doing an evening show on BBC Radio 5 Live in 2005, and I'll never forget the night we went down to Hove to cover Sussex's 2006 County Championship triumph. With Sussex certain to take the title, we decided to do a live broadcast from the Sussex Arms next door to their ground. All the players and fans were bound to be in there at the end of play, so we could give listeners a flavour of the celebrations. What we didn't allow for was the possibility that the game might end early.

Sure enough Sussex win their game at two in the afternoon. My show starts at 9pm. By the time we walk in the pub at half six, the place is absolutely rammed and Sussex's all-conquering heroes and supporters are already well oiled.

We dutifully start to set up, but soon realise it's a nonstarter. We fear the show's listeners may not appreciate the sound of people running up to the microphones and screaming 'Waaaarrrrrgggghhh' every two seconds.

Instead, we beat a tactical retreat to the OB van and decide to broadcast the show from there, dragging out players from the pub as and when we need them.

The show gets under way and my first guests are the victorious captain Chris Adams and batsman Murray Goodwin. Well, they are absolutely lashed.

As I try in vain to ask them questions, Chris is grabbing my bollocks while Murray Goodwin raucously belts out the club anthem at the top of his voice:

Me: 'So what was the key to your . . . ow! . . . success this season, Chris?'

Murray: '. . . GOOD OLD SUSSEX BY THE SEA, YOU CAN TELL THEM ALL THAT WE STAND OR FALL, FOR SUSSEX BY THE SEA!'

I persist and manage to get a bit of sense out of Chris and

Murray between gonad crunches, nipple pinches and songs.

At one point, Chris grabs me in a headlock.

'No, honestly, Chris . . . no, it's really funny, but, honestly, we're live on air.'

In the background, I can hear a growing hubbub outside. Clearly, the Sussex fans have discovered where we are. Then the van starts rocking back and forth. Cups and papers fly off the desk. What the . . . ?

The producer opens the back door: 'Can you stop doing that, please?'

'WHHHHHHHAAAAAAYYYYY!!'

We'll take that as a no, then . . .

The van continues to rock as if we're doing a pirate broadcast from the North Sea. Occasionally, another pickled Sussex player is escorted in through the cheering hordes and I try to ask some sensible questions.

Absolute mayhem – and it remains the most terrifying thirty minutes of my radio presenting career.

Funnily enough, I haven't heard of anyone trying anything similar to mark the end of the county cricket season since.

WE ARE ANDY'S ARMY

Keeping to the *TMS* impartiality rule on air can be tricky, especially when it comes to an Ashes series, so when I got a chance to record a song and video in support of Andrew Strauss and the boys before the 2009 series, I was well up for it. And that's how I ended up dressed up as a glam rocker, 'playing' an inflatable guitar, and trying to sing like Johnny Rotten alongside a Queen Elizabeth-lookalike at Kew Cricket Club. The video got 50-odd thousand hits on YouTube, but like Marmite, who sponsored the record, you might love it or hate it . . .

The Ashes Song
by Tuffers & The Wooden Urns
(To the tune of 'When We Were Two Little Boys'; new lyrics by
Keith Bunker and Richard Melvin)

We are Andy's Army
Here to make the Aussie's blue
Love 'em, or hate 'em, we're gonna beat 'em
Probably 3–2!

'Hey Ponting . . . Lend us your brain . . . We're building an
idiot!'

Two cricket teams, with one cricket dream
Fighting for a wooden urn
One is crude, rude and lewd
The other is En-ger-land. ENGLAND!

We are Andy's Army
There's no room in this ground for you
GET OUT OF HERE! You'll soon be crying
When we beat you 3–2. PROBABLY!
Put Marmite on your sarnie
That other stuff is wrong
We are Andy's Army
And this is our Ashes song

England are men, proud, strong but then
Aussies are just little boys
Out at the crease their fears will increase
Hearing the home crowd's noise

EXTRAS

Cos, we are Andy's Army
There's no room in this ground for you
GET OUT OF HERE! You'll soon be crying
When we beat you 3–2. PROBABLY!
Cos, we are Andy's Army
We're here to make a noise
GET BACK, to the pavilion
And send in your next little boy!

The Aussies have Priscilla, but we've had a real Queen
Andy's Army love their women, not something in between!

They've got Ricky, we've got KP
This is the land of plenty, not a desert in the sea!

They drink weak lager, and love a barbecue
We prefer a cup of tea, and a piece of toast or two

So put Marmite on your sarnie, that other stuff is wrong
We are Andy's Army, and this is our Ashes song.

REPEAT CHORUS

THE END

CHAPTER 20

TEAM ENGLAND

Having played in a few losing England sides myself, the success of our Test team under the captaincy of Michael Vaughan and now Andrew Strauss has been great to watch. From talking to the boys, seeing them in action through my work with *TMS*, and thinking back on my own England experience, I can see a few reasons for the change of fortunes:

1. England is now the central priority

I earned eighteen grand for my last tour of South Africa. The following year they introduced central contracts and suddenly it was a case of here's a quarter of a million quid, and you don't even have to play! Bad luck for me, but a huge turning point for English cricket, because international matches became the priority.

Without central contracts, someone like Gus Fraser could be bowling against Glamorgan in Wales the whole of the last day of a County Championship game to try and get a win for Middlesex.

He'd do 30 overs, drive back to London, have a kip, wake up and drive all the way up to Headingley and the following morning open the bowling for England.

That sort of schedule, week in, week out, leaves you absolutely shattered. Rather than having a build-up to playing for England, with time to prepare, it was almost like being on a treadmill going from one match to the next. Eventually that catches up with you. You start to think, 'Oh God, I've got to go and play for England'.

There was no crescendo and it shouldn't be like that.

Central contracts have made players feel that there is a prestige to playing for England, like they are part of an élite. Before, players turned out for both county and country, and it was a case of doing well for your county, and if you were good enough, you'd get into the Test team. Now, you are an England player, full stop. You don't look at Kevin Pietersen as a county player at all – he's an England player who only turns out for a county if he and the England coach Andy Flower think he'll benefit from some more time at the crease. That's a crucial man-management aspect of the job: making sure people are match-sharp, ready for Tests but not overworked.

Compare that to the England football team, which is amateurishly run in comparison. English football is club-oriented and the top players meet up for international games just a few days beforehand. The players earn far more money playing for their clubs, and the stakes are so high in the Premier League and European competitions that there is no likelihood of that changing. So we should be thankful in cricket that such radical changes have been made.

The only danger of central contracts is that things become too cosy and players relax too much because they don't feel their place is under any threat. 'Team England' must not become 'Club England' where the centrally contracted players keep their place whether they are delivering or not, when there are other talented players on the sidelines who could do better.

Things can go wrong very quickly if the players are not kept on their toes. Since India won the World Cup in 2011 and topped the world rankings, they have been destroyed in England and Australia, and yet their selectors have kept blindly faithful to established players. Their attitude is that the players themselves should decide when they retire from international cricket and they'll keep on picking them until they do. Crazy.

2. Selectors and players recognise each other

One of the problems used to be how alienated selectors and players were from each other. Before we went on one tour, the squad were invited to the House of Commons for lunch and a drink.

While we're there a chap comes up to Mark Ramprakash and starts making small talk with him.

'So which constituency do you represent?' says Ramps after a little while.

The guy looks at him, baffled: 'Er, I'm an England selector.'

It was Brian Bolus.

On the other side, there's that great story about 'Lord' Ted Dexter, when he was chairman of selectors, and Mike Atherton was parking his car at Lord's.

Athers opens the boot so the dressing-room attendant can get his cricket bag and heads inside. The attendant picks up the coffin, 'MA' embossed on the side.

Ted walks by and seeing the bag says, 'Good luck today, Athers.'

The attendant says, 'Thanks very much!'

It was a very élitist culture, and becoming a selector seemed to be more about securing a parking space at Lord's than working with the players. That's why for years you were better off playing for Middlesex, Surrey or Essex, because none of them wanted to travel up north to watch cricket. Playing for Middlesex was definitely an advantage for me, because they all liked coming to Lord's.

The lack of relationship between selectors and players is summed up by the fact that we often found out whether or not we'd been picked by looking it up on Ceefax (remember that?). Wake up in the morning, put on Ceefax page 340 . . . I'm in! . . . Oh shit, I'm a bit late, I've got to get up to Old Trafford!

Other times I'd turn up at Lord's for a Middlesex game, and all the press would be waiting there, saying, 'Congratulations, Phil.'

'Er, what for?'

3. No more yo-yo selection

In my time as a player, it was more 'Cut-throat England' than Club England. I didn't feel any security in my England career because the selection process was so erratic. Consequently, you felt under so much pressure when you played that something had to give.

The criticism thrown at me was that I didn't respect playing for England. If I did seem flippant about it, it was only because I didn't feel respected myself and I had no idea what the selectors were judging me on. For instance, in February 1997 I played in a One-Day International against New Zealand in Christchurch. I got my best-ever ODI bowling figures of 4/22, dismissed four of the Kiwis' top five batsmen and we won by four wickets. That was the last ODI I ever played!

If you keep getting kicked in the bollocks no matter what you do, you might as well at least try and have a good time while you are in the squad, because you might not be there for long. I think a lot of the boys took the same attitude.

Yo-yo selection was very damaging to the careers of a number of players in my time, most notably Graeme Hick and Mark Ramprakash, two of the most talented batsmen of their generation. My *TMS* colleague Malcolm Ashton dug out an interesting statistic for me on the ins and outs of their England careers and mine. While Hicky played 65 Tests (1991–2001), he missed 41; Ramps had 52 appearances (1991–2002) but missed 68. Meanwhile, I played 42 Tests (1990–2001) but missed 76. As a spinner, I was liable to be dropped more often than other bowlers because pitch conditions may favour seamers, but that's a lot of games to miss during a decade in which I was generally regarded as England's best left-arm spinner.

It's easiest for me to talk about Ramps because I know him particularly well from playing with him for Middlesex and England. Odd couple we were – extrovert/introvert, drinker/non-drinker, smoker/non-smoker – but we always got on. I think we were both seen as potential trouble in different ways. With Ramps, he could blow a fuse, hence his 'Bloodaxe' nickname, but that was because he's passionate about his cricket and desperately wanted to do well.

I can remember me and Ramps having a lot of chats during our Test career about this feeling of not being wanted, of the selectors looking down their noses at us. All right, I know we both played 40, 50 Tests, but we were never supported like they are today.

Ramps started his Test career in a home series against the West Indies in 1991, and he made a start in each innings without scoring over 30, and averaged 23. On paper, that doesn't look good, but you have to put it in context. He was facing Curtly Ambrose, Courtney Walsh, Patrick Patterson and Malcolm Marshall. He'd applied himself well, and having gone through the hell of facing that lot, he might have expected to be on the next tour to New Zealand where he could build up his average and his confidence against a weaker bowling attack. So what happens? He gets left out, only to be recalled the following summer to face Pakistan's Waqar Younis and Wasim Akram with no runs in the bank, the guillotine hanging over his head, and he 'fails' again.

Batting was hard work then. Today, the nearest an England batsman will get to facing that quality of searingly fast bowlers is South Africa's Morkel–Steyn combo, but the battery of proper legendary quicks you saw in my generation (and just before my time) doesn't exist today.

You can't tell me that Mark Ramprakash didn't have the skill to be much more successful than he was at Test level, so you have to question the reasons why he didn't fulfil his potential. People say he was brittle mentally, but I wonder what would have happened if he'd been given the same support as current England players?

Yes, Ramps played a decent number of Tests in the end, but he was dropped so many times, it must have dented his confidence. It did with me. Every time you come back to the side, you feel like it's your first Test match and you have to prove yourself again.

With England, when things were going badly, you knew you would be dropped straight away. I can remember Ramps and Hicky coming off after making a low score and saying, 'Boys, I'll see you later. That's me gone.' Ridiculous pressure. It was shocking, really. And they wondered why we weren't successful.

Even the more established players weren't immune to the flight-of-fancy selection methods. Robin Smith got dropped when he was averaging well over 40. What annoyed him was the reason given was that he couldn't play Shane Warne, to which Judge rightly replied, 'Well not many people ****ing can!'

Thankfully, the selectors now take a longer-term view. Look at Ian Bell, who I compare very much with Ramps – both technically strong, heavy run scorers, but both needed time to build the mentality of a Test batsman. I remember Bell being criticised for not looking imposing enough. What was he going to do? Grow six inches? Is Lionel Messi not big enough to be a brilliant footballer?

Under old regimes, Bell would have yo-yoed in and out of the squad like Ramps did, but he's been consistently backed and England have reaped the benefits.

4. Players who are selected are made to feel wanted

Looking at the current England squad, I get the impression that they all feel valued and wanted. Bizarrely, that was not my experience at all. Being selected for the squad was often just the start of the battle. The most striking example of that was in India in 1993.

John Emburey and I are the two spinners selected for the touring squad, but leg-spinner Ian Salisbury is brought over as net bowler to help our batsmen to prepare for India's leggie Anil Kumble. Me and Embers are not great net bowlers – we just like to warm up, get loose, get a rhythm and then go – so having Sals there is a great help. And he bowls really well in the nets. So well, in fact that they pick him for the First Test, and Embers and I miss out!

To go to India, where spin is king, and be dropped for the First Test for the net bowler who wasn't even in the tour squad is a stunning blow. It's not like I've had a bad Test, I haven't played!

As well as dropping me, they pick left-arm seamer Paul Taylor who has a bit of a problem with running on the pitch on his follow-through. Good news for India, because while England have dropped their two alleged top spinners, India have picked three, of which two are right-armers – Kumble and an offie, Rajesh Chauhan.

We lose the toss, bowl first, and the game's done the first over PT bowls. Sure enough, he follows through down the pitch – bang, bang, bang. As he's walking back to his mark, the Indian batsmen are smiling and giving the thumbs-up to the dressing room. By the end of the innings, PT has created a crater of rough, just outside off stump on a pitch that was turning anyway.

Genius selection – how to gift the opposition the advantage before you start.

Surprise, surprise, we're bowled out, have to follow on and eventually lose by eight wickets. Their three spinners take 17 wickets in the match. On our side, our ace batsman/part-time spinner Graeme Hick manages five wickets in total and Sals takes one, so I'd like to think Embers and I might have done all right on that pitch. Instead, I don't know about Embers, but my confidence is shattered from day one.

This became a bit of a pattern in my England career. I never felt like the powers-that-be actually wanted me there. It seemed more a case of, 'We've got to pick Tufnell because he keeps getting everyone out in the County Championship.' At the time, I tried to put such thoughts to the back of my mind – no, it can't be that. Don't be paranoid, Philip.

I didn't help myself with my behaviour at times, but the feeling that if anyone might be able to do better, they'd drop me like a stone never faded away.

5. Smarter thinking

The England team not only play as a unit now, they look like one. We used to wear all sorts of gear on the pitch. Some of us would be wearing baseball caps, some old-fashioned caps, blue floppies from the one-day game, white floppies. In the warm-up, it was even worse. We'd be wearing our own tops and shorts, some would be wearing Billabong beach shorts.

This came to a head when we got thrashed on that tour of India in 1993. A picture was taken of us afterwards, which was splashed all over the papers the next day. We were slumped in chairs, all wearing different gear, unshaven, some shoeless, some changed, some not. We looked an absolute shower, so it had to be addressed.

I'm glad to see that people are allowed to express their individuality in other ways, though. For instance, Jade Dernbach being covered in tattoos hasn't stopped him getting called up, whereas I had to cut off my ponytail to get in!

I think that incident stayed with me through my whole career. It made me uneasy because I didn't really understand what the selectors were looking for. Am I being overlooked because I didn't bowl well enough or is it because my face doesn't fit?

In the end, rather than worry about something I couldn't control, I just thought, '**** you lot, if you pick me it's because I force you to by getting more wickets than anyone else, and I'll live my own way.'

6. Not knackering players in the warm-up

England cricketers today are athletes and their training between matches is so much more intensive and scientific than it was ten, twenty years ago. In the early part of my England career, any success we achieved was through ability and fighting spirit rather than preparation, despite the best efforts of pioneers like Graham Gooch to bring in better diet, nutrition and fitness. He had all the right intentions, but got it wrong when it came to matchdays.

Watching the England boys now, they seem to do short, sharp, skills-specific stuff to loosen up. All I felt I needed was to do some sharp catching practice, a little twenty-minute bowl in the nets and then go and have a cup of tea. But we'd be doing an hour and a quarter of running about before a day's play. In a hot climate on tour where I used to get itchy heat rashes, I'd be feeling horrible before we started. While the toss was being done, we'd sit down and stiffen up, and if we were fielding, I'd be thinking, 'Oh God, I'm knackered already!' It was like doing a fourth session each day.

Over the seasons, those warm-ups became so boring and I used to dread them. Now they break up the monotony with games of football and other little games and try to preserve energy for the match itself.

7. Making the most of what we have (and ending the search for the new Beefy)

When I was a kid in the English set-up, the emphasis seemed always to be on trying to turn players into something they were not rather than on their positive attributes. That was the culture. And they destroyed people. We had a generation of cricketers who had all the flair knocked out of them. Take Devon Malcolm. He was picked to run in and bowl as fast as he could. Then at a training camp a couple of weeks before the 1994 West Indies tour they dismantled his action and told him to bowl top of off stump! Well that wasn't him.

The shadow of the mighty Ian Botham also hung heavy over English cricket for many years. Derek Pringle? Chris Lewis? Craig White? Oh, none of them are Botham. Let's look for someone else. Well, hold on, they were still pretty good!

Putting aside what's happened to him since his career ended, Chris Lewis's story as a cricketer is particularly sad. Chris was an enigma and he seemed to rub some people up the wrong way, but I always got on well with him. Despite his enormous all-round talent, he seemed to lack confidence as a cricketer and the England set-up as it was back then was not a place for someone unsure of himself. Everyone thought he was physically capable of bowling a bit quicker, and everyone thought he was capable of scoring more runs. And it's true he could be an explosive batter and very fast bowler at times, which made people think he should do that all the time. When he didn't, they accused him of being lazy.

He appeared to have everything and became a victim of, one, people's expectations of his ability and, two, the search for 'the new Botham', which was an obsession back then. Chris was one of a generation of players who were slated for what they were not, rather than being nurtured to get the best out of them. Unlike Beefy, Chris probably needed people to help him gain confidence, but that kind of support was absent at the time. If he had been encouraged to bowl fast-medium with the odd express delivery thrown in, to become a more consistent lower-order batter and continue being a brilliant fielder, he could have been as effective as Stuart Broad is today for England.

It was the same for the spinners. When Warne started the 'mystery bowler' trend, I was buggered. No matter what I did – even on the rare occasions I outbowled him – I couldn't win. 'He's no Warney.'

I used to get nervous because we had no support staff telling me to play to my strengths.

Every time I bowled I had to get wickets. It used to wind me up when I'd done a great job on a flat wicket, taken two for 80 off 35 overs, kept it tight, allowing the seamers to rest, only to read in the next day's papers: 'Tufnell was ineffectual.' I'd bowled beautifully, kept the ball on a string, just to hang on by my fingernails to international batsmen, and it was still not good enough in comparison with Warne.

When the Aussies started to dominate, the England selectors were trying to find players who could play the Aussie way. It took a very long time for it to click that we have players with their own style and it would be to build a team to our own strengths.

Nowadays, players are freer to develop their own game. Take Broad. I think he is a fantastic cricketer. He hasn't been saddled with Botham comparisons and is showing what a great player he is in his own right. Then you have someone like Alastair Cook, who plays a very limited range of shots, but does what he does brilliantly and is allowed to get on with it.

No more square pegs in round holes, but a team built on excellent individuals encouraged to play to their strengths.

8. More care for the players

International cricket is not a very forgiving arena and nor should it be. It's a results business, so you have to go out there and perform. To a certain degree, pressure comes with the job and if you don't fancy that way of life, do something else. But when you grow up wanting to be a cricketer, there are certain factors you don't think about.

For instance, are you the sort of person who doesn't mind being away from home for four or five months of the year? When I first started touring, it was like a five-star 18–30 holiday, with some famous cricketers going all the way around the world, playing a little bit of cricket and enjoying themselves. And I certainly did. It was like a roadshow. You turned up in town, you bowled and did your stuff, then you partied at night. All good fun, until you get married and start a family at which time it becomes very hard to keep all the different strands of your life connected.

In the course of my career, I went through three major relationship break-ups – awful times, but I still had to get on and play for fear of losing my place in the team. Now they concentrate more on that side of things, reducing the length of tours, letting the wives and girlfriends come away too, and encouraging the players to see their families.

In my case, I had more than my share of off-pitch dramas, but there was precious little compassion in the England set-up. The Ashes tour of 1994/95 is a prime example.

I take up my place in the squad despite having recently gone through a very public break-up, a court case, and been cut off from access to my daughter. Then when I get out there, I discover my new partner back home is receiving threatening phone calls. Everything gets on top of me and I end up being taken to a psychiatric unit for overnight observation. I discharge myself after little more than an hour, mind. By the time I get back to the team hotel, the management are already nominating a replacement spinner, Min Patel. That's fair enough, because when they last saw me I looked in no fit state to take any further part in the tour. It's harder to understand when I later get fined £1,000 – 'We can't have conduct like that on a cricket tour,' I'm told.

I was actually punished for having a terrible time! But attitudes to mental and emotional issues were different then. It used to be: 'What's wrong with you, roll your sleeves up and get on with it.' In later years, they did bring sports psychologist Steve Bull into the England set-up, and I have to admit I was resistant to that. I guess those old-school attitudes were ingrained in me, too.

I don't know whether I ever had clinical depression, but I definitely had insecurities, where sometimes I needed support. But there really wasn't any, apart from the senior pro offering a word of advice. Instead, my solution was to go out and get pissed without dealing with the root of my problems, which then just built up. However, there is much more support within the England set-up now to help players cope with problems, on and off the field. And top players such as Marcus Trescothick and Steve Harmison talking about the problems they've had will only help to reduce those issues in future.

THAT'S WHAT I LIKE TO SEE

One of the pleasures of remaining involved in cricket as a pundit in the years since I played is to see up close how the game continues to evolve. Test match cricket has become more entertaining in the last decade or so because of the willingness of batsmen to take greater risks. Especially the openers. In my day, the normal mentality was for them to dig in, keep the ball on the ground and see off the new ball steadily. Now they often look to smash the shine off it, hit the ball over the infield and knock the bowlers out of their stride.

Clayton Lambert and Philo Wallace were two of the pioneers of this approach. Not the greatest opening partnership of all time, but mental to watch because they just attacked from ball one. A good example is West Indies' first innings at the Kensington Oval back in March 1998.

Andrew Caddick is bowling the first over and I'm stationed at deep mid-off. First ball, Clayton lamps it hard as he can, doesn't quite middle it, and it steeples up into the air landing about a foot in front of me!

It was kamikaze stuff, but also very unnerving for the fielding side. With a conventional opener such as Mike Atherton, he'd play each ball on its merits, you'd have the odd maiden and he'd accumulate runs gradually. The Clayton/Filo combo paved the way for a different approach, which Australia took to another level. The Aussies had such a strong top-seven batting line-up – from

Matthew Hayden to Adam Gilchrist – they realised that they could all go out and play their natural attacking game without getting bogged down. Even if the opposition did manage to nick off three or four wickets, their sheer aggression would still knock the stuffing out of the bowlers so that some of the batters would score heavily. Hayden did it to me in my last Test match at The Oval in 2001.

Just come back into the side, feeling quite confident before my first ball. Got my field set. Lovely. Do my usual little hop at the start of my run-up, and before I can even skip, I can see Matty holding his bat up like a baseball player, walking down the pitch.

Grrrr. He swings at it, top-edges it for two runs.

Second ball. Same again. Walks down the pitch, smashes me.

****ing hell. I've got no rhythm.

Nasser Hussain, bless him, as captains tend to do in this situation, runs up to me and says: 'Don't worry, Tuffers. That's what we like to see.'

'Yeah, but you won't like to see that if he keeps ****ing hitting them!'

Of course, what Nass said was right, because by gambling, he was giving me a chance, and it can work against the batting side if they overegg the positivity. For instance, in 1991 the Windies boys tried to hit me out of the attack at The Oval and I ended getting six-fer. And I think you do see more spectacular collapses at Test level now because batters are prepared to take more risks, hitting across the line, attacking good-length balls and taking the aerial route.

However, international coaches have realised that the odds favour the brave and have taken the view that it is better to go out and try to dominate and dictate the play. On flat pitches, if the best batsmen in the world start trying to tonk you indiscriminately, and succeed, the bowlers can get a bit wobbly. That's why international Test openers are encouraged to take more risks now, an approach that Oz's great new prospect David Warner took to the extreme against India in January 2011 when he scored a century off 69 balls.

A BIT OF CRICKET, NOW AND THEN

MAYBE I'M A DINOSAUR?

Some of the credit for the faster scoring at Test level has to go to the rise and rise of the Twenty20 format of the game. Teams have found ways to score 200-plus in 20 overs and the innovations in shotmaking have filtered up.

Twenty20 cricket is great, but I do think we have to be very mindful of its effect on the game as a whole for the future. At the moment, the balance is just about right. Test cricket is the main event, Twenty20 brings some light relief – coloured clothing, music, dancing girls and general razzmatazz – and then you've got 50-over cricket in the middle of that.

If there's much more Twenty20, I can see people getting bored with it, though. It's already being shown that if you don't make Twenty20 into a real event, you don't get the people coming through the gate. Twenty20 competitions should be something people look forward to as a treat every now and then. It's like fast food – sometimes you just really fancy a Big Mac and fries and eaten occasionally that won't do you any harm, but if all you're offered is fast food, you'll get lethargic and bored. There needs to be variety for the overall health of the game and it's very important to me that Test cricket remains top dog because it is still the ultimate format. The clue's in the name – it is the ultimate test of every aspect of a cricketer's game.

Twenty20 has been a great way to get more bums on seats and bring a new audience to cricket. I just hope that new interest filters into Test cricket, so people understand that this is what the game's really about.

I love Test cricket. I *love* it. I don't know if I'm becoming a traditionalist in my old age, but I love the to and fro of Test matches, the character that it brings out in players, and I don't think any other form of the game offers that.

People say that attention spans are shorter these days and Test matches are too long, but I don't buy that. Even if people don't have time to sit and watch all five days, they can enjoy following the game's progress in other ways. Often when I'm working on television shows and an England game's on, I'll see people on the production team checking up on the score on their iPads or phones throughout the day. Test matches suck you in.

Twenty20 undoubtedly is drawing young players into the game and that's a great thing, but I want cricketers to grow up wanting to play Test cricket for their country, rather than honing their skills to become a biffer in Twenty20 cricket. What I'd hate to happen is for players with the potential to become Test players, settling for becoming a Twenty20 specialist.

When you see top players, such as Chris Gayle and Lasith Malinga, giving up Tests to focus on Twenty20 when they are still capable of playing Test cricket, that is a real loss.

I do understand, when you are getting towards the end of your career and you've only got so many games in your body, why it makes sense to play the games you get a million quid for, rather than do a four-month tour. And Gayle can rightly say he's done his bit, playing 91 Tests, 228 ODIs, in difficult times for West Indies. Even Malinga, who played his last Test for Sri Lanka before his 27th birthday, appeared in 30 Tests and 106 ODIs.

However, the key thing that drove me as a cricketer was to play for my country. I can't see how playing for Sydney Thunder or Mumbai Indians could compare to that. If the financial rewards of playing Twenty20 come off the back of Test cricket, that's a bonus, but I couldn't imagine that replacing the pride and excitement of playing for my country.

It depends how much a player loves cricket, which is no different from other professions in that some people see it purely as a job. I think the vast majority of players come into the game with a passion for it, but over the years that love of the game can get ground down. When the game becomes a chore, the Twenty20 option is very attractive because it's more money for less work.

I wonder whether they will regret missing out on the feelings you can get only by playing for your country at the highest level? Maybe I'm a dinosaur, but when I look back at my career, my greatest memories are of Test cricket. Maybe the odd 50-over game sticks in the mind, but the games that remain in my heart and keep my passion for the game alive are Test matches. You don't remember a game of biff, boff, bash.

Who won the IPL last year? No idea, but I can recall almost every wicket that fell in an England Test match.

Carving out a century in four hours against a brilliant bowling attack with the whole country behind you, pushing yourself to the limit, has to have more lasting meaning for a batsman than going out and bashing 44 off 16 balls in Twenty20. Taking three wickets and keeping the batsmen down to seven an over in a Twenty20 game can't possibly be as satisfying as eking out a five-fer on a flat one against the Aussies. Twenty20 is a fun, one-night stand, but Test cricket offers a more fulfilling long-term romance.

You have to be careful because if all the top players migrate to Twenty20, as has started to happen in the West Indies, it could affect the standard of Test cricket. Okay, these guys can earn a six- or even seven-figure salary for a few weeks' work every now and then, and swish about living the life, driving Ferraris, but meanwhile your country gets beaten left, right and centre at Test level because their best players aren't available for selection. I see that as a worry for the game as whole.

Look what happened when Kerry Packer came in and took all of the good boys for his World Series, and left the Test arena with a load of second-rate players. Test cricket is still the core of the game and should be contested between the best players in the world at any given time. It has been fantastic to watch in recent years, so we don't want that progress to be jeopardised.

THE MONEY GAME

Cricketers were not getting paid very well and that had to change. If you were a decent county player who played a handful of times for England without things going your way, you could end up after a fifteen- or twenty-year career with very little money in the bank.

You'd hopefully get a couple of hundred grand tax-free in your benefit year and leave the game in your mid- to late-thirties, possibly having no other career lined up. You may have worked the winters doing odd jobs, worked on your game, then you're out on your ear aged 38 still with half your life to live and no qualifications and little prospect of a new career apart from within cricket where there are limited jobs. When I finished, I still had a mortgage and a lot of other regular bills to pay.

A good county player can earn well now. You can nick yourself a hundred grand a year without having to find alternative winter employment, so if you can do that for ten years, with a benefit year, you can realistically hope to pay off your mortgage and be well set for the future. The Professional Cricketers' Association now also offer courses to assist the transition into other work.

As for the top players, there is big money to be earned in the Test arena (let alone the riches on offer in Twenty20). I was the best spinner in England for a while and I was getting two bob. I got the kudos, which was great, and I could network off the back of that, but the financial rewards weren't there for actually playing. When I won the Championship with Middlesex in 1993, I got a three-grand bonus.

In American sport, with the college draft picks, a young bloke can be given $20 million on the basis that he has the potential to be a great professional player. When I played for England, I was still playing for my living. It was another pressure. If they'd seen me get seven-fer as a Second XI player and given me £1 million for my first contract, it might have been different.

A BIT OF CRICKET, NOW AND THEN

A lot of people may have been happy to sit on the bench and take the money. But I can't play sport like that. One thing I did have was gritty competitiveness. In my case, I think having some financial security would have eased the pressure without reducing my hunger one bit.

The money coming into the game is now trickling down to the players at a fairer level as they are the ones who put bums on seats. A top England international can expect to earn upwards of half a million a year including endorsements. No need to network. Five years of that and you are a very wealthy boy.

If you play for England in the Ashes and beat Australia, a series that generates millions of pounds, it is only correct you are rewarded. Now the players are getting life-changing amounts as bonuses, which will pay a good lump off their mortgages and rightly so.

I'M NOT BITTER, BUT . . .

. . . sitting at home watching Monty Panesar bowling against Pakistan in their second innings in Abu Dhabi one morning in January 2012, I was jumping off the sofa in disbelief.

He bowls the left-armer's stock delivery – round the wicket, decent length, pitching on and straightening a bit – the batsman takes a massive stride forward, ball hits pad and bat apparently (to the naked eye) simultaneously. Appeal. Go to the Decision Review System (DRS). Hawkeye shows the ball will go on to hit the stumps, but the evidence from Hotspot is not wholly conclusive as to whether it was bat or pad first. Decision given: out.

Now, I don't mean to sound bitter – and I'm pleased for Monty and the modern-day spinners – but ten years ago you would not have had a hope in hell of the batsman being given out for that. The umpire would dismiss the possibility of lbw out of hand because of the batsman's big stride and the doubt about whether the ball has hit bat or pad first.

And batsmen would deliberately play pad first to four balls out of the six like that, safe in the knowledge that they would not be given out. If I even appealed, the umpire would look at me as if I'm mad. And if I continued to appeal, they'd say, 'Can you please stop hassling me?'

'Well, I dunno, I think that looked pretty close to me . . .'

'Tuffers, please. That's just not out.' And they'd walk off shaking their heads at my insubordinate behaviour.

For years and years, umpires got it wrong, because they said that when the batsman made a big stride forward, the ball would need to turn appreciably to hit the stumps. The consensus was that if a left-arm spinner pitched it on the stumps and the ball only straightened slightly, it would still be going down legside because of the angle it had been delivered from. It is only with the introduction of Hawkeye that it's been appreciated that the ball only needs to 'hold its own', as they say, to hit the stumps.

And whenever the ball squeezed between the bat and pad, the umpire would routinely give the batsman the benefit of the doubt that it was bat first. Hotspot has changed all that, but what amazes me is that even when the evidence that Hotspot provides is not wholly conclusive, the bowler rather than the batsman often gets the benefit of the doubt.

There's a lot of talk nowadays about the need for an off-spinner to have a doosra, and the doosra is a great innovation because it gives you more chance of getting edges, but DRS means that you don't really need to be able to bowl one. All you need to do is spin one and then bowl one that doesn't turn. The batsmen are now having to play with their bats much more. So if you bowl one where they play for a bit of turn, and instead it skids on – not through your trickery, it's just the way it comes out of your hand or the pitch it lands on – that can be as effective as a doosra.

Nasser Hussain was commentating on the Pakistan–England game, and he made the point that there is nothing in the laws of cricket that says the benefit of the doubt should go to the batsman. Well, for thirty years I was led to believe the exact opposite – the benefit of the doubt always went to the batsmen. Of my 121 Test wickets, just nine (7.4 per cent) were lbw decisions. Compare that to Monty's record in the Pakistan–England series in the UAE – in two Tests eight of his 14 wickets (54 per cent) were lbw. Perhaps people will understand why I got so stressed out with umpires now!

ELEVEN THOUSAND TWO HUNDRED AND EIGHTY-EIGHT BALLS BOWLED IN TEST CRICKET. NINE LBWS. HMM . . .

Opponents	M	balls	wkts	bowled	caught	ct wkt	ct field	c&b	hit wkt	LBW	stumped
1 Australia	12	3230	36	7	26	4	20	2	0	1	2
2 India	2	483	4	0	3	0	3	0	0	1	0
3 New Zealand	10	2703	37	5	26	3	22	1	0	3	3
4 Pakistan	1	204	1	0 .	1	0	0	1	0	0	0
5 South Africa	4	1360	10	2	6	1	4	1	0	0	2
6 Sri Lanka	2	493	8	2	4	1	3	0	0	1	1
7 West Indies	9	2318	18	1	14	2	12	0	0	2	1
8 Zimbabwe	2	497	7	0	6	1	5	0	0	1	0

There has been a fundamental change in the game, and I think it is a positive one because, aside from debatable Hotspot decisions like the one mentioned above, batsmen who should be given out are being given out. Also, cricket pitches are generally flatter and more batsman-friendly these days, and they've got the big bats with enlarged sweet spots and thicker edges, so DRS helps to level the playing field.

As a spin bowler a decade or two ago, you had to be much craftier because batsmen could pad you away all day, or play the sweep shot, with little fear of being given lbw. If you were bowling really tightly, the sweep shot was their 'get out of jail' card to score some runs. If they planted their front foot down the pitch, swung across the line and missed it, so what? Now they haven't got that option because they know that if they miss the ball and it hits their front pad, it doesn't matter how far they've stretched forward – if Hawkeye shows the ball would go on to hit the stumps, they're gone. A gifted player such as Kevin Pietersen, who takes risks on hitting across the line of the ball and relies on fantastic timing, is now that much more vulnerable to lbw decisions when he makes a misjudgement.

DRS also adds another tactical element for players and drama for spectators. First the batsmen or fielding side have to make a decision whether or not to go for the DRS, and then everyone watches the virtual reality replays on the big screen to see whether it's out or not, which always creates a buzz.

In the Third Test of that Pakistan–England series, Jonathan Trott asked his batting partner and captain Andrew Strauss whether he should go for the DRS and Strauss told him, you're dead, don't bother. So he didn't, but Hawkeye subsequently showed he wasn't out. Then, in the second innings, Strauss was out plumb lbw, and Alastair Cook was criticised for not telling his captain that it wasn't worth going to DRS. He went for it, it showed the ball was hitting and they'd wasted a review.

But this raises another question in the DRS debate: if you're always looking to get the correct decision, why limit the number of times a team can ask for a decision to be reviewed? Currently, the system allowing each team two unsuccessful reviews per innings favours the top-order batsmen. They can effectively have two knocks if they get a DRS decision in their favour, but what about those lower down the order who don't get the benefit when the team's run out of reviews? On the other hand, if you allow unlimited reviews for batters and bowlers, you might end up with much lower scores and Test matches ending in a couple of days.

One quirk of the DRS referral system is the fact that the same delivery can still lead to two different results – if the umpire thought it was out lbw, and it's shown on Hawkeye that the ball would have gone on to clip the stumps, it's out, but if he hasn't given it, it's not out. I don't mind that because it gives the umpires a little bit of credit, a reason to be there. Otherwise, you may as well stick a hatstand in their place for the bowler to put his cap and jumper on before bowling the ball and then appealing to the umpire in the sky. And there have been doubts raised about the accuracy of Hawkeye, so I think we have got to be careful not to take all the decisions out of the hands of the umpire.

DRS has brought spin bowling back as a more potent weapon, so as a member of the spinners' union, I've got to be pleased about that, but I'm reminded of the *Terminator* films – the machines are taking over the world – and part of the charm of sport is the human aspect. I don't want us to move too far away from that.

So it is a tricky balance between striving for correct decisions, trying to make it fairer for bowlers on batting-friendly pitches and not undermining the umpires completely. What is for sure is that innovations like DRS make a mockery of any attempts to compare cricketers of different generations through statistics. Cricket is a stats game and many people enjoy that side of it, but the onus now is going to be on the evidence of what you see. You can't compare across eras based purely on wickets, runs and averages, because there are too many variables at play. You have to look within the DRS era alone.

It used to be a good effort to get a Test side out for 300 on a decent pitch. But, for instance, in the Third Test of Pakistan–England in Dubai, you were looking at first innings totals of 99 against 141. In my day, you'd see scores like that on a nightmare pitch, but that was a good cricket wicket.

When the Australians came to dominate world cricket, scoring rates went up to four, five an over, but perhaps that will change again with DRS. It certainly did in the Pakistan–England series as batsmen were forced to grind out runs.

Over the years, I think bowlers have been the ones forced to find more tricks up their sleeves to adapt to new conditions and improved equipment, but with DRS the onus is on the batters.

It's a totally different game with DRS, but I'm sure players will adapt their techniques to cope as they have done in the past. Batsmen will have to play with the bat more. As Michael Vaughan said following England's 3–0 series defeat by Pakistan, the answer was not necessarily to drop all the underperforming batsmen, but for them to work on their techniques.

I just wish I'd had DRS when I was playing because I would have saved myself (and the umpires who had to listen to my rants) a whole lot of stress and bagged another 100 Test wickets!

MY FANTASY DINNER PARTY

Tommy Cooper

Tommy would be perfect to provide the entertainment if we had to wait between courses. He wouldn't have to say anything – just the look on his face used to make me laugh.

Dalai Lama

I actually bumped into the Dalai Lama in Port Elizabeth on my last tour with England. Vaughanie and I had got the early bus back from training and we were dropped off round the back of our hotel. As we're about to walk in through the tradesman's entrance, these two huge guys in black suits come out followed by an unmistakable figure in orange and red robes, wearing his little glasses.

'Oi, you're the Dalai Lama!' I comment subtly.

'Yes, I am.'

'Very nice to meet you. I'm Phil Tufnell,' I say, shaking his hand. 'This is my mate, Michael Vaughan.'

'Hello Lama!' says Michael.

He smiles beatifically and asks, 'What are you doing here?'

'We're here playing cricket for England versus South Africa.'

'Well, good luck, good luck.'

'Come and watch if you fancy it. We'll leave you some tickets.'

'Yes, okay. Thank you.'

And off he toddled.

When we were fielding during the Second Test at PE, as we crossed between overs, Vaughanie and I would say, 'It's the Lama! The Lama's with us! We've been touched by the Lama! We're going to win!'

We didn't, but we got a draw, which was an improvement on the First Test, which we lost by an innings.

To this day, Vaughanie and I will often greet each other by asking: 'Where's the Lama?'

Oliver Reed

I loved a story I was told about him owning a great big house, which he was getting renovated. Every lunchtime, he used to take the builders down the pub, they'd all get absolutely smashed and he'd tell them not to worry about the house. The bathroom, which should have taken two weeks, took three years. Something tells me we'd get on famously.

Red Rum

He's the only horse I've ever bet on that won, so I owe him a feed. It will be like that police horse in a Barbados rum shack all over again.

Dawnie

I've got to have my Dawnie there. Wouldn't be the same without her. Mind you, it's a miracle we ever met. It happened at a six-a-side benefit game for Darren Gough down in Finchley on Friday, 13 July 2001.

I'm fielding down at fine-leg, sipping on a pint of beer (it's a very relaxed match), when a guy walks past talking to someone on the phone. He cuts off his conversation to say hello.

'Hello, mate,' I reply.

He continues his conversation: 'Phil Tufnell . . . yeah, he's right here . . . yeah, all right . . . [to me] Excuse me, Phil, can you say hello to my mate? He's a fan of yours.'

'Sure.'

He hands me his mobile and I have a little chat with his friend.

'Where are you standing?' says the voice at the other end of the line.

'I'm down on the boundary.'

'Can you see the Gotaas-Larsen hospitality tent? A girl I work with is in there. She's lovely. You should go and say hello.'

'Got arse what?'

'Gotaas-Larsen.   G-o-t-a-a-s-l-a-r-s-e-n . . . It's a shipping company.'

'Gotaas-Larsen, Gotaas-Larsen . . . oh, yeah, there it is.'

I put my beer down, wander off the pitch and head to the tent as directed with the bloke whose phone I've borrowed following behind.

'What's her name?' I ask my phone-a-new-friend.

'Dawn. She's blonde. Five foot eight, five foot nine.'

'Dawn? Is there a Dawn here?'

I see a beautiful blonde girl putting her hand over her face, looking very embarrassed.

'I think I've found Dawn, thanks,' I say into the receiver, and hand the phone back to its owner.

'Hello, Dawn!'

'Oh my God, who are you?'

Meanwhile, out on the pitch, a ball has been clipped down to fine leg: 'Get it in, Tuffers . . . er, Tuffers? Where the hell is Tufnell?'

I don't hear about that till later though, because I've only got eyes for Dawn. It turns out she's not into cricket, has no idea who I am, and only bothered to come along to the event at the last minute after persuasion from her work colleagues.

I pursue her for the next couple of weeks, and finally she agrees to a date.

We meet at a pub after a Middlesex game, so I'm wearing my club blazer and tie. When Dawn arrives, there's a couple of people asking for my autograph. She tells me later it was lucky they were. I'd been wearing a cap and wraparound sunglasses at the match and she couldn't remember what I looked like!

Four years later we got married. Just goes to prove my point that cricket has given me so much.

TUFFERSAURUS

A brief at-a-glance guide to commonly used words and phrases in the Tufnell lexicon . . .

Audi
a term used to describe a batsman scoring four noughts in a row (see also 'Olympic').
'*Tuffers is on an Audi here . . .*'

Bunsen
a wicket that will take a bit of spin (i.e. Bunsen burner – turner).
'*It's a raging Bunsen, Tuffers. You can fill your boots.*'

cherry
the new ball.
'*We aren't offered a new ball when we're fielding in a Sport Relief game against Mohammad Azharuddin's team, but Azhar's team miraculously find a brand new cherry when it's their turn to bowl.*'

coffin
cricket bag.
'"*Hello Athers,*" *says chairman of the selectors Ted Dexter to the bemused dressing-room attendant carrying Mike Atherton's coffin.*'

don't change the fly (courtesy of Allan Lamb)
refers to a left-arm spinner bowling perfect line and length tempting a batsman into a mistake, like an angler dangling the bait in front of the nose of a fish.
'"*Don't change the fly, Tuffers. They're rising!*" *said Lamby.*'

featherbed
a flat pitch that does nothing for bowlers – also known as a 'pudding'.
'"*How the **** am I supposed to get a wicket on this featherbed,*" *grumbled Tufnell.*'

feng shui
to clean bowl a batsman or be clean bowled (i.e. rearrange the furniture/have your furniture rearranged).
'*Ooh, he's just been feng shuied.*'

fill your boots time
a time when either batsmen or bowlers are dominant and there is a chance for lots more runs/wickets.
See 'Bunsen' example above.

filth
poor bowling that gets carted to/over the boundary.
'"*That's absolute filth, Tuffers,*" *said Goochy.*'

flan
a medium-pace delivery that is easy to hit – also known as 'phantom bowling' or 'dobbers' or 'dolly-drops'.
'That was a flan of the highest flan order.'

full bung
another way of describing a full toss – see 'filth'.
'The miserly Gus Fraser bowled his annual full bung to the grateful batsman.'

happy days
catch-all phrase to herald a positive outcome.
'"Happy days," said Tuffers as Lord Gower sabred open another bottle of champagne.'

he'll be disappointed with that . . .
tactful phrase to describe one of the worst shots/deliveries/dropped catches in the history of mankind during *Test Match Special* commentary to avoid speaking the ugly truth.
'He'll be disappointed with that . . . massive heave across the line, particularly now his middle stump is catapulting towards the wicketkeeper and he's going to have to walk back into the dressing room and face his teammates.'

jaffa
an unplayable delivery.
'Oh, and that's an absolute jaffa from Swanny . . .'

jazz hat
posh boy.
'Straussy was a bit of a jazz hat as a youngster, but I could see he was England captain material.'

knock one off the stump
to masturbate.
'*His roommate mistakenly thought Tufnell was knocking one off the stump when in fact he was trying to work out how to bowl out Justin Langer.*'

lose my/your/his whooper
to lose one's nerve, to bottle it.
'*Tufnell totally lost his whooper throwing darts up on the famous stage at Lakeside.*'

Majorca
yorker.
'*What a Majorca there by Jimmy Anderson!*'

Michelle
to take five wickets in an innings (i.e. Michelle Pfeiffer – five-fer).
'*He's bagged a lovely Michelle.*'

marmalise
to destroy/make marmalade of a bowler/bowling attack through aggressive batting.
'*Tuffers sat back in the dressing room and chuckled as captain Gatt marmalised the opposition's spinners.*'

moose
to drive fast.
'*I absolutely moosed it round the Goodwood track, and later I watched as the written-off Maserati was winched back to the pits on a crane.*'

muppet

useful derogatory term to intimidate a debutant batsman.

'*"Who's this ****ing muppet?" said the fearsome David Smith as debutant batsman Tufnell trembled.*'

Olympic

term used to describe an alleged batsman scoring five noughts in a row (see also 'Audi').

'*Bloody hell, Tuffers has only got an Olympic.*'

omelette

the rough outside of the leg stump (or the off stump of a left-handed batsman) in the second innings of a game.

'*Plop it in the omelette, Tuffers.*'

overs kadovers

used when a game is effectively over even if the final ball is yet to be bowled.

'*It's overs kadovers here at Headingley.*'

penguin

to engage in deep mental analysis of batsmen in preparation for a game. Usually conducted while lying on one's back under the bed covers, arms by one's sides flapping involuntarily, like a penguin on its back. Not to be confused with 'knocking one off the stump' (see above).

'*The main reason I was a good spinner was because I did a lot of late-night penguining.*'

ponce

to beg, steal, borrow.

'*Luckily, Catalina had smuggled some ciggies into the jungle in her hair, so I ponced a couple from her.*'

rock & roll

to lose a lot of wickets in quick succession.

'England have got to be careful not to get rock and rolled here.'

seed

a beautifully bowled delivery.

'Oh, that's a good seed by Monty P.'

strangle

a wicket taken with a poor delivery.

'Always nice to get a strangle once in a while.'

spangled

to be very, very drunk.

'By the time the show starts, my interviewees Chris Adams and Murray Goodwin are absolutely spangled.'

timber

to fall over like a felled tree in a bar due to excessive alcohol intake.

'As Lara leaves the bar, I look round just in time to see Athers timbering over.'

twat

to strike the ball hard (note to self: this term is not suitable for usage during a live TV/radio cricket commentary).

'He's twatted that through the offside . . . Sorry, what was that? I'm not allowed to say that on Sky?'

touched by the Lama

to feel lucky (particularly after shaking hands with the Dalai Lama).

'"We're going to win," says Vaughanie. "We've been touched by the Lama."'

unit
a very big man.
'*Patrick Patterson was a sizeable unit.*'

wickets in the hutch
wickets in hand.
'*England have wickets in the hutch and look to be marching to victory.*'

INDEX

INDEX

INDEX

INDEX

INDEX

INDEX